HOUGHTON ★ MIFFLIN ★ HISTORY PROGRAM

■ *Life in America* Series

General Editor: **Richard C. Wade**
Editorial Adviser: **Howard R. Anderson**

HOUGHTON MIFFLIN COMPANY / Boston

REVISED EDITION

IMMIGRANTS IN AMERICAN LIFE

Selected Readings

ARTHUR MANN
The University of Chicago

Atlanta / Dallas / Geneva, Ill. / Hopewell, N.J. / Palo Alto

■ About the Author and Editors

ARTHUR MANN

A graduate of Brooklyn College, Dr. Mann received his Ph. D. in history from Harvard University. Currently Preston and Sterling Morton Professor of American History at the University of Chicago, he has also taught at the Massachusetts Institute of Technology and Smith College. Dr. Mann is the author of Yankee Reformers in the Urban Age, La Guardia: A Fighter Against His Times, 1882–1933, and La Guardia Comes to Power, 1933. He has also edited a book of readings called The Progressive Era, Liberal Renaissance or Liberal Failure?

RICHARD C. WADE

General editor for the LIFE IN AMERICA series, Dr. Wade is Professor of American History at the Graduate Center, City University of New York. He is the author of Slavery in the Cities and The Urban Frontier.

HOWARD R. ANDERSON

Dr. Anderson, consulting editor for the Houghton Mifflin Social Studies program, has taught in the secondary schools of Michigan, Iowa, and New York. He has also taught at the University of Iowa and at Cornell University, and has served as Provost of the University of Rochester and as President of the National Council for the Social Studies.

Copyright © 1974, 1968 by Houghton Mifflin Company
All rights reserved. No part of this work may be reproduced or transmitted in any form or by any means, electronic or mechanical, including photocopying and recording, or by any information storage or retrieval system, without permission in writing from the publisher.
Printed in the United States of America
Library of Congress Catalog Card Number: 73–3055
ISBN: 0–395–17011–7

■ Contents

· *The Life in America Series*   ix

PART ONE · The Peopling of America   1

I. The Colonial Background
1. The Crossing / Gottlieb Mittelberger   8
2. Passage from Africa / Olaudah Equiano   13
3. Jews and Christians in Colonial New York / Peter Kalm   19
4. Variety and Harmony in Pennsylvania / *William Winterbotham*   21
5. Common Social and Economic Backgrounds / Benjamin Franklin   23
6. The American, a New Man / J. Hector St. John de Crèvecoeur   29

II. Migrations of the Nineteenth and Twentieth Centuries
1. A Numerical Overview / *Statistical Abstract*   32
2. Europe Watched Them Go / Oscar Handlin   34
3. Crossing the Atlantic by Steam / Michael Pupin   36
4. They Came in Waves / Marcus L. Hansen   38
5. North from Mexico / Carey *McWilliams*   43
6. Gift of the Black Tropics / *W. O. Domingo*   47
7. Why They Came   51
    A. A Trinity of Forces / John F. Kennedy   51
    B. The Lure of America / Emma Lazarus   55

III. Some Personal Testimonies
1. A German Revolutionist / Carl Schurz   56
2. A Scottish Weaver's Son / Andrew Carnegie   59

3. A Swedish Soldier / Hans Mattson — 62
4. A Daughter from Ireland / Anonymous — 64
5. A French-Canadian Farmer / Jacques Ducharme — 68
6. A Jewish Girl from Russia / Mary Antin — 71
7. A Jamaican Schoolboy / William Scott — 74
8. A Mexican Storekeeper / Pablo Mares — 76

PART TWO · The Immigrants Adjust to America — 79

IV. Jobs and Housing

1. Farming in Missouri / Anonymous — 84
2. A Skilled Artisan in New York City / Samuel Gompers — 87
3. Tenement Factories / Jacob A. Riis — 89
4. Pick and Shovel / Constantine M. Panunzio — 92
5. Killed in a Foundry / Antoni Butkowski — 97
6. A Servant Girl / Aleksandra Rembieńska — 98
7. Loss in Status / An Anonymous Black Teacher — 100
8. Tenement House Evils / Robert DeForest and Lawrence Veiller — 102

V. Community Life

1. The Lack of Community / E. V. Smalley — 104
2. Sociability in East Harlem / Edward Corsi — 108
3. The Church / Robert E. Park and Herbert A. Miller — 110
4. Mutual Aid Societies / Robert E. Park and Herbert A. Miller — 112
5. The Press / Winifred Rauschenbusch — 115
6. Conflict Between Generations — 116
   A. Bohemians in Chicago / Mary E. McDowell — 116
   B. Cubans in Miami / The New York Times — 119
7. Black Immigrant Communities / Ira De A. Reid — 122

VI. Politics

1. Ward Politics / George Washington Plunkitt 127
2. Tammany Attacked / Lincoln Steffens 130
3. Tammany Defended / William T. Stead 132
4. Issue Politics / Fiorello H. La Guardia 136
5. Foreign Affairs / Survey 139

VII. The Achievement

1. An Expanding Economy / President's Commission on Immigration and Naturalization 143
2. Culture / Ernst Frederick Philblad 145
3. Wartime Loyalty / Josephine Roche 147

PART THREE · America Adjusts to the Immigrants 152

VIII. Cycles of Bigotry

1. Know-Nothing Prejudice in the 1850's / "One of 'Em" 157
2. World War I Persecutions of German Americans / Gerald L. Wendt 159
3. The Ku Klux Klan in the 1920's / Hiram Wesley Evans 161
4. An American Catholic Answers Back / Alfred E. Smith 167
5. Japanese Americans Interned During World War II / Ted Nakashima 168

IX. Concepts of Americanism and Americanization

1. The Melting Pot 172
   A. A Nineteenth Century View / Ralph Waldo Emerson 172
   B. A Twentieth Century View / Israel Zangwill 173
2. Cultural Pluralism / Emily Greene Balch 175
3. Assimilation / Theodore Roosevelt 179
4. Obstacles to Becoming an American / Emily Greene Balch 182

5. A Freedom Fighter Views His Own Adjustment / Janos Hollo — 184

X. Immigration Policy

1. Chinese Exclusion / American Federation of Labor — 189
2. The Literacy Test Vetoed / Woodrow Wilson — 192
3. The National Origins Plan / Ellison DuRant Smith — 195
4. The McCarran-Walter Immigration Bill / Time — 197
5. The Repeal of Racism / Lyndon B. Johnson — 201

XI. The Contemporary Scene

1. Changing Ethnic Profile / Bill Kovach — 205
2. Successful Adjustment in Miami / Bryan O. Walsh — 208
3. Multiple Problems of the Poor — 212
   A. In the Southwest / Inter-Agency Committee on Mexican-American Affairs — 213
   B. In New York City / José Morales, Jr. — 218
4. The Response of Government / Inter-Agency Committee on Mexican-American Affairs — 222
5. The Question of Identity / Albert Pena — 229
6. A Plea for Bilingual Education / Nick E. Garza — 231
7. Uprising in the Barrios / Charles A. Erickson — 236
8. White Ethnic Revival / Roman C. Pucinski — 242
9. Who Are We? / Arthur Mann — 245

The Student's Paperback Library — 249

Questions for Study and Discussion — 251

Acknowledgments — 256

Index — 257

■ *Life in America Series*

Almost a half century ago the philosopher George Santayana, writing about his fellow Americans in *Character and Opinion in the United States*, had this to say:

> ... if there are immense differences between individual Americans ... yet there is a great uniformity in their environment, customs, temper, and thoughts. They have all been uprooted from their several soils and ancestries and plunged together into one vortex, whirling irresistibly in a space otherwise quite empty. To be an American is of itself a moral condition, an education, and a career....

One might express this idea another way by saying that there is indeed broad diversity in American life and yet enough similarity in the American experience to enable us profitably to explore that experience in its various facets — whether we are speaking of its rich cultural heritage or of the development of its political and social institutions. For "this soil is propitious to every seed," wrote Santayana. And it will be the purpose of the LIFE IN AMERICA SERIES — of which the present volume is one — to trace the planting and the growth of those many seeds that go to make up American civilization as we know it today.

Coming originally from different — often disparate — national and social backgrounds, speaking a multiplicity of languages, our colonial forebears found on this broad continent the room and the freedom they sought. Here they shaped a new society while yet preserving much of their older heritage. From this interaction between the old and new, between the land and the people, a distinctively American civilization emerged.

For nearly two hundred years the mainstream of American life has remained sufficiently broad and open to contain a great variety of views and experience while continuing to add to — and thereby to enrich — our total cultural heritage.

This series examines what has come to be known as the American way of life by looking into the separate aspects of the American experience. It not only emphasizes the crises in the American past but traces the continuities as well. It discovers meaning in the life of ordinary people as well as in the achievements of their leaders. It illumines the great movements of history by viewing them first hand through the eyes of contemporaries. Most of all, it puts the student on the stage of history, making him a companion of the generations and the groups that have gone before.

Each volume in the LIFE IN AMERICA SERIES deals with a particular facet of the American experience. In each, the story will begin by examining the way in which the people most involved with that aspect of national life have become part of the American story. Other selections will trace their development, chronicle their troubles and achievements and, finally, suggest present problems and prospects.

In this way the student will receive a balanced picture of the growth of his country. Instead of seeing American history as a series of crises and conflicts only, he will perceive also the continuing, if sometimes uneven, development of a free society. Instead of trying to find in Washington all the keys to understanding the American achievement, he will be encouraged to seek them as well in the many other sections of the country. And in searching for the significance of events, he will focus his attention not only on the prominent figures of history but on the experiences of ordinary citizens as well. He will be invited to participate vicariously, as he reads, in their struggles, hopes, aspirations, failures, and successes.

The present volume concerns the immigrants in American life — those millions of people who came from many different lands to make a new life for themselves and who, in doing so, helped to build a great nation. The story of how and why these people came to America, how they adjusted to their strange surroundings, and how America adjusted to them is a vital part of this country's history.

Part One

Introduction
I. The Colonial Background
II. Migrations of the Nineteenth and Twentieth Centuries
III. Some Personal Testimonies

The Peopling of America

Part One: Introduction

It was just a little more than a hundred years ago that Walt Whitman, the poet of democracy, hailed the United States as a "nation of nations." No phrase better sums up this country's history in cosmopolitanism. America was discovered from Europe by Scandinavians, named by a German mapmaker in honor of a Florentine explorer, and opened for colonization by a Genoese sea captain in the Spanish service. Captain Columbus's crew was a preview of things to come. It included an Englishman, a Negro, an Irishman, a Pole, and a Jew.

Origins of the American People

Non-Europeans got here long before Columbus. Will Rogers liked to say that his ancestors met the *Mayflower* when it docked. The Oklahoma humorist was part Cherokee. Yet, like the Pilgrims, the first Indians were foreign to America. They immigrated to North America from Siberia across the Bering Strait around 11,500 years ago — and perhaps even earlier than that, according to some anthropologists.

But the question of who came first is irrelevant. The important thing is that, whether one traces his family back to Ellis Island, Plymouth Rock, or the Bering Strait, every American discovers that his ancestors came here from somewhere else. That is what President Franklin D. Roosevelt (who was of Dutch ancestry) meant when he reminded the Daughters of the American Revolution: "Remember, remember always, that all of us . . . are descended from immigrants. . . ."[1]

Roosevelt had in mind the great migrations that have made America. In the more than 350 years since the English established their first permanent settlement at Jamestown, over forty million people have immigrated to these shores. This figure is sixteen times greater than the American population in 1776. It is five times the number of people who now live in the eight Rocky Mountain states.

[1] Quoted in John F. Kennedy, *A Nation of Immigrants*, Revised and Enlarged Edition (New York: Harper & Row, 1964), p. 3.

Introduction to Part One 3

It dwarfs in magnitude all other population movements before or since. The peopling of America adds up to the greatest migration in recorded history.

But Americans have come not only from somewhere else — they also have come from almost everywhere. Therein lies still another key to the American identity. Immigration explains why the people of this nation are unique in the diversity of their ancestors. The Americans spring from a multitude of stocks that have made their way to this land from Europe, Asia, Africa, the Middle East, and the Americas. (*See Section II, selection 1.*) That is why Walt Whitman called the United States a "nation of nations."

Effect of Immigration on American History

Our diversity has affected almost every aspect of our history. Like the westward movement, to which it was related, immigration acted as one of the great creative forces in the shaping of American society. Our culture emerged from the interplay between immigrant heritages and the New World environment. Our language; our government, politics, and economy; our religions, music, arts, literature, and sciences; our educational systems; our sports, entertainment, even the foods we eat — all testify, in one way or another, to immigrant backgrounds.

Impact of America on Immigrants

But immigration was, and remains, a two-way process. To know that the immigrants altered America is not enough. We also have to see how America altered the immigrants. Otherwise, we shall fail to understand the meaning of the journey for the immigrant and for his children as well. That dimension to the story, the human dimension, saves history from being a tale of cold abstractions.

The Ethnic Mosaic of Early America

This book opens with an account of a German immigrant's crossing of the Atlantic in 1750. Immediately following there is a description by an Ibo[2] of his own slave passage in the same decade. According to the law, slaves were not immigrants — that is to say, aliens who voluntarily left their native lands in order to settle in America. Notwith-

[2] The Ibo inhabited a territory that is now part of the state of Nigeria. They were one of several tribes in West Africa from which most slaves came to America.

standing that legal distinction, hundreds of thousands of reluctant African migrants formed an important element in the ethnic mosaic of early America.

When the first United States census was taken in 1790, close to a fourth of the enumerated 3,929,000 inhabitants were black. They were second in size only to the English and their descendants, who constituted just under half the population. The remaining fourth or so consisted of persons of German, Scotch-Irish, Dutch, French, Scottish, Spanish, Swedish, Welsh, Swiss, Irish, and still other ethnic origins.

Clearly, by the time the American republic was founded, this nation was already a "nation of nations." One Revolutionary leader, Tom Paine, stated unequivocally that England was not "the parent country of America." Still another contemporary, J. Hector St. John de Crèvecoeur, commented on "that strange mixture of blood, which you will find in no other country." (*See Section I, selection 6.*)

The mixture varied, however, from one part of the country to the other. French Huguenots were conspicuous in South Carolina, Dutch Calvinists in New York, and Swedish Lutherans in Delaware. New England, which had been relatively unaffected by the 18th-century migrations from Africa and continental Europe, was the most homogeneously English region in America. Pennsylvania, in contrast, was the most multi-ethnic state in the new nation. (*See Section I, selection 4.*) The southern frontier was heavily peopled by Germans, Scotsmen, Scotch-Irish, and Welsh, whereas the southern seaboard was predominantly English and African. As early as 1750, as is revealed in *Section I, selection 3*, New York City was on its way toward being the most cosmopolitan city in the world.

America an Ideal

Yet, however varied in ancestry, the Americans of the colonial and early national periods had much in common. It would be impossible to overestimate the unifying power of the English language, of English law, and of English political institutions. Then, too, everyone had to work hard to earn a living, for men with inherited incomes rarely came here. America appealed, as Benjamin Franklin pointed out, to lower- and middle-class immigrants. (*See Section I, selection 5.*) People of that background helped to lay the foundations of American equality.

It is here that we touch on a major problem. According to Crèvecoeur (*Section I, selection 6*), the Americans were a nation before they won their independence from England and framed their Constitution. What was the source, and the meaning, of their nationality? Unlike the citizens of the great European nation-states, the Americans did not have a long history, fixed territorial boundaries, the same religion, or — what is most relevant here — a common descent. They got around this problem by defining their identity in terms of the democratic principles by which they lived. Blood was irrelevant to this concept of nationality. America was an ideal.

Confident of the ability of all people to respond to this ideal, Americans kept their doors open to immigration for the next century and a half. More than that, remembering their own origins, Americans believed that they had a responsibility to keep the doors open. In his best-selling pamphlet *Common Sense* (1776), Tom Paine prophesied that the land of liberty would "receive the fugitive, and prepare in time an asylum for mankind." In 1783 George Washington wrote: "The bosom of America is open to receive not only the Opulent and Respectable Stranger, but the oppressed and persecuted of all Nations and Religions. . . ."

All nations? Not quite, to begin with. In the first Naturalization Law, enacted in 1790, Congress limited citizenship to *"any alien, being a free white person. . . ."* The framers meant to exclude not only immigrants from Africa, but also persons of African origin no matter where they came from. After the Civil War Amendments, however, which emancipated the slaves and made them citizens, Congress amended the original prohibition against black immigrants. The Act of July 14, 1870, reads: "The naturalization laws are hereby extended to aliens of African nativity, and to persons of African descent."

The Flood Tide of Immigration

And so, in the nineteenth and twentieth centuries, tens of millions of immigrants came. (*See Section II.*) Moreover, the end is not in sight. It is undeniable that the lure of America has been powerful. Yet, before the development of modern transportation, the long, hard, and dangerous Atlantic crossing discouraged some people from leaving Europe. (*See Section I, selection 1.*) More important, until the last two centuries or so, people traditionally had lived in the places where they — and their fathers and their fathers' fathers before them — had been born.

What, then, made them move? And in such huge numbers? For one thing, an industrial and agricultural revolution threw artisans out of work and uprooted peasants from the land. That cause was a push. For another, information spread throughout the world about the possibility of making a fresh start in America. That cause was a pull. In almost every instance, moreover, emigrating countries experienced a huge increase in population that their economies could not absorb.

Whatever the combination of causes, they operated in different areas at different times. That is why immigrants came in waves. They first predominated from the British Isles, then from western Europe, later from central Europe, and still later from eastern Europe, southern Europe, and the Middle East. (*See Section II, selection 4.*) In Asia the first newcomers arrived from China, followed by those from Japan and Korea. After the restriction of mass immigration from the Old World in the 1920's, the Americas provided the chief waves of immigration. (*See Section II, selections 1, 5, and 6.*)

Immigrants as Individuals

But such words as *pulls*, *pushes*, and *waves* are abstractions. And *industrial and agricultural revolutions* are the historian's terms for describing vast, impersonal forces operating on masses of people. Masses were of course involved, but the decision to move from one country to another was — except for Africans — an individual decision. In England and Ireland, in Russia and Italy, in Norway, Greece, and Poland — no matter where — a man or a woman or a whole family said: "It is better over there than here; let's go." The documents in Section III tell about some of these personal decisions.

"To know America," President John F. Kennedy wrote, ". . . it is necessary to know why over 42 million people gave up their settled lives to start anew in a strange land."[2] Part Two of this book will deal with how the immigrants adjusted to America, and Part Three with how America adjusted to the immigrants. Here, in Part One, we start with the sources of America's diversity — namely, with Americans who came from somewhere else. ■

---

[2] John F. Kennedy, *A Nation of Immigrants*, Revised and Enlarged Edition (New York: Harper & Row, 1964), p. 3.

(*Note:* The readings in this book have been reproduced as they appeared in the original sources, save that in certain instances paragraph indentations have been added, punctuation altered, spellings modernized, or italics removed, in order to facilitate comprehension.)

I. The Colonial Background

Theodore Roosevelt once said that the word "settler" was "a euphemistic name for an immigrant who came over in the steerage of a sailing vessel in the seventeenth century instead of the steerage of a steamer in the nineteenth century."[1] Roosevelt was not only deflating snobs who claimed to be better than other Americans because their ancestors had arrived in this country a long time ago. He was also calling attention to the plain historical fact that immigration began with the beginning of America. What were the backgrounds of those early newcomers? And how did they get on with each other? These questions are crucial for understanding the kind of society that had come into being in the New World by the end of the eighteenth century. ■

1. The Crossing[2]
♣ Gottlieb Mittelberger

Even the slowest airplane today crosses the Atlantic in a matter of hours. In the day of the sailing vessel, it took months to cross the ocean. But the voyage was not only long; it was also wearing, degrading, and perilous. In the following account, by a German

---

[1] Quoted in Stanley J. Tracy, et al., *A Report on World Population Migrations as Related to the United States of America* (Washington, D.C.: George Washington University, 1956), p. 47.

[2] *Gottlieb Mittelberger's Journey to Pennsylvania in the Year 1750 and Return to Germany in the Year 1754* (Frankfurt, Germany, 1756). Reprinted by permission of the publishers from Gottlieb Mittelberger, *Journey to Pennsylvania*, Oscar Handlin and John Clive, translators (Cambridge, Mass.: The Belknap Press of Harvard University Press, Copyright 1960 by the President and Fellows of Harvard College), pp. 11–16.

The Crossing **9**

organist and teacher who immigrated to Pennsylvania in 1750, we have a vivid but not overdrawn description of how immigrants came to these shores more than two hundred years ago. ■

This journey lasts from the beginning of May until the end of October, that is, a whole six months, and involves such hardships that it is really impossible for any description to do justice to them. The reason for this is that the Rhine boats must pass by thirty-six different customs houses between Heilbronn[3] and Holland. At each of these all the ships must be examined, and these examinations take place at the convenience of the customs officials. Meanwhile, the ships with the people in them are held up for a long time. This involves a great deal of expense for the passengers; and it also means that the trip down the Rhine alone takes from four to six weeks.

Stopovers in Holland and England

When the ships with their passengers arrive in Holland they are there held up once again for from five to six weeks. Because everything is very expensive in Holland the poor people must spend nearly all they own during this period. In addition various sad accidents are likely to occur here. I have, for instance, seen with my own eyes two of the children of a man trying to board ship near Rotterdam meet sudden death by drowning.

In Rotterdam, and to some extent also in Amsterdam, the people are packed into the big boats as closely as herring, so to speak. The bedstead of one person is hardly two feet across and six feet long, since many of the boats carry from four to six hundred passengers, not counting the immense amount of equipment, tools, provisions, barrels of fresh water, and other things that also occupy a great deal of space.

Because of contrary winds it sometimes takes the boats from two to four weeks to make the trip from Holland to Cowes.[4] But, given favorable winds, that voyage can be completed in eight days or less. On arrival everything is examined once more and customs duties paid. It can happen that ships have to ride at anchor there from eight to fourteen days, or until they have taken on full cargoes. During this

[3] [**Heilbronn:** a city in southwestern Germany.]
[4] [**Cowes:** a seaport in southern England.]

time everyone has to spend his last remaining money and to consume the provisions that he meant to save for the ocean voyage, so that most people must suffer tremendous hunger and want at sea where they really feel the greatest need. Many thus already begin their sufferings on the voyage between Holland and England.

When the ships have weighed anchor for the last time, usually off Cowes in Old England, then both the long sea voyage and misery begin in earnest. For from there the ships often take eight, nine, ten, or twelve weeks sailing to Philadelphia, if the wind is unfavorable. But even given the most favorable winds, the voyage takes seven weeks.

Sickness

During the journey the ship is full of pitiful signs of distress — smells, fumes, horrors, vomiting, various kinds of sea sickness, fever, dysentery, headaches, heat, constipation, boils, scurvy, cancer, mouth-rot, and similar afflictions, all of them caused by the age and the highly-salted state of the food, especially of the meat, as well as by the very bad and filthy water, which brings about the miserable destruction and death of many. Add to all that shortage of food, hunger, thirst, frost, heat, dampness, fear, misery, vexation, and lamentation as well as other troubles. Thus, for example, there are so many lice, especially on the sick people, that they have to be scraped off the bodies. All this misery reaches its climax when in addition to everything else one must also suffer through two to three days and nights of storm, with everyone convinced that the ship with all aboard is bound to sink. In such misery all the people on board pray and cry pitifully together.

In the course of such a storm the sea begins to surge and rage so that the waves often seem to rise up like high mountains, sometimes sweeping over the ship; and one thinks that he is going to sink along with the ship. All the while the ship, tossed by storm and waves, moves constantly from one side to the other, so that nobody aboard can either walk, sit, or lie down and the tightly packed people on their cots, the sick as well as the healthy, are thrown every which way. One can easily imagine that these hardships necessarily affect many people so severely that they cannot survive them.

I myself was afflicted by severe illness at sea, and know very well how I felt. These people in their misery are many times very much in want of solace, and I often entertained and comforted them with singing, praying, and encouragement. Also, when possible, and when wind and waves permitted it, I held daily prayer meetings with them on deck, and, since we had no ordained clergyman on board, was forced to administer baptism to five children. I also held services, including a sermon, every Sunday, and when the dead were buried at sea, commended them and our souls to the mercy of God.

Misery, Malice, Regrets, Despair

Among those who are in good health impatience sometimes grows so great and bitter that one person begins to curse the other, or himself and the day of his birth, and people sometimes come close to murdering one another. Misery and malice are readily associated, so that people begin to cheat and steal from one another. And then one always blames the other for having undertaken the voyage. Often the children cry out against their parents, husbands against wives and wives against husbands, brothers against their sisters, friends and acquaintances against one another.

But most of all they cry out against the thieves of human beings! Many groan and exclaim: "Oh! If only I were back at home, even lying in my pig-sty!" Or they call out: "Ah, dear God, if I only once again had a piece of good bread or a good fresh drop of water." Many people whimper, sigh, and cry out pitifully for home. Most of them become homesick at the thought that many hundreds of people must necessarily perish, die, and be thrown into the ocean in such misery. And this in turn makes their families, or those who were responsible for their undertaking the journey, oftentimes fall almost into despair — so that it soon becomes practically impossible to rouse them from their depression. In a word, groaning, crying, and lamentation go on aboard day and night; so that even the hearts of the most hardened, hearing all this, begin to bleed.

Death

One can scarcely conceive what happens at sea to women in childbirth and to their innocent offspring. Very few escape with their lives; and mother and child, as soon as they have died, are thrown into the water. On board our ship, on a day on which we had a great storm, a woman about to give birth and unable to deliver under the circumstances, was pushed through one of the portholes into the sea because her corpse was far back in the stern and could not be brought forward to the deck.

Children between the ages of one and seven seldom survive the sea voyage; and parents must often watch their offspring suffer miserably, die, and be thrown into the ocean, from want, hunger, thirst, and the like. I myself, alas, saw such a pitiful fate overtake thirty-two children on board our vessel, all of whom were finally thrown into the sea. Their parents grieve all the more, since their children do not find repose in the earth, but are devoured by the predatory fish of the ocean. It is also worth noting that children who have not had either measles or smallpox usually get them on board the ship and for the most part perish as a result.

On one of these voyages a father often becomes infected by his wife and children, or a mother by her small children, or even both parents by their children, or sometimes whole families one by the other, so that many times numerous corpses lie on the cots next to those who are still alive, especially when contagious diseases rage on board.

Many other accidents also occur on these ships, especially falls in which people become totally crippled and can never be completely made whole again. Many also tumble into the sea.

Wretched Food and Drink

It is not surprising that many passengers fall ill, because in addition to all the other troubles and miseries, warm food is served only three times a week, and at that is very bad, very small in quantity, and so dirty as to be hardly palatable at all. And the water distributed in these ships is often very black, thick with dirt, and full of worms. Even when very thirsty, one is almost unable to drink it without loathing. It is certainly true that at sea one would often spend a great deal of money just for one good piece of bread, or one good drink of water — not even to speak of a good glass of wine — if one could only obtain them. I have, alas, had to experience that myself. For toward the end of the voyage we had to eat the ship's biscuit, which had already been spoiled for a long time, even though in no single piece was there more than the size of a thaler[5] that was not full of red worms and spiders' nests. True, great hunger and thirst teach one to eat and drink everything — but many must forfeit their lives in the process. It is impossible to drink sea water, since it is salty

---

[5] [**thaler**: a German coin.]

and bitter as gall. If this were not the case, one could undertake such an ocean voyage with far less expense and without so many hardships.

Land Ahead!

When at last after the long and difficult voyage the ships finally approach land, when one gets to see the headlands for the sight of which the people on board had longed so passionately, then everyone crawls from below to the deck, in order to look at the land from afar. And people cry for joy, pray, and sing praises and thanks to God. The glimpse of land revives the passengers, especially those who are half-dead of illness. Their spirits, however weak they had become, leap up, triumph, and rejoice within them. Such people are now willing to bear all ills patiently, if only they can disembark soon and step on land.

2. Passage from Africa[1]
✚ Olaudah Equiano

Around 350,000 black slaves were brought to colonial America literally in chains. Whites were not alone in profiting from this inhumane traffic. The odyssey of a slave began when he was kidnapped by Africans or captured by them in war. If they themselves did not keep him as a slave, they might sell him on the West African coast to European or American traders. The latter then transported him to the Western Hemisphere for resale.

The author of the piece below, an Ibo from what is now the state of Nigeria, was kidnapped at the age of eleven by Africans and sold to a British slaver bound for the West Indies. The year was 1756. A decade later, after serving masters in the Barbados, Virginia, and Philadelphia, he purchased his freedom and went to live in England. There he became active in the British antislavery movement. In the following extract from his memoirs, which he wrote in his forties, he recreates the terror that he experienced as a child aboard an 18th-century slave ship. ■

---

[1] Olaudah Equiano, *The Life of Olaudah Equiano, or Gustavus Vassa, the African* (Boston: Isaac Knapp, 1837), pp. 20–21, 43–52.

The first object which saluted my eyes when I arrived on the coast was the sea, and a slaveship, which was then riding at anchor, and waiting for its cargo. These filled me with astonishment, which was soon converted into terror, which I am yet at a loss to describe, nor the then feelings of my mind.

Fear of Being Eaten

When I was carried on board I was immediately handled, and tossed up, to see if I were sound, by some of the crew; and I was now persuaded that I had got into a world of bad spirits, and that they were going to kill me. Their complexions too differing so much from ours, their long hair, and the language they spoke, which was very different from any I had ever heard, united to confirm me in this belief. Indeed, such were the horrors of my views and fears at the moment, that, if ten thousand worlds had been my own, I would have freely parted with them all to have exchanged my condition with that of the meanest slave in my own country.

When I looked round the ship too, and saw a large furnace or copper boiling, and a multitude of black people of every description chained together, every one of their countenances expressing dejection and sorrow, I no longer doubted of my fate; and, quite overpowered with horror and anguish, I fell motionless on the deck and fainted. When I recovered a little, I found some black people about me, who I believed were some of those who brought me on board, and had been receiving their pay; they talked to me in order to cheer me, but all in vain. I asked them if we were not to be eaten by those white men with horrible looks, red faces, and long hair. They told me I was not.... Soon after this, the blacks who brought me on board went off, and left me abandoned to despair....

I even wished for my former slavery[2], in preference to my present situation, which was filled with horrors of every kind, still heightened

---

[2] Equiano is here referring to the fact that, as a kidnapee, he was a slave. Elsewhere in his memoirs he contrasts the mildness of African slavery with the harshness of New World slavery. "With us they [slaves] do no more work than other members of the community, even their master. Their food, clothing, and lodging were nearly the same as theirs, except that they were not permitted to eat with those who were free born; and there were scarce any other difference between them than a superior degree of importance which the head of a family possesses in our state, and that authority which, as such, he exercises over every part of his household. Some of these slaves have even slaves under them, as their own property, and for their own use."

by my ignorance of what I was to undergo. I was not long suffered to indulge my grief; I was soon put down under the decks, and there I received such a salutation in my nostrils as I had never experienced in my life; so that, with the loathsomeness of the stench, and crying together, I became so sick and low that I was not able to eat, nor had I the least desire to taste anything. I now wished for the last friend, death, to relieve me; but soon, to my grief, two of the white men offered me eatables; and, on my refusing to eat, one of them held me fast by the hands, and laid me across, I think, the windlass, and tied my feet while the other flogged me severely.

I had never experienced anything of this kind before; and, although not being used to the water, I naturally feared that element the first time I saw it; yet, nevertheless, could I have got over the nettings, I would have jumped over the side; but I could not; and, besides, the crew used to watch us very closely who were not chained down to the decks, lest we should leap into the water: and I have seen some of these poor African prisoners most severely cut for attempting to do so, and hourly whipped for not eating. This indeed was often the case with myself.

The Savagery and Magic of White People

In a little time after, amongst the poor chained men, I found some of my own nation, which in a small degree gave ease to my mind. I inquired of them what was to be done with us. They gave me to understand we were to be carried to these white people's country to work for them. I then was a little revived, and thought, if it were no worse than working, my situation was not so desperate: but still I feared I should be put to death, the white people looked and acted, as I thought, in so savage a manner; for I had never seen among any people such instances of brutal cruelty; and this not only shown towards us blacks, but also to some of the whites themselves. One white man in particular I saw, when we were permitted to be on deck, flogged[3] so unmercifully with a large rope near the foremast, that he died in consequence of it; and they tossed him over the side as they would have done a brute. This made me fear these people the more; and I expected nothing less than to be treated in the same manner.

---

[3] "Such brutal floggings were at this time considered essential to the maintenance of discipline in the British navy and on ships engaged in the slave trade." Philip D. Curtin (ed.), *Africa Remembered: Narratives by West Africans from the Era of the Slave Trade* (Madison: University of Wisconsin Press, 1967), p. 94.

I could not help expressing my fears and apprehensions to some of my countrymen: I asked them if these people had no country, but lived in this hollow place the ship? They told me they did not, but came from a distant one. "Then," said I, "how comes it in all our country we never heard of them?" They told me, because they lived so very far off. I then asked, where were their women? Had they any like themeslves? I was told they had. "And why," said I, "do we not see them?" They answered, because they were left behind. I asked how the vessel could go? They told me they could not tell; but that there were cloth put upon the masts by the help of the ropes I saw, and then the vessel went on; and the white men had some spell or magic they put in the water when they liked in order to stop the vessel. I was exceedingly amazed at this account, and really thought they were spirits. I therefore wished much to be from amongst them, for I expected they would sacrifice me: but my wishes were vain; for we were so quartered that it was impossible for any of us to make our escape....

Filth, Stench, Pestilence, Chains, Floggings

At last, when the ship we were in had got in all her cargo, they made ready with many fearful noises, and we were all put under deck, so that we could not see how they managed the vessel. But this disappointment was the least of my sorrow. The stench of the hold while we were on the coast was so intolerably loathsome, that it was dangerous to remain there for any time, and some of us had been permitted to stay on the deck for the fresh air; but now that the whole ship's cargo were confined together, it became absolutely pestilential. The closeness of the place, and the heat of the climate, added to the number in the ship, which was so crowded that each had scarcely room to turn himself, almost suffocated us. This produced copious perspirations, so that the air soon became unfit for respiration, from a variety of loathsome smells, and brought on a sickness amongst the slaves, of which many died, thus falling victims to the improvident avarice, as I may call it, of their purchasers. This wretched situation was again aggravated by the galling of the chains, now become insupportable; and the filth of the necessary tubs, into which the children often fell, and were almost suffocated. The shrieks of the women, and the groans of the dying, rendered the whole a scene of horror almost inconceivable.

Happily perhaps for myself I was soon reduced so low here that it was thought necessary to keep me almost always on deck; and from my extreme youth I was not put in fetters. In this situation I expected every hour to share the fate of my companions, some of whom were almost daily brought upon deck at the point of death, which I began to hope would soon put an end to my miseries. Often did I think many of the inhabitants of the deep much more happy than myself; I envied them the freedom they enjoyed, and as often wished I could change my condition for theirs.

Every circumstance I met with served only to render my state more painful and heighten my apprehensions and my opinion of the cruelty of the whites. One day they had taken a number of fishes; and when they had killed and satisfied themselves with as many as they thought fit, to our astonishment who were on the deck, rather than give any of them to us to eat, as we expected, they tossed the remaining fish into the sea again, although we begged and prayed for some as well as we could, but in vain; and some of my countrymen, being pressed by hunger, took an opportunity, when they thought no one saw them, of trying to get a little privately; but they were discovered, and the attempt procured them some very savage floggings.

Attempted Suicides

One day, when we had a smooth sea, and moderate wind, two of my wearied countrymen, who were chained together (I was near them at the time), preferring death to such a life of misery, somehow made through the nettings, and jumped into the sea; immediately another quite dejected fellow, who, on account of his illness, was suffered to be out of irons, also followed their example; and I believe many more would very soon have done the same, if they had not been prevented by the ship's crew, who were instantly alarmed. Those of us that were the most active were in a moment put down under the deck; and there was such a noise and confusion amongst the people of the ship as I never heard before, to stop her, and get the boat out to go after the slaves. However, two of the wretches were drowned, but they got the other, and afterwards flogged him unmercifully, for thus attempting to prefer death to slavery. . . .

Final Destination: Sold

At last, we came in sight of the island of Barbados, at which the whites on board gave a great shout, and made many signs of joy to us. We did not know what to think of this; but, as the vessel drew nearer, we plainly saw the harbor, and other ships of different kinds and sizes: and we soon anchored amongst them off Bridge Town. Many merchants and planters now came on board, though it was the evening. They put us in separate parcels, and examined us attentively. They also made us jump, and pointed to the land, signifying we were to go there.

We thought by this we should be eaten by these ugly men, as they appeared to us; and when, soon after we were all put down under the deck again, there was much dread and trembling among us, and nothing but bitter cries to be heard all the night from these apprehensions, insomuch that at last the white people got some old slaves from the land to pacify us. They told us we were not to be eaten, but to work, and were soon to go on land where we should see many of our country people. This report eased us much; and sure enough, soon after we landed, there came to us Africans of all languages. We were conducted immediately to the merchant's yard, where we were all pent up together like so many sheep in a fold, without regard to sex or age.... We were not many days in the merchant's custody, before we were sold after their usual manner, which is this: on a signal given (as the beat of a drum), the buyers rush at once into the yard where the slaves are confined, and make choice of that parcel they like best. The noise and clamor with which this is attended, and the eagerness visible in the countenances of the buyers, serve not a little to increase the apprehension of the terrified Africans, who may well be supposed to consider them as the ministers of that destruction to which they think themselves devoted. In this manner, without scruple, are relations and friends separated, most of them never to see each other again. I remember in the vessel in which I was brought over, in the men's apartment, there were several brothers, who, in the sale, were sold in different lots; and it was very moving on this occasion to see and hear their cries at parting.

A New Refinement in Cruelty

O, ye nominal Christians! might not an African ask you, learned you this from your God? who says unto you, Do unto all men as you would men should do unto you. Is it not enough that we are torn from our country and friends to toil for your luxury and lust of gain? Must every tender feeling be likewise sacrificed to your avarice? Are the dearest friends and relations, now rendered more dear by their separation from their kindred, still to be parted from each other, and thus preventing from cheering the gloom of slavery with the small comfort of being together, and mingling their sufferings and sorrows? Why are parents to leave their children, brothers their sisters, or husbands their wives? Surely this is a new refinement in cruelty, which, while it has no advantage to atone for it, thus aggravates distress, and adds fresh horrors even to the wretchedness of slavery.

3. Jews and Christians in Colonial New York[1]
✣ Peter Kalm

Ever since Columbus's letters to the Spanish monarchs, foreign travelers have been describing the New World as different from the Old. That is why their observations are invaluable for studying America's uniqueness. In the eighteenth century none of these travelers was more perceptive than Professor Peter Kalm, a Swedish naturalist. Arriving in America in 1784 at the age of thirty-two, the young scientist noted that, in contrast to Sweden, America had a variety of churches and peoples. Below is what Kalm observed about New York City in his diary (originally published in Swedish and then in German, Dutch, French, and English) a quarter of a century before the American Revolution. ■

Besides the different sects of Christians there are many Jews settled in New York, who possess great privileges. They have a synagogue and houses, and great country seats of their own property, and are allowed to keep shops in town. They have likewise several ships, which they freight, and send out with their own goods; in fine, they enjoy all the privileges common to the other inhabitants of this town and province.

During my residence at New York this time, and in the next two years, I was frequently in company with Jews. I was informed, among other things, that these people never boiled any meat for themselves

[1] Peter Kalm, *Travels into North America* (London, 1772, second English edition). Reprinted in John Pinkerton, ed., *A General Collection of the Best and Most Interesting Voyages and Travels in All Parts of the World* (London: Longman, Hurst, Rees, Orme, and Brown, 1812), Vol. XIII, pp. 455–457.

on Saturday, but that they always did it the day before; and that in winter they kept a fire during the whole Saturday. They commonly eat no pork; yet I have been told by several men of credit, that many of them (especially among the young Jews) when traveling, did not make the least difficulty about eating this or any other meat that was put before them; even though they were in company with Christians.

An Evening in the Synagogue

I was in their synagogue last evening for the first time, and this day at noon I visited it again, and each time I was put into a particular seat, which was set apart for strangers or Christians. A young rabbi read the divine service, which was partly in Hebrew, and partly in the rabbinical dialect. Both men and women were dressed entirely in the English fashion; the former had all of them their hats on, and did not once take them off during service. The galleries, I observed, were appropriated to the ladies, while the men sat below. During prayers the men spread a white cloth over their heads; which perhaps is to represent sackcloth; but I observed that the wealthier sort of people had a much richer cloth than the poorer ones. Many of the men had Hebrew books, in which they sang and read alternately. The rabbi stood in the middle of the synagogue, and read with his face turned towards the east: he spoke, however, so fast as to make it almost impossible for any one to understand what he said.[2] . . .

New York Originally a Dutch Town

The town was first founded by the Dutch: this, it is said, was done in the year 1623, when they were yet masters of the country; they called it New Amsterdam, and the country itself New Holland. The English, towards the end of the year 1664, taking possession of it . . . and keeping it by the virtue of the next treaty of peace, gave the name of New York to both the town and the province belonging to it; in size it comes nearest to Boston and Philadelphia. But with regard to its fine buildings, its opulence, and extensive commerce, it disputes the preference with them: at present it is about half as big again as Gothenburg[3] in Sweden. . . .

---

[2] As there are no Jews in Sweden, Prof. Kalm was an utter stranger to their manners and religious customs, and therefore relates them as a kind of novelty. [Footnote from 1812 edition.]

[3] [**Gothenburg**: Göteborg, a city in Sweden.]

Various Protestant Churches

There are several churches in the town, which deserve some attention. 1. The English church, built in the year 1695, at the west end of the town, consisting of stone, and has a steeple with a bell. 2. The new Dutch church, which is likewise built of stone, is pretty large, and is provided with a steeple; it also has a clock, which is the only one in the town. This church stands almost due from north to south. No particular point of the compass has here been in general attended to in erecting sacred buildings. Some churches stand as is usual from east to west, others from south to north, and others in different positions. In this Dutch church there is neither altar, vestry, choir, sconces, nor paintings. Some trees are planted round it, which make it look as if it was built in a wood. 3. The old Dutch church, which is also built of stone; it is not so large as the new one. It was painted in the inside, though without any images, and adorned with a small organ, of which Governor Burnet made them a present. The men, for the most part, sit in the gallery, and the women below. 4. The Presbyterian church, which is pretty large, and was built but lately; it is of stone, and has a steeple and a bell in it. 5. The German Lutheran church. 6. The German Reformed church. 7. The French church, for Protestant refugees. 8. The Quakers' meeting-house. 9. To these may be added the Jewish synagogue, which I mentioned before.

4. Variety and Harmony in Pennsylvania[1]
✢ William Winterbotham

European reformers often held up America as a model for their own countries. Their writings therefore contain insights similar to those of foreign travelers. Take, for example, William Winterbotham, an English Baptist minister who was jailed in 1793 for claiming, like the Americans in 1776, that a king's authority derives from the people. While in prison Winterbotham wrote a four-volume history of the United States. In the fragment below, concerning Pennsylvania, he describes a society varied yet free and harmonious. ■

[1] William Winterbotham, *An Historical, Geographical, Commercial and Philosophical View of the United States, and the European Settlements in America and the West Indies* (London: Ridgway, Symonds, and Holt, 1795, 4 vols.), Vol. II, pp. 437–440.

The Colonial Background

Religious Liberty for All

The situation of religion and religious rights and liberty in Pennsylvania is a matter that deserves the attention of all sober and well-disposed people, who may have thoughts of seeking the enjoyment of civil and religious liberty in America. This state always afforded an asylum to the persecuted sects of Europe. No church or society ever was established here, no tithes[2] or tenths can be demanded; and though some regulation of the crown of England excluded two churches from a share in the government of the province, these are now done away with regard to every religious society whatever. A convention of special representatives of the citizens of Pennsylvania have had under consideration all the errors that had inadvertently crept into their constitution and frame of government, and, in the act they have published for the examination of the people, they have rejected the *detestable half-way* doctrine of Toleration, and have *established*, upon firm and perfectly equal ground, *all* denominations of religious men. By the provisions of the new code, a Protestant, a Roman Catholic, and a Hebrew, may elect or be elected to any office in the state, and pursue any lawful calling, occupation, or profession.

Religious Diversity a Product of Ethnic Diversity

The inhabitants of Pennsylvania are principally the descendants of the English, Irish and Germans, with some Scotch, Welsh, Swedes and a few Dutch. There are also many of the Irish and Germans who emigrated when young or middle-aged. The Friends [Quakers] and Episcopalians are chiefly of English extraction, and compose about one-third of the inhabitants. They live principally in the city of Philadelphia, and in the counties of Chester, Philadelphia, Bucks and Montgomery. The Irish are mostly Presbyterians, but some Catholics. Their ancestors came from the north of Ireland, which was originally settled from Scotland; hence they have sometimes been called Scotch Irish, to denote their double descent; but they are commonly and more properly called Irish, or the descendants of people from the north of Ireland. They inhabit the western and frontier counties, and are numerous.

The Germans compose about one quarter of the inhabitants of Pennsylvania. They are most numerous in the north parts of the city

[2] [**tithe:** a tenth part of one's income, when paid as a tax for the support of a church.]

of Philadelphia, and the counties of Philadelphia, Montgomery, Bucks, Dauphin, Lancaster, York, and Northampton, mostly in the four last, and are spreading in other parts. They consist of Lutherans (who are the most numerous sect), Calvinists or Reformed Church, Moravians, Catholics, Mennonists, Tunkers (corruptly called Dunkers) and Zwingfelters, who are a species of Quakers. These are all distinguished for their temperance, industry, and economy.

The Germans have usually fifteen of sixty-nine members in the Assembly; and some of them have arisen to the first honors in the state, and now fill a number of the higher offices; yet the body of them want education. A literary spirit has however of late been increasing among them.

Variety and Harmony

The Baptists, except the Mennonist and Tunker Baptists, who are Germans, are chiefly the descendants of emigrants from Wales, and are not numerous. A proportionate assemblage of the national prejudices, the manners, customs, religions, and political sentiments of all these, will form the Pennsylvanian character. As the leading traits in this character, thus constituted, we may venture to mention industry, frugality, bordering in some instances on parsimony, enterprise, a taste and ability for improvements in mechanics, in manufactures, in agriculture, in public buildings and institutions, in commerce, and in the liberal sciences; temperance, plainness, and simplicity in dress and manners; pride and humility in their extremes; inoffensiveness and intrigue; and in regard to religion, VARIETY and HARMONY. Such appear to be the distinguishing traits in the collective Pennsylvanian character.

5. Common Social and Economic Backgrounds[1]
✦ Benjamin Franklin

Benjamin Franklin lived in Pennsylvania most of his life and therefore knew first-hand the human variety described by the

[1] "Information to Those Who Would Remove to America," taken from Jared Sparks, ed., *The Works of Benjamin Franklin* (Boston: Tappan & Whittemore, 1836, 10 vols.), Vol. II, pp. 467–477.

Reverend Winterbotham. He further knew, as the son of an immigrant candlemaker from England, the common lower- and middle-class backgrounds that most immigrants shared. No one appreciated better than he the opportunities that existed in America for hardworking people to get ahead. Franklin left Boston for Philadelphia as a penniless boy and became an outstanding businessman, printer, writer, scientist, inventor, civic reformer, Revolutionary leader, and diplomat. Here, in an essay that he wrote shortly after the War for Independence, he tells people who want to immigrate to America what they can expect for themselves and their children. ■

Many persons in Europe, having directly or by letters expressed to the writer of this, who is well acquainted with North America, their desire of transporting and establishing themselves in that country; but who appear to have formed, through ignorance, mistaken ideas and expectations of what is to be obtained there; he thinks it may be useful, and prevent inconvenient, expensive, and fruitless removals and voyages of improper persons, if he gives some clearer and truer notions of that part of the world than appear to have hitherto prevailed.

Misconceptions About America

He finds it is imagined by numbers, that the inhabitants of North America are rich, capable of rewarding, and disposed to reward, all sorts of ingenuity; that they are at the same time ignorant of all the sciences, and, consequently, that strangers, possessing talents in the belles-lettres;[2] fine arts, etc., must be highly esteemed, and so well paid, as to become easily rich themselves; that there are also abundance of profitable offices to be disposed of, which the natives are not qualified to fill; and that, having few persons of family among them, strangers of birth must be greatly respected, and of course easily obtain the best of those offices, which will make all their fortunes; that the governments too, to encourage emigrations from Europe, not only pay the expense of personal transportation, but give lands gratis [free] to strangers, with Negroes to work for them, utensils of husbandry,[3] and stocks of cattle. These are all wild imaginations; and

[2] [**belles-lettres:** literature as a fine art.]
[3] [**utensils of husbandry:** agricultural tools.]

SETTLING THE NEW LAND: *Despite the hardships of the wilderness, Old World emigrants planted durable colonies in America. Among these ancestors of future Americans were some who came unwillingly — Africans who were captured and forced into slavery. Above, left, Englishmen in Jamestown, Virginia, the first permanent English colony, with new arrivals from Africa. Lutherans from Salzburg in Austria were representative of the many people who sought religious liberty in America. Persecuted by a Catholic ruler, they left their homeland in 1732 (below) to settle in Georgia. The amazing career of Benjamin Franklin (above, right), son of an immigrant candlemaker, illustrated how talented men of humble origin could make full use of opportunities offered by the new country.*

those who go to America with expectations founded upon them will surely find themselves disappointed.

The Misconceptions Corrected

The truth is, that though there are in that country few people so miserable as the poor of Europe, there are also very few that in Europe would be called rich; it is rather a general happy mediocrity that prevails. There are few great proprietors of the soil, and few tenants; most people cultivate their own lands, or follow some handicraft or merchandise; very few rich enough to live idly upon their rents or incomes, or to pay the highest prices given in Europe for painting, statues, architecture, and the other works of art, that are more curious than useful. Hence the natural geniuses, that have arisen in America with such talents, have uniformly quitted that country for Europe, where they can be more suitably rewarded. . . .

America Is Not for Idlers

. . . It cannot be worth any man's while, who has a means of living at home, to expatriate himself, in hopes of obtaining a profitable civil office in America; and, as to military offices, they are at an end with the war,[4] the armies being disbanded. Much less is it advisable for a person to go thither, who has no other quality to recommend him but his birth. In Europe it has indeed its value; but it is a commodity that cannot be carried to a worse market than that of America, where people do not inquire concerning a stranger, *What is he?* but, *What can he do?* . . .

The people have a saying, that God Almighty is himself a mechanic, the greatest in the universe; and he is respected and admired more for the variety, ingenuity, and utility of his handiworks, than for the antiquity of his family. . . . According to these opinions of the Americans, one of them would think himself more obliged to a genealogist,[5] who could prove for him that his ancestors and relations for ten generations had been ploughmen, smiths, carpenters, turners,[6] weavers, tanners, or even shoemakers, and consequently that they were useful members of society; than if he could only prove

---

[4] [War for Independence.]
[5] [**genealogist:** one who traces a person's ancestors.]
[6] [**turner:** a workman who uses a lathe.]

that they were gentlemen, doing nothing of value, but living idly on the labors of others. . . .

With regard to encouragements for strangers from government, they are really only what are derived from good laws and liberty. Strangers are welcome, because there is room enough for them all, and therefore the old inhabitants are not jealous of them; the laws protect them sufficiently, so that they have no need of the patronage of great men; and every one will enjoy securely the profits of his industry. But, if he does not bring a fortune with him, he must work and be industrious to live. One or two years' residence gives him all the rights of a citizen; but the government does not, at present, whatever it may have done in former times, hire people to become settlers, by paying their passages, giving land, Negroes, utensils, stock, or any other kind of emolument [payment] whatsoever. In short, America is the land of labor. . . .

Who then are the kind of persons to whom an emigration to America may be advantageous? And what are the advantages they may reasonably expect?

Farmers, Artisans, Men of Moderate Fortunes

Land being cheap in that country, from the vast forests still void of inhabitants, and not likely to be occupied in an age to come, insomuch that the propriety [ownership] of an hundred acres of fertile soil full of wood may be obtained near the frontiers, in many places, for eight or ten guineas, hearty young laboring men, who understand the husbandry of corn and cattle, which is nearly the same in that country as in Europe, may easily establish themselves there. A little money saved of the good wages they receive there, while they work for others, enables them to buy the land and begin their plantation, in which they are assisted by the goodwill of their neighbors, and some credit. Multitudes of poor people from England, Ireland, Scotland, and Germany, have by this means in a few years become wealthy farmers, who, in their own countries, where all the lands are fully occupied, and the wages of labor low, could never have emerged from the poor condition wherein they were born.

From the salubrity [healthfulness] of the air, the healthiness of the climate, the plenty of good provisions, and the encouragement to early marriages by the certainty of subsistence in cultivating the earth, the increase of inhabitants by natural generation is very rapid in America, and becomes still more so by the accession of strangers; hence there is a continual demand for more artisans of all the necessary and useful kinds, to supply those cultivators of the earth with houses, and with furniture and utensils of the grosser sorts, which cannot so well be brought from Europe. Tolerably good workmen in any of those mechanic arts are sure to find employ, and to be well paid for their work, there being no restraints preventing strangers from exercising any art they understand, nor any permission necessary. If they are poor, they begin first as servants or journeymen; and if they are sober, industrious, and frugal, they soon become masters, establish themselves in business, marry, raise families, and become respectable citizens.

Also, persons of moderate fortunes and capitals, who, having a number of children to provide for, are desirous of bringing them up to industry, and to secure estates for their posterity, have opportunities of doing it in America, which Europe does not afford. There they may be taught and practise profitable mechanic arts, without incurring disgrace on that account, but on the contrary acquiring respect by such abilities. There small capitals laid out in lands, which daily become more valuable by the increase of people, afford a solid prospect of ample fortunes thereafter for those children. . . .

A Fresh Start for the Children of the Poor

In the long-settled countries of Europe, all arts, trades, professions, farms, etc., are so full, that it is difficult for a poor man, who has children, to place them where they may gain, or learn to gain, a decent livelihood. The artisans, who fear creating future rivals in business, refuse to take apprentices, . . . [except] upon conditions of money, maintenance, or the like, which the parents are unable to comply with. Hence the youth are dragged up in ignorance of every gainful art, and obliged to become soldiers, or servants, or thieves, for a subsistence.

In America, the rapid increase of inhabitants takes away that fear of rivalship, and artisans willingly receive apprentices from the hope of profit by their labor, during the remainder of the time stipulated, after they shall be instructed. Hence it is easy for poor families to get their children instructed; for the artisans are so desirous of apprentices, that many of them will even give money to the parents, to have boys from ten to fifteen years of age bound apprentices to them till the age of twenty-one; and many poor parents have, by that means, on their arrival in the country, raised money enough to buy land sufficient to establish themselves, and to subsist the rest of their family by agriculture.

These contracts for apprentices are made before a magistrate, who regulates the agreement according to reason and justice, and, having in view the formation of a future and useful citizen, obliges the master to engage by a written indenture [contract], not only that, during the time of service stipulated, the apprentice shall be duly provided with meat, drink, apparel, washing, and lodging, and, at its expiration, with a complete new suit of clothes, but also that he shall be taught to read, write, and . . . [keep] accounts; and that he shall be well instructed in the art or profession of his master, or some other, by which he may afterwards gain a livelihood, and be able in his turn to raise a family. A copy of this indenture is given to the apprentice or his friends, and the magistrate keeps a record of it, to which recourse may be had, in case of failure by the master in any point of performance.

This desire among the masters, to have more hands employed in working for them, induces them to pay the passages of young persons, of both sexes, who, on their arrival, agree to serve them one, two, three, or four years; those, who have already learned a trade, agreeing for a shorter term, in proportion to their skill, and the consequent immediate value of their service; and those, who have none, agreeing for a longer term, in consideration of being taught an art their poverty would not permit them to acquire in their own country.

6. The American, a New Man[1]
✣ *J. Hector St. John de Crèvecoeur*

J. Hector St. John de Crèvecoeur was born in France and lived in America from the 1760's to 1780. He recognized that it was one thing for America to welcome many different kinds of people but still another for those people to constitute a single nation. What, in short, was an American? Crèvecoeur's answer below,

---

[1] J. Hector St. John de Crèvecoeur, *Letters from an American Farmer* (London, 1782; Philadelphia, 1793; New York: Fox, Duffield & Company, 1904), pp. 52–56.

that the American stands for a new way of life and a new set of values, is a classic statement of American nationality. It shows how immigration gives meaning to the motto on the Great Seal of the United States: E. Pluribus Unum, "From many, one." ■

In this great American asylum, the poor of Europe have by some means met together, and in consequence of various causes; to what purpose should they ask one another what countrymen they are? Alas, two thirds of them had no country. Can a wretch who wanders about, who works and starves, whose life is a continual scene of sore affliction or pinching penury; can that man call England or any other kingdom his country? A country that had no bread for him, whose fields procured him no harvest, who met with nothing but the frowns of the rich, the severity of the laws, with jails and punishments; who owned not a single foot of the extensive surface of this planet? No! urged by a variety of motives, here they came.

The American Alchemy

Everything has tended to regenerate them; new laws, a new mode of living, a new social system; here they are become men: in Europe they were as so many useless plants, wanting vegetative mould, and refreshing showers; they withered, and were mowed down by want, hunger, and war; but now by the power of transplantation, like all other plants they have taken root and flourished! Formerly they were not numbered in any civil lists of their country, except in those of the poor; here they rank as citizens. By what invisible power has this surprising metamorphosis been performed? By that of the laws and that of their industry. The laws, the indulgent laws, protect them as they arrive, stamping on them the symbol of adoption; they receive ample rewards for their labors; these accumulated rewards procure them lands; those lands confer on them the title of freemen, and to that title every benefit is affixed which men can possibly require. This is the great operation daily performed by our laws. From whence proceed these laws? From our government. Whence the government? It is derived from the original genius and strong desire of the people ratified and confirmed by the crown.[2] . . .

[2] [Crèvecoeur wrote this before the Thirteen Colonies had won their independence.]

The American Is a Man of New Opinions

What then is the American, this new man? He is either an Europian, or the descendant of an European, hence that strange mixture of blood, which you will find in no other country. I could point out to you a family whose grandfather was an Englishman, whose wife was Dutch, whose son married a French woman, and whose present four sons have now four wives of different nations. *He* is an American, who, leaving behind him all his ancient prejudices and manners, receives new ones from the new mode of life he has embraced, the new government he obeys, and the new rank he holds. He becomes an American by being received in the broad lap of our great *Alma Mater*.

Here individuals of all nations are melted into a new race of men, whose labors and posterity will one day cause great changes in the world. Americans are the western pilgrims, who are carrying along with them that great mass of arts, sciences, vigor, and industry which began long since in the east; they will finish the great circle. The Americans were once scattered all over Europe; here they are incorporated into one of the finest systems of population which has ever appeared, and which will hereafter become distinct by the power of the different climates they inhabit.

The American ought therefore to love this country much better than that wherein either he or his forefathers were born. Here the rewards of his industry follow with equal steps the progress of his labor; his labor is founded on the basis of nature, *self-interest;* can it want a stronger allurement? Wives and children, who before in vain demanded of him a morsel of bread, now, fat and frolicsome, gladly help their father to clear those fields whence exuberant crops are to arise to feed and to clothe them all; without any part being claimed, either by a despotic prince, a rich abbot, or a mighty lord. Here religion demands but little of him; a small voluntary salary to the minister, and gratitude to God; can he refuse these?

The American is a new man, who acts upon new principles; he must therefore entertain new ideas, and form new opinions. From involuntary idleness, servile dependence, penury, and useless labor, he has passed to toils of a very different nature, rewarded by ample subsistence. This is an American.

II. Migrations of the Nineteenth and Twentieth Centuries

The wars growing out of the American and French revolutions slowed down immigration for about fifty years. In the 1820's the movement resumed and reached fantastic proportions over the next hundred years. The arrivals totaled forty times as many people as during the colonial period — and represented almost that many different kinds of people. By World War I, newspapers were being published in this country for immigrants in two dozen and more different foreign languages. Yet, even though they were vaster in size and variety, the migrations of the nineteenth and twentieth centuries were in certain ways like those of the seventeenth and eighteenth centuries. They involved ordinary people who left the ancestral hearth for a strange land in the hope of making a fresh start for themselves and their children. ■

1. A Numerical Overview[1]
♣ *Statistical Abstract*

In 1820 the Federal government began to count the number of immigrants annually admitted to the United States. Thanks to that practice, we have an accurate record of the volume of immigration over the past 152 years. By 1971 the total passed the 45-million mark. In the following table, prepared from official sources, there is a breakdown by continent and country

---

[1] *Statistical Abstract of the United States*, 1972 (Washington, D.C., Superintendent of Documents, United States Government Printing Office), page 92.

A Numerical Overview

of America's world-wide sources of immigration. The first column of figures records the volume by number, and the second by percentage. Together they give us a statistical overview of the size, the variety, and the relative proportions of the migrations that have peopled America in this and the last century. ■

IMMIGRANTS, BY COUNTRY OF LAST PERMANENT RESIDENCE, 1820–1971

Country	Total (152 yrs.)	Per Cent
All countries	45,533,116	100.0
Europe	35,630,398	78.2
Austria / Hungary	4,304,302	9.4
Belgium	198,738	0.4
Czechoslovakia	133,285	0.3
Denmark	361,095	0.8
Finland	31,544	0.1
France	733,009	1.6
Germany	6,925,736	15.2
Great Britain	4,804,520	10.5
Greece	588,160	1.3
Ireland	4,715,041	10.3
Italy	5,199,304	11.4
Netherlands	352,594	0.8
Norway	853,783	1.9
Poland	487,778	1.1
Portugal	369,665	0.8
Spain	229,235	0.5
Sweden	1,267,574	2.8
Switzerland	343,421	0.8
U.S.S.R. (Europe and Asia)	3,347,118	7.4
Yugoslavia	90,234	0.2
Other Europe	294,262	0.6
Asia	1,782,711	3.9
China	450,900	1.0
Hong Kong	98,511	0.2
India	53,852	0.1
Japan	370,033	0.8
Korea	54,463	0.1
Philippines	145,371	0.3
Turkey	376,842	0.8
Other Asia	232,739	0.5
America	7,641,268	16.8
Argentina	71,746	0.2
Brazil	45,209	0.1
Canada	3,991,417	8.8
Colombia	56,539	0.2
Cuba	309,225	0.7
Dominican Rep.	115,835	0.3
Ecuador	51,616	0.1
Haiti	45,977	0.1
Honduras	22,870	0.1
Mexico	1,642,916	3.6
West Indies	544,688	1.2
Other America	703,230	1.5
Africa	82,317	0.2
Australia and New Zealand	101,762	0.2
Pacific Islands	23,207	0.1
All other countries	271,453	0.6

Because of boundary changes and changes in list of countries separately reported, data for certain countries are not comparable throughout.

2. Europe Watched Them Go[1]
✤ *Oscar Handlin*

It is easy enough to say that 36 million Europeans immigrated to America. It is still another thing for the human mind to grasp the immensity of that movement. Of the many writers who have told the story, none has done it as well as Professor Oscar Handlin of Harvard University, who is America's outstanding historian of immigration. The succinct and vivid account that follows is from Professor Handlin's Pulitzer-prize winning book about the peopling of America. ■

So Europe watched them go . . . well over thirty-five million of them from every part of the continent. In this common flow were gathered up people of the most diverse qualities, people whose rulers had for centuries been enemies, people who had not even known of each other's existence. Now they would share each other's future.

Irishmen

Westward from Ireland went four and a half million. On that crowded island a remorselessly rising population, avaricious absentee landlords, and English policy that discouraged the growth of industry early stimulated emigration. Until 1846 this had been largely a movement of younger sons, of ambitious farmers and artisans. In that year rot destroyed the potato crop and left the cotters[2] without the means of subsistence. Half a million died and three million more lived on only with the aid of charity. No thought then of paying rent, of holding on to the land; the evicted saw their huts pulled down and with bitter gratitude accepted from calculating poor-law officials the price of passage away from home. For decades after, till the end of the nineteenth century and beyond, these peasants continued to leave, some victims of later agricultural disasters, some sent for by relatives already across, some simply unable to continue a way of life already thoroughly disrupted.

---
[1] Copyright ©, 1951, by Oscar Handlin. From *The Uprooted* by Oscar Handlin, by permission of Atlantic–Little, Brown and Co. Pp. 35–36.
[2] [**cotters**: tenant farmers.]

Britons

Westward from Great Britain went well over four million. There enclosure[3] and displacement had begun back in the eighteenth century, although the first to move generally drifted to the factories of the expanding cities. By 1815, however, farmers and artisans in substantial numbers had emigration in mind; and after midcentury they were joined by a great mass of landless peasants, by operatives from the textile mills, by laborers from the potteries, and by miners from the coal fields. In this number were Scots, Welsh, and Englishmen, and also the sons of some Irishmen, sons whose parents had earlier moved across the Irish Sea.

Germans

From the heart of the continent, from the lands that in 1870 became the German Empire, went fully six million. First to leave were the free husbandmen[4] of the southwest, then the emancipated peasants of the north and east. With them moved, in the earlier years, artisans dislocated by the rise of industry, and later some industrial workers.

Scandinavians

From the north went two million Scandinavians. Crop failures, as in 1847 in Norway, impelled some to leave. Others found their lots made harsher by the decline in the fisheries and by the loss of the maritime market for timber. And for many more, the growth of commercial agriculture, as in Sweden, was the indication no room would remain for free peasants.

Italians

From the south went almost five million Italians. A terrible cholera epidemic in 1887 set them moving. But here, as elsewhere, the stream was fed by the deeper displacement of the peasantry.

---

[3] [enclosure: The fencing off of common land to make possible more efficient agriculture. The enclosure movement in England deprived many small farmers of traditional land rights. As a result, many hired themselves out as agricultural laborers or moved to the cities.]

[4] [husbandmen: farmers.]

From Eastern Europe, the Balkans, Asia Minor

From the east went some eight million others — Poles and Jews, Hungarians, Bohemians, Slovaks, Ukrainians, Ruthenians — as agriculture took new forms in the Austrian and Russian Empires after 1880.

And before the century was out perhaps three million more were on the way from the Balkans and Asia Minor: Greeks and Macedonians, Croatians and Albanians, Syrians and Armenians.

In all, thirty-five million for whom home had no place fled to Europe's shores and looked across the Atlantic.

3. Crossing the Atlantic by Steam[1]
✤ Michael Pupin

Many of the immigrants just described by Oscar Handlin endured the horrors of an ocean crossing similar to Gottlieb Mittelberger's in the middle of the eighteenth century. In the 1840's, however, larger ships powered by steam began to replace the smaller sailing vessels. By the end of the century the time of a transatlantic journey had dropped to a week or so. Yet traveling by steerage (the place below the deck for immigrant passengers) was so unpleasant that few persons ever forgot the experience. In the following account, a Serbian immigrant who became a famous physicist at Columbia University tells about the crossing he made in 1874 at the age of sixteen. ■

The ship sailed with a full complement of steerage passengers, mostly Germans. As we glided along the River Elbe the emigrants were all on deck, watching the land as it gradually vanished from our sight. Presently the famous German emigrant song rang through the air, and with a heavy heart I took in the words of its refrain:

---

[1] Adapted and reprinted with the permission of Charles Scribner's Sons from *From Immigrant to Inventor*, pp. 35–37, by Michael Pupin. Copyright 1922 Charles Scribner's Sons; renewal copyright 1950. Copyright 1923 Charles Scribner's Sons; renewal copyright 1951 Varvara Pupin Smith.

Oh, how hard it would be to leave the homeland shores
If the hope did not live that soon we shall see them again.
Farewell, farewell, until we see you again.

Homesickness

I did not wait for the completion of the song, but turned in, and in my bare bunk I sought to drown my sadness in a flood of tears. Idvor, with its sunny fields, vineyards, and orchards; with its grazing herds of cattle and flocks of sheep; with its beautiful church-spire and the solemn ringing of church-bells; with its merry boys and girls dancing to the tune of the Serbian bagpipes the Kolo on the village green — Idvor, with all the familiar scenes that I had ever seen there, appeared before my tearful eyes, and in the midst of them I saw my mother listening to my sister reading slowly the letter which I had sent to her from Hamburg. Every one of these scenes seemed to start a new shower of tears, which finally cleared the oppressiveness of my spiritual atmosphere. I thought that I could hear my mother say to my sister: "God bless him for his affectionate letter. May the spirit of St. Sava guide him in the land beyond the seas! I know that he will make good his promises." Sadness deserted me then and I felt strong again.

Steerage

He who has never crossed the stormy Atlantic during the month of March in the crowded steerage of an immigrant ship does not know what hardships are. . . . To stand the great hardships of a stormy sea when the rosy picture of the promised land is before your mind's eye is a severe test for any boy's nerve and physical stamina; but to face the same hardships as a . . . penniless immigrant with no cheering prospect in sight is too much for any person, unless that person is entirely devoid of every finer sensibility.

The Cold

Many a night I spent on the deck of that immigrant ship hugging the warm smoke-stack and adjusting my position so as to avoid the force of the gale and the sharpness of its icy chilliness. All I had was the light suit of clothes which I carried on my back. Everything else I had converted into money with which to cover my transportation expenses. There was nothing left to pay for a blanket and mattress for my steerage bunk. I could not rest there during the cold nights of March without much shivering and unbearable discomfort. If it had not been for the warm smoke-stack I should have died of cold. At first I had to fight for my place there in the daytime, but when the immigrants understood that I had no warm clothing they did not disturb me any longer. I often thought of my yellow sheepskin coat and the black sheepskin cap, and understood more clearly than ever my mother's far-sightedness when she provided that coat and cap for my long journeys. A blast of the everlasting gales had carried away my hat, and a Turkish fez such as the Serbs of Bosnia wear was the only head-gear I had. It was providential that I had not succeeded in selling it in Prague.

Loneliness

Most of my fellow emigrants thought that I was a Turk and cared little about my discomforts. But, nevertheless, I felt quite brave and strong in the daytime; at night, however, when, standing alone alongside of the smoke-stack, I beheld through the howling darkness the white rims of the mountain-high waves speeding on like maddened dragons toward the tumbling ship, my heart sank low. It was my implicit trust in God and in his regard for my mother's prayers which enabled me to overcome my fear and bravely face the horrors of the angry seas.

4. They Came in Waves[1]
♣ Marcus L. Hansen

Along with its continuity, immigration flowed heaviest first from one region of the world, then from another. The heaviest flow, as you can see at a glance from the opening selection of this section, originated in Europe. But that old continent consisted of many different countries, and each country followed its own

[1] Reprinted by permission of the publishers from Marcus L. Hansen, *The Atlantic Migration, 1607–1860: A History of the Continuing Settlement of the United States* (Cambridge, Mass.: The Belknap Press of Harvard University Press, Copyright 1940 by the President and Fellows of Harvard College), pp. 8–11, 16–17.

immigration timetable. That is the point of the selection below. Written by Marcus L. Hansen, the father of immigration history, it describes the three major waves of migration that rolled across Europe to America in the century between 1815 and 1914. ■

Though the thirteen American colonies owed their growth and prosperity largely to the recurrent additions of population from Europe, the century from 1815 to 1914 marked the most significant period in the foreign peopling of the United States. The years from the fall of Napoleon to the outbreak of the World War spanned exactly one hundred seasons of migration in which a great flood of humanity rolled westward across the Atlantic and swept over the waiting continent. To that flood every nation, every province, almost every neighborhood, contributed its stream. . . .

Quite as marked as its universality was the periodicity of the movement. It advanced in a series of waves, each greater than the preceding. After a period of flow there followed an interval during which the current hesitated or seemed to reverse itself, only to be followed by a sudden rush of even greater volume. For an understanding of the underlying factors the ebb is no less important than the flow. The source of each gives the significant clue to a solution of the puzzling problem of cause.

The 1830–1860 Wave

Three distinct stages of migration marked the nineteenth century. The first . . . began in the 1830's and continued until 1860, reaching its crest in the years 1847–1854. To this exodus the adjective "Celtic" may properly be applied. The emigrants came from Ireland, the Highlands of Scotland and the mountains of Wales — regions where the language and blood were predominantly Celtic and where the land system grew directly out of the agrarian customs of the early tribes. Though many came also from the upper Rhine Valley of Germany and the adjoining districts, these newcomers may in a sense also be regarded as Celtic, for the first peoples to cultivate their hills and valleys had been Celts and, when the conquering German tribes occupied the villages and fields, they took over the divisions and the customs which in primitive times formed such an important feature of the agricultural routine. As elsewhere, the centuries had wrought changes; but the transformed rural economy had more in common with the prevailing system in Ireland than it did with the conditions in the purely German lands to the east. The Belgian and Dutch farmers who sought America also had inherited an economic organization descended from the Celts, and even the Norwegian pioneers of the time came from the districts along the coast to which the Celts had clung long after being expelled from the Continent as a whole.

The 1860–1890 Wave

The next great period of migration covered the decades between 1860 and 1890. Now Englishmen predominated numerically — yeoman farmers and their sons, and agricultural laborers — but the biggest Scandinavian emigration of all time took place within these years, and Germany was represented by Prussians and Saxons, and Austria by Bohemians. As before, the diverse national groups possessed a common denominator, and again that denominator was the system by which land was held. Its origin was Germanic, for the emigrants came from regions where the early Teutonic tribes had fixed the customs that governed agricultural practice and land succession. These Germanic regions stand out on the map with distinct prominence: England from north of the Thames to the Scotch Highlands, Germany east of the Elbe, Austria west of the mountain range that divides its territories, the plains of Denmark and southern Sweden, and the interior valleys of Norway. This exodus was Teutonic in blood, in institutions, and in the basis of its language, forming the most homogeneous of all the migrations to America.

The 1890–1914 Wave

In the third period, that from 1890 to 1914, two distinct geographic regions mingled their diverse currents in the New World. One was Mediterranean in origin, the other Slavic. The latter possessed the same unifying element of land as had the Celtic and Germanic newcomers. Finns, Latvians, Lithuanians, Poles, Karelians and Ukrainians — most of them were subjects of the Russian Empire and all of them enjoyed a common agricultural inheritance. But the Mediterranean peoples present a more complex spectacle, one impossible to simplify. Too many civilizations and cultures had flourished one after the other, too many populations had been swept away by wars and

NINETEENTH CENTURY ARRIVALS: The stream of immigrants to America swelled into a mass movement in the 1800's. The Europeans in the photograph above crossed the Atlantic in the steerage of the S.S. Pennland in 1893. Below, newcomers from many lands mingled as they landed at New York City. Posters advertising western land (above, right) drew some immigrants to take up farming on the plains, while others settled in the eastern cities.

pestilence, to leave intact and distinct the original agrarian unity that may once have existed in Italy and Greece and the countries of the Near East. Commerce and politics remained as binding threads.

Each Wave Had a Peak

The magnitude of this century-long movement, involving the transplantation of thirty-five million people, becomes even more impressive when viewed at the moments of greatest intensity. In the first of the three periods fully half of the migrants arrived in America between 1847 and 1854; in the second, the decade from 1880 to 1890 accounted for a similar percentage; in the third, the years 1909 to 1914 brought an equal proportion. More than seventeen millions crossed the sea in the space of these twenty-five years! This horde of human beings overshadows all other population movements in peace or war. The barbarian invasions of the late Roman Empire and the transportation of American troops in . . . World War [I] fade into numerical insignificance. . . .

Immigration, the Business Cycle, and the Westward Movement

The periodicity evident in the flow of migration over the Atlantic is reflected in the wavelike motion with which population crossed the continent to the Pacific. Among the few generalizations that can be made regarding immigration from Europe is that the periods of greatest volume corresponded with the eras of liveliest industrial activity in the United States. With a regularity which, however, does not exhibit perfect co-ordination, the westward movement was strongest at times of industrial depression. If these two circumstances are put together they illuminate the relationship between the two movements. Good business demanded labor, and Europe provided an abundant source of supply; but when the canals, railroads, factories and warehouses had been built to a point exceeding profitable returns, business came to a standstill and the workmen were discharged. Equipped with their savings, they continued the broken journey to the West, where they bought up the lands of those who had preceded them. This fluctuating inflow of Europeans and their subsequent dispersion over the continent furnish the main chapters in the history of American immigration.

5. North from Mexico[1]
✢ Carey McWilliams

Of the 45 million immigrants to reach these shores since 1820, 20 per cent came from outside Europe. The proportion is small, but the actual number — 9¼ million — is huge. America's largest city, New York, does not have quite that many people. Some countries have much less. The combined populations of Denmark and Israel today, for example, fall below the number of non-European immigrants who made their way to this country.

If you go back to the statistical table that opens this section, you'll see that the New World provided the United States with three-fourths of its non-European immigrants. Notice, too, that the two largest suppliers were Canada and Mexico. Contiguous to the United States, their nationals migrated to the United States by foot, wagon, horseback, train, bus, or car. Also because of the closeness of their native lands, Mexican and Canadian immigrants have never felt as cut off from their roots as immigrants from more distant countries. They were further special in that they arrived in largest number after Congress, in the 1920's, restricted immigration from all parts of the world except the Americas. Why such laws were enacted is the subject of Section X in Part Three. Below, in a study by a careful scholar of the movement, there is an account of migrations north from Mexico. ■

Of the various ethnic elements that make up the American population, Mexicans belong in a special category, for (1) they have a special relation to a specific region of the United States, that is, to the Southwest; (2) in significant respects their history is unlike that of European and Asiatic immigrant groups, and (3) immigration from Mexico exhibits marked differences from the familiar European pattern.

The Southwest Arc, a Homeland Reclaimed

Most Mexicans in the United States today live within an arc or fan of settlement which extends from Southern California through Arizona and New Mexico (and portions of Colorado), and includes a

[1] Carey McWilliams, *The Mexicans in America, A Students' Guide to Localized History* (New York: Teachers College Press, 1968), pp. 2, 4–7, 9, 13–15.

stretch of territory running from El Paso to Brownsville which extends inland several hundred miles north of the present border. This arc or fan of territory is essentially the same area which was first discovered and settled, after a fashion, by the Spanish. It embraces most of the area we wrested from Mexico at the time of the Mexican-American War....

It is not surprising, therefore, that Mexicans in moving "north from Mexico" have always felt that they were moving within an environment that was geographically, culturally, and historically familiar. They have not crossed an ocean to a new and wholly unfamiliar land. In the borderlands, Mexicans have always had a feeling of being close to their ancestral roots, of being very much a part of the landscape. In one sense, it would not be far-fetched to say that no Mexican is ever an immigrant in the Southwest; he is more like a native returning to his homeland. Until recent times, it was very easy for Mexicans to cross the border into the United States. The Border Patrol was not established until 1924 and there was no quota on Mexican immigration until 1965. Nor did it cost much for Mexicans to move north. Once in the Southwest, the immigrant could return to Mexico just as easily as he crossed the border into the United States....

A Special Kind of Bitterness

But there is still another reason why the Mexican belongs in a special category in our roster of immigrants. The first Mexicans to become citizens did not "acquire" their citizenship; the United States acquired them — by forceful annexation. They did not come to the United States; the United States, through a war with Mexico, simply extended its boundaries to include a large territory, about the size of present-day Mexico, in which some 75,000 Spanish-speaking were then living. Our conquest of the borderlands was less brutal than the process by which we seized Indian lands, but it was not dissimilar....

Later, when thousands of Mexican immigrants surged into the borderlands — drawn there by the Anglo-initiated economic development of the region — they encountered patterns of hostility and ill-will which dated from the period of the Mexican-American War and the embittered aftermath. And by then, too, a pattern of Anglo dominance had been established. Naturally the immigrants resented the attitudes they encountered. What Mexican could forget that the United States had acquired — on the eve of the discovery of gold in

California — the entire vast territory of the Southwest for the token payment of $15,000,000 which was stipulated in the Treaty of Guadalupe Hidalgo? Immigrants from Europe and Asia often encountered intense prejudice in this country, witness, among other groups, the Irish, the Italians, and the Japanese. But the countries from which these groups came had not been defeated in a war of conquest by the United States, hence the prejudice against them was not like the mutual hostility and resentment between Anglos and Hispanos which prevailed in the Southwest for many years after 1848.

Two Great Waves of Mexican Immigration

. . . there had been a slow but steady influx of Mexican immigrants prior to 1900. In that year, the Mexican immigrant population of Texas was estimated at 71,061, of Arizona at 14,172, of California at 8,096, and of New Mexico at 6,649. But between 1900 and 1964, 1.3 million Mexicans entered the regions in two great waves; the first from 1900 to 1920, the second from 1920 to 1930. It has been estimated that the number of Mexicans entering the United States between 1900 and 1920 was roughly the equivalent of one-tenth of the population of Mexico. . . .

The first great wave, of 224,706, crossed the border between 1910 and 1920. The next large wave, of roughly 436,733 swept north between 1920 and 1930. Still a third wave, of 293,000, was recorded in the period from 1950 to 1960. But in the 1930–1940 decade, only 27,937 immigrants crossed the border and from 1940 to 1950 the number was 54,290. There is, of course, an explanation for the relative decline registered in these decades. The 1930's marked a period of depression. It was in this period, also, that tens of thousands of dust bowl migrants, the so-called Okies and Arkies, came to Arizona and California and, to some extent, displaced the Mexicans in certain types of work. In the period from 1940 to 1950, with the demand for labor soaring, the number of Mexican "wetbacks,"[2] or illegal entrants, greatly increased, and this increase was not included in the immigration totals.

The Bracero Program

In fact, the demand for labor during World War II and the Korean War became so great that the governments of the United States and

[2][**wetback:** a Mexican laborer who enters the United States illegally, as by wading the Rio Grande.]

Mexico entered into an agreement under which Mexican labor was imported, known as the *bracero* program. The *braceros*, or imported workers, were not included in the immigration total. They were imported, under contract, to work in certain crops and returned to Mexico once the crops were harvested. Generally speaking, when the demand for labor in the Southwest has increased, the volume of Mexican immigration has increased, but in depression years immigration has tapered off and, in some years, many immigrants have returned to Mexico. For example, during the depression years welfare agencies in California deported thousands of Mexican aliens.

The Wetback Problem

The "wetback" situation requires a word of comment. There have always been wetbacks in the border states and, in some periods, very large numbers indeed. During World War II, with the dust bowl migrants being drawn into the shipyards and industrial plants, and with the Japanese-Americans being removed from the West Coast, the number of "wetbacks" zoomed. At the same time, thousands of *braceros* were imported (the first contingent arrived in Stockton, California, in September, 1942).

The demand for labor was so great that the wetback situation soon got out of control; the Border Patrol was not in a position to stop the influx even if it had wanted to stop it. For every Mexican legally imported under the *bracero* program, at least four alien Mexicans or "wetbacks" were apprehended by the Border Patrol. Of the 875,000 apprehended in 1953, thousands were found to hold non-agricultural jobs. In fact, the wetback influx had such a demoralizing effect on wages and labor standards, and drained off so much purchasing power from local communities in the form of remittances sent to relatives in Mexico, that a determined effort was finally made to stop it. In 1953, the number of wetbacks rose to 1,035,282, but the next year the Border Patrol reported that the influx had been greatly reduced. Since then the border has been under fairly tight control. The *bracero* program continued, in one form or another, until it was permitted to lapse in December, 1964. The number of workers imported under this program varied from year to year; 447,000 were imported in 1959, only 183,000 in 1964. The wetback problem, so troublesome and complex, is merely one of numerous aspects of Mexican immigration not to be found in the pattern of European immigration.

A Late and Continuing Saga in Immigration

The years of heaviest Mexican immigration occurred *after* the peak of European immigration. Mexican immigration, in a word, has been a late chapter in the saga of immigration. The first restrictive immigration acts in the 1920's made an exception for immigration from the Western Hemisphere, so that Mexican immigration continued long after European immigration had, for all practical purposes, ceased to be important. Legislation adopted in 1965 for the first time fixed a quota of 120,000 per year for Mexican immigration. Mexican immigration, of course, continues. In 1965 it was estimated that in five of the eleven years since 1954, permanent visas issued to immigrants born in Mexico exceeded the number of immigrants from any other country. In the fiscal year ending June 30, 1965, 55,253 immigrants born in Mexico entered the United States under permanent immigrant visas. There is also a high and steadily mounting movement of peoples back and forth across the border; more Mexicans visit the United States, more Americans visit Mexico. And since the Southwest is still expanding, it is reasonable to assume that Mexican immigration, in substantial volume, will continue for a long time.

6. Gift of the Black Tropics[1]
✤ W. O. Domingo

> *The overwhelming majority of black Americans today are the descendants of southern slaves. But not all are. In the century since Congress in 1870 changed the naturalization law to include "persons of African descent," the United States has admitted several hundred thousand immigrant Negroes. Like other newcomers from the Americas, they began to arrive in significant numbers after World War I. Most of them settled in New York City. Below, in an article written in the mid-1920's by an intellectual from the British West Indies, there is a survey of Harlem's varied and growing foreign-born population.* ■

Within Harlem's seventy or eighty blocks, for the first time in their lives, colored people of Spanish, French, Dutch, Arabian,

[1] W. O. Domingo, "The Tropics in New York," *Survey Graphic*, No. LIII (March 1, 1925), pp. 648–650.

Danish, Portuguese, British and native African ancestry or nationality meet and move together.

Black Harlem: A Fifth Foreign-Born

A dusky tribe of destiny seekers, these brown and black and yellow folk, eyes filled with visions of their heritage — palm fringed sea shores, murmuring streams, luxuriant hills and vales — have made their epical march from the far corners of the earth to Harlem. They bring with them vestiges of their folk life — their lean, sunburnt faces, their quiet, halting speech, fortified by a graceful insouciance,[2] their light, loose-fitting clothes of ancient cut telling the story of a dogged, romantic pilgrimage to the El Dorado of their dreams.

Here they have their first contact with each other, with large numbers of American Negroes, and with the American brand of race prejudice. Divided by tradition, culture, historical background and group perspective, these diverse peoples are gradually hammered into a loose unit by the impersonal force of congested residential segregation. Unlike others of the foreign-born, black immigrants find it impossible to segregate themselves into colonies; too dark of complexion to pose as Cubans or some other Negroid but alien-tongued foreigners, they are inevitably swallowed up in black Harlem. Their situation requires an adjustment unlike that of any other class of the immigrant population; and but for the assistance of their kinsfolk they would be capsized almost on the very shores of their haven.

According to the census for 1920 there were in the United States 73,803 foreign-born Negroes; of that number 36,613, or approximately 50 per cent lived in New York City, 28,184 of them in the Borough of Manhattan. They formed slightly less than 20 per cent of the total Negro population of New York. . . . These people are, therefore, a formidable minority whose presence cannot be ignored or discounted. It is this large body of foreign born who contribute those qualities that make New York so unlike Pittsburgh, Washington, Chicago and other cities with large aggregations of American Negroes.

English-, Spanish-, French-, African-speaking

The largest number came from the British West Indies and were attracted to New York by purely economic reasons. The next largest group consists of Spanish-speaking Negroes from Latin America. Dis-

[2] [**insouciance**: the quality of being free from concern; carefree.]

tinct because of their language, and sufficiently numerous to maintain themselves as a cultural unit, the Spanish element has but little contact with the English speaking majority. For the most part they keep to themselves and follow in the main certain definite occupational lines. A smaller group, French-speaking, have emigrated from Haiti and the French West Indies. There are also a few Africans, a batch of voluntary pilgrims over the old track of the slave-traders.

Virgin Islanders

Among the English-speaking West Indian population of Harlem are some 8,000 natives of the American Virgin Islands. A considerable part of these people were forced to migrate to the mainland as a consequence of the operation of the Volstead Act which destroyed the lucrative rum industry and helped to reduce the number of foreign vessels that used to call at the former free port of Charlotte Amalie for various stores. Despite their long Danish connection these people are culturally and linguistically English, rather than Danish. Unlike the British Negroes in New York, the Virgin Islanders take an intelligent and aggressive interest in the affairs of their former home and are organized to cooperate with their brothers there who are valiantly struggling to substitute civil government for the present naval administration of the islands.

British West Indians

To the average American Negro all English-speaking black foreigners are West Indians, and by that is usually meant British subjects. There is a general assumption that there is everything in common among West Indians, though nothing can be further from the truth. West Indians regard themselves as Antiguans or Jamaicans as the case might be, and a glance at the map will quickly reveal the physical obstacles that militate against homogeneity of population; separations of many sorts, geographical, political and cultural tend everywhere to make and crystallize local characteristics. . . .

West Indians have been coming to the United States for over a century. The part they have played in Negro progress is conceded to be important. As early as 1827 a Jamaican, John Brown Russwurm, one of the founders of Liberia, was the first colored man to be graduated from an American college and to publish a newspaper in this country; sixteen years later his fellow countryman, Peter Ogden, organized in New York City the first Odd-Fellows Lodge for Negroes.

Prior to the Civil War, West Indian contribution to American Negro life was so great that Dr. W. E. B. DuBois, in his *Souls of Black Folk*, credits them with main responsibility for the manhood program presented by the race in the early decades of the last century. Indicative of their tendency to blaze new paths is the achievement of John W. A. Shaw of Antigua who, in the early 90's of the last century, passed the civil service tests and became deputy commissioner of taxes for the County of Queens.

It is probably not realized, indeed, to what extent West Indian Negroes have contributed to the wealth, power and prestige of the United States. Major-General Goethals, chief engineer and builder of the Panama Canal, has testified in glowing language to the fact that when all other labor was tried and failed it was the black men of the Caribbean whose intelligence, skill, muscle and endurance made the union of the Pacific and the Atlantic a reality.

A Leaven in American Life

Coming to the United States from countries in which they had experienced no legalized social or occupational disabilities, West Indians very naturally have found it difficult to adapt themselves to the tasks that are, by custom, reserved for Negroes in the North. Skilled at various trades and having a contempt for body service and menial work, many of the immigrants apply for positions that the average American Negro has been schooled to regard as restricted to white men only with the result that through their persistence and doggedness in fighting white labor, West Indians have in many cases been pioneers and shock troops to open a way for Negroes into new fields of employment. . . .

In facing the problem of race prejudice, foreign born Negroes, and West Indians in particular, are forced to undergo considerable adjustment. Forming a racial majority in their own countries and not being accustomed to discrimination, expressly felt as racial, they rebel against the "color line" as they find it in America. For while color and caste lines tend to converge in the islands, it is nevertheless true that because of the ratio of population, historical background and traditions of rebellions before and since their emancipation, West Indians of color do not have their activities, social, occupational and otherwise, determined by their race. Color plays a part but it is not the prime determinant of advancement; hence, the deep feeling of resentment when the "color line," legal or customary, is met and found to be a barrier to individual progress. For this reason the West Indian has thrown himself whole-heartedly into the fight against lynching, discrimination and the other disabilities from which Negroes in America suffer....

The outstanding contribution of West Indians to American Negro life is the insistent assertion of their manhood in an environment that demands too much servility and unprotesting acquiescence from men of African blood. This unwillingness to conform and be standardized, to accept tamely an inferior status and abdicate their humanity, finds an open expression in the activities of the foreign-born Negro....

Their dominant characteristic is that of blazing new paths, breaking the bonds that would fetter the feet of a virile people — a spirit ... expressed in the defiant lines of Jamaican poet, Claude McKay:

> Like men we'll face the murderous, cowardly pack,
> Pressed to the wall, dying, but fighting back.

7. Why They Came

One of the most stubborn problems in history is the problem of causation. Why do people do the things that they do? The complexity of human beings makes it terribly hard to answer that question. Our problem is further compounded by the fact that we are trying to understand the behavior of tens of millions of people. Why did the immigrants leave their homelands? And why did they come to America? The two questions are of course related. For the sake of analysis, however, it is best to examine them separately. ■

A. A TRINITY OF FORCES[1]

✦ *John F. Kennedy*

At some point in his life a man might decide that he no longer cared to live in the country where he had been born. The reasons

[1] John F. Kennedy, *A Nation of Immigrants* (New York: Anti-Defamation League of B'nai B'rith, 1959), pp. 7–10. Copyright © 1964 by Anti-Defamation League of B'nai B'rith. (A revised and enlarged edition of *A Nation of Immigrants* was published in 1964 by Harper & Row.)

for coming to that decision varied, of course, from one person to another. Yet certain causes of dissatisfaction affected large numbers of people. That is the central point of the following selection. It was written by the first Catholic President of the United States, whose great-grandfather, Patrick Kennedy, immigrated to Boston from famine-stricken Ireland in 1850. ■

It is almost impossible for Americans today to comprehend the power of the forces that moved our forebears to leave their old life and start a new one. Try to understand what would be necessary to cause you to leave America and go to Italy to live. Your family and friends live in America and you have lived here all of your life. What force could be strong enough to cause you to give up this life and move thousands of miles to a land where life is different, where you do not speak the language, where you have no friends?

Historian Oscar Handlin, in his book *The Uprooted*, describes this sensation in this way: "The crossing immediately subjected the emigrant to a succession of shattering shocks and decisively conditioned the life of every man that survived it. This was the initial contact with life as it was to be. For many peasants it was the first time away from home, away from the safety of the circumscribed little villages in which they had passed all their years. Now they would learn to have dealings with people essentially different from themselves. Now they would collide with unaccustomed problems, learn to understand alien ways and alien languages, manage to survive in a grossly foreign environment."[2]

In truth, we can never recapture this sensation. Even one who has never left his home town "knows" the world through his schooling or, failing that, through the newspapers, radio, television, and the movies. The innocence, and consequently the shock, of the European peasant or craftsman encountering his first experiences in the outside world can never be fully duplicated by an American in the middle of the twentieth century.

Yet, the exercising of imagination may give some idea of the power of the reasons that drove forty million people from their old lives and the power of the attractions that drew them to America.

There were probably as many reasons for coming to America as

[2] Copyright ©, 1951, by Oscar Handlin. From *The Uprooted* by Oscar Handlin, by permission of Atlantic–Little, Brown and Co. P. 38.

there were people who came — every man sees his own lot and his own prospects as just a little different from that of his neighbor. There were some things that these people had in common, however, and these were more important than their differences.

Religious Persecution

Starting with the first settlers of America, there has been a steady flow of people who [have] come to the New World to escape religious persecution and to practice their own creed without interference. It has always been a central theme in American immigration from the days of the Puritans to the twentieth century. In the 1880's czarist Russia embarked on a policy of Russian nationalism. Jews were persecuted and forced to emigrate. In more recent years the anti-Semitism and anti-Catholicism of Hitler's Germany and Stalin's Russia — and religious persecution under Communist regimes in eastern Europe — drove many people to leave their homes and flee to America.

It would be false to say that all of these people were met in a spirit of tolerance and understanding. Only blindness to the facts or self-delusion could lead us to overlook the religious intolerance that has characterized some periods of American history starting with some of the Puritans of Massachusetts Bay. When that is said, however, the fact still remains that America has shown the greatest amount of religious tolerance and the highest degree of religious freedom of any nation in the modern world. That is the important fact and it is due in very large measure to the variety of religious denominations brought to this country and to the insistence of each succeeding group that it had a *right* to practice its religion as it saw fit. It is no accident that freedom of religion has always been a central part of the American creed. People who crossed oceans for the right to believe in their own God were not lightly going to surrender that right in their new life.

Political Tyranny

Not only has America been a haven for victims of religious persecution, from Puritan Englishmen to Russian Jews; it has attracted also the victims of political tyranny. The violent upheavals in Europe in the middle of the nineteenth century set off a wave of migration. These were not the first political refugees to come to America, nor were they the last. The Russian Revolution, the terrors of Hitler's Germany, and most recently the Russian plunder of Hungary all brought new thousands seeking the freedom of the New World.

Economic Restrictions

The first two parts of the great trinity of forces that mold history are religion and politics. The third part is economics. America was, for millions, the land of economic opportunity. For some, this meant the chance to get rich quick; for most it meant a chance to earn a better living for themselves and their families.

The economic motive was perhaps even more complex than the other two. Some were no doubt led to this country by wild stories of fabulous riches. But more were driven by the economic hardships of their native lands. Disasters like the Irish potato famine of 1846 drove millions to America. The Irish famine brought almost three-quarters of a million in five years. Still others were brought to America on the promise of jobs in growing American industries. The demands of an expanding economy for labor seemed insatiable and it was common for a manufacturer or a railroad builder to advertise in European newspapers and offer to pay the passage of any man willing to come to America.

These, then, were the major forces that triggered this explosive migration. They affected different people in different ways and there was some of each of these factors in the motivation of almost every immigrant. Only one thing is certain — every immigrant served to reinforce and strengthen those elements in American society that had attracted him in the first place. The motives of some were commonplace — the motives of others were noble. Taken together they add up to the strengths and weaknesses of America.

B. THE LURE OF AMERICA[3]

✣ Emma Lazarus

Once a man decided to move, he might go to another part of his native country. Quite a few did that. There was also the alternative of immigrating to Canada, Australia, New Zealand, South America, Africa, or some other place. People did that, too. But the greatest number of immigrants chose the United States. They came because of this country's reputation as an asylum or refuge. The most striking symbol of that reputation is the Statue of Liberty on Liberty Island (formerly Bedloe's Island) in New York City's harbor. A gift from the French people to the United States, it was unveiled in 1886. On the pedestal of the statue is inscribed the sonnet which appears below. It was written by Emma Lazarus, a poet who was descended from an old Jewish family in America. ■

THE NEW COLOSSUS

Not like the brazen giant of Greek fame,
With conquering limbs astride from land to land;
Here at our sea-washed, sunset gates shall stand
A mighty woman with a torch, whose flame
Is the imprisoned lightning, and her name
Mother of Exiles. From her beacon-hand
Glows world-wide welcome; her mild eyes command
The air-bridged harbor that twin cities frame.

"Keep, ancient lands, your storied pomp!" cries she
With silent lips. "Give me your tired, your poor,
Your huddled masses yearning to breathe free,
The wretched refuse of your teeming shore.
Send these, the homeless, tempest-tossed to me.
I lift my lamp beside the golden door!"

---

[3] "The New Colossus" (1883), from *The Poems of Emma Lazarus* (Boston: Houghton Mifflin Company, 1889, 2 vols.), Vol. I, pp. 202–203.

III. Some Personal Testimonies

Historians and statisticians are indispensable for providing the overall picture of the mass migrations that made America. But to appreciate the personal dimensions of the story, we have to read what the immigrants themselves wrote. The libraries are full of such accounts but we have space to reprint only a few of them. Altogether, though, they suggest the range of motives that led people to America. ■

1. A German Revolutionist[1]
✣ Carl Schurz

From the English civil wars of the seventeenth century to the Communist suppressions of the twentieth, immigrants have come to America for political reasons. The big European political upheavals of the nineteenth century were the revolutions of 1848. Their goals — personal liberty, representative government, and national unity — had been the goals of the American Revolution. The uprisings of 1848 failed, and many leaders had to flee. One of them, Carl Schurz of Germany, escaped to England, where he laid plans for a second round. But late in 1851 Schurz decided to give up those plans and go to America. In this country he distinguished himself as a journalist, reformer, minister to Spain, Civil War general, senator, and Cabinet officer in President Hayes' administration. In the following selection Schurz tells how events in France led him to make his decision to leave Europe. ■

The reports which we had received from our friends in Paris made us believe that Louis Napoleon, the president of the French republic,

[1] *The Reminiscences of Carl Schurz* (New York: The McClure Company, 1907, 3 vols.), Vol. I, pp. 398–402, 406.

was an object of general contempt, that he played a really ridiculous figure with his manifest ambition to restore the empire in France and to mount the throne, and that every attempt to accomplish this by force would inevitably result in his downfall and in the institution of a strong and truly republican government. . . . Suddenly, on the 2d of December, 1851, the news arrived in London that Louis Napoleon had actually undertaken the long-expected *coup d'etat*.[2] . . .

Insurrection in France

Exciting reports arrived in rapid succession. Members of the national assembly had met in considerable numbers and tried to organize resistance to the *coup d'etat*, but were soon dispersed by military force. At last the news came that the people, too, were beginning to "descend into the streets" and to build barricades. Now the decisive battle was to be fought.

Early Reports of Victory

It is impossible to describe the state of mind produced among the exiles by these reports. We Germans ran to the meeting-places of the French clubs, because we expected to receive there the clearest and most reliable tidings, perhaps from sources which might not be open to the general public. In these clubs we found a feverish excitement bordering upon madness. Our French friends shouted and shrieked and gesticulated and hurled opprobrious names at Louis Napoleon. . . . All were sure of a victory of the people. The most glorious bulletins of the progress of the street fight went from mouth to mouth. Some of them were proclaimed by wild-looking revolutionary exiles, who had jumped upon tables, and frantic screams of applause welcomed them. So it went on a night, a day and again a night. Sleep was out of the question. There was hardly time for the necessary meals.

The Insurrection Crushed

The reports of victory were followed by others that sounded less favorable. They could not and would not be believed. They were

[2] [Louis Napoleon, the nephew of Napoleon I, had been elected president of the Second French Republic in 1848. In the *coup d'etat* referred to here, he declared an extension of his presidency and imposed military rule. A year later he took the title of Emperor Napoleon III.]

"the dispatches of the usurper and his slaves"; "they lied"; . . . but the messages continued more and more gloomy. The barricades which the people had erected . . . had been taken by the army without much trouble. On the 4th a serious battle occurred on the streets of the Faubourgs St. Martin and St. Denis, but there, too, the troops had remained masters of the field. Then the soldiery rushed into the houses and murdered without discrimination or compassion. At last there was the quiet of the graveyard in the great city.

The popular rising had been comparatively insignificant and powerless. . . . There was no doubt the republic was at an end, and with its downfall vanished also the prospect of the new revolutionary upheaval, which, on the impulse coming from France, was expected to spread over the whole European continent.

Farewell to Revolution

Stunned by all these terrible reports, and mentally as well as physically exhausted, we quietly returned to our quarters. After I had recuperated from this consuming excitement by a long sleep, I tried to become clear in my mind about the changed situation of things. It was a foggy day, and I went out because I found it impossible to sit still within my four walls. Absorbed in thought, I wandered on without any definite aim, and found myself at last in Hyde Park, where, in spite of the chilly air, I sat down on a bench. In whatever light I might consider the downfall of the republic and the advent of a new monarchy in France, one thing seemed to me certain: All the efforts connected with the revolution of 1848 were now hopeless; a period of decided and general reaction was bound to come, and whatever the future might bring of further developments in the direction of liberal movement must necessarily have a new starting-point.

To America!

With this conviction my own situation became equally clear to me. It would have been childish to give myself up to further illusory hopes of a speedy return to the Fatherland. To continue our plottings and thereby bring still more mischief upon others, appeared to me a reckless and wicked game. I had long recognized the exile's life to be empty and enervating. I felt an irresistible impulse not only to find for myself a well-regulated activity, but also to do something really and truly valuable for the general good. But where, and how? The fatherland was closed to me. England was to me a foreign country, and would always remain so. Where, then? "To America," I said to myself. "The ideals of which I have dreamed and for which I have fought I shall find there, if not fully realized, but hopefully struggling for full realization. In that struggle I shall perhaps be able to take some part. It is a new world, a free world, a world of great ideas and aims. In that world there is perhaps for me a new home." *Ubi libertas ibi patria*[3] — I formed my resolution on the spot. I would remain only a short time longer in England to make some necessary preparations, and then — off to America!

... I went my way home to inform my parents at once, by letter, of the resolution I had taken on that bench in Hyde Park. Some of my fellow-exiles tried to dissuade me from it, picturing to me all sorts of wonderful things which would happen very soon on the European continent and in which we refugees must take an active part; but I had seen too thoroughly through the unreality of these fantastic imaginings to be shaken in my resolve. . . .

My young wife and myself sailed from Portsmouth in August, 1852, and landed in the harbor of New York on a bright September morning. With the buoyant hopefulness of young hearts, we saluted the new world.

[3] ["Where there is liberty, there is my home."]

2. A Scottish Weaver's Son[1]
✦ Andrew Carnegie

At about the same time that nineteenth-century Europe was undergoing political upheaval, mechanical inventions were transforming the economy. In manufacturing, for example, the introduction of the steam engine made the skills of artisans obsolete in many trades. Since Great Britain was the first to experience this industrial revolution, many skilled British workers came to America in the nineteenth century. Andrew Carnegie's father, a Scottish weaver, was one of them. Below, in a selection from his autobiography, Carnegie tells why his family left their home for the New World. Carnegie was to make his mark in America as a steel industrialist and philanthropist. ■

[1] *Autobiography of Andrew Carnegie* (Boston: Houghton Mifflin Company, 1920), pp. 2, 8–13, 25.

To begin, then, I was born in Dunfermline . . . on the 25th of November, 1835, and, as the saying is, "of poor but honest parents, of good kith and kin." Dunfermline had long been noted as the center of the damask trade in Scotland. My father, William Carnegie, was a damask weaver. . . .

His Father Succeeds

As my father succeeded in the weaving business we [moved] . . . to a much more commodious house. . . . My father's four or five looms occupied the lower story; we resided in the upper, which was reached, after a fashion common in the older Scottish houses, by outside stairs from the pavement. It is here that my earliest recollections begin, and, strangely enough, the first trace of memory takes me back to a day when I saw a small map of America. It was upon rollers and about two feet square. Upon this my father, mother, Uncle William, and Aunt Aitken were looking for Pittsburgh and pointing out Lake Erie and Niagara. Soon after my uncle and Aunt Aiken sailed for the land of promise. . . .

Radical Dunfermline

The denunciations of monarchical and aristocratic government, of privilege in all its forms, the grandeur of the republican system, the superiority of America, a land peopled by our own race, a home for freemen in which every citizen's privilege was every man's right — these were the exciting themes upon which I was nurtured. As a child I could have slain king, duke, or lord, and considered their deaths a service to the state and hence an heroic act. . . .

Dunfermline has long been renowned as perhaps the most radical town in the Kingdom, although I know Paisley has claims. This is all the more creditable to the cause of radicalism because in the days of which I speak the population of Dunfermline was in large part composed of men who were small manufacturers, each owning his own loom or looms. They were not tied down to regular hours, their labors being piece work.[2] They got webs[3] from the larger manufacturers and the weaving was done at home. . . .

---

[2] [**piece work:** work paid for at a certain rate per unit.]
[3] [**webs:** skeins of fibers to be woven into cloth.]

A Disastrous Innovation

The change from hand-loom to steam-loom weaving was disastrous to our family. My father did not recognize the impending revolution, and was struggling under the old system. His looms sank greatly in value, and it became necessary for that power which never failed in any emergency — my mother — to step forward and endeavor to repair the family fortune. She opened a small shop in Moodie Street and contributed to the revenues which, though slender, nevertheless at that time sufficed to keep us in comfort and "respectable."

I remember that shortly after this I began to learn what poverty meant. Dreadful days came when my father took the last of his webs to the great manufacturer, and I saw my mother anxiously awaiting his return to know whether a new web was to be obtained or that a period of idleness was upon us. It was burnt into my heart then that my father, though neither "abject, mean, nor vile," as Burns has it, had nevertheless to

> "Beg a brother of the earth
> To give him leave to toil."

And then and there came the resolve that I would cure that when I got to be a man. We were not, however, reduced to anything like poverty compared with many of our neighbors. I do not know to what lengths of privation my mother would not have gone that she might see her two boys wearing large white collars, and trimly dressed....

Forced to Leave

With the introduction and improvement of steam machinery, trade grew worse and worse in Dunfermline for the small manufacturers, and at last a letter was written to my mother's two sisters in Pittsburgh stating that the idea of our going to them was seriously entertained — not, as I remember hearing my parents say, to benefit their own condition, but for the sake of their two young sons. Satisfactory letters were received in reply. The decision was taken to sell the looms and furniture by auction. And my father's sweet voice sang often to mother, brother, and me:

> "To the West, to the West, to the land of the free,
> Where the mighty Missouri rolls down to the sea;

Where a man is a man even though he must toil
And the poorest may gather the fruits of the soil."

The proceeds of the sale were most disappointing. The looms brought hardly anything, and the result was that twenty pounds more were needed to enable the family to pay passage to America. Here let me record an act of friendship performed by a lifelong companion of my mother — who always attracted stanch friends because she was so stanch herself — Mrs. Henderson, by birth Ella Ferguson, the name by which she was known in our family. She boldly ventured to advance the needful twenty pounds, my Uncles Lauder and Morrison guaranteeing repayment. Uncle Lauder also lent his aid and advice, managing all the details for us, and on the 17th day of May, 1848, we left Dunfermline. My father's age was then forty-three, my mother's thirty-three. I was in my thirteenth year, my brother Tom in his fifth year. . . .

3. A Swedish Soldier[1]
✛ Hans Mattson

Military rank in Europe depended not on merit but on social class. This system was frustrating to lower-class young men of ability who wanted to be professional soldiers. It was for this reason that Hans Mattson, the teen-aged son of a Swedish farmer, made up his mind to go to America, as he tells us in the following account. This was about the same time that Carnegie and Schurz immigrated. During the Civil War, when he was a resident of Minnesota, Mattson rose to the rank of colonel in the Union army. ∎

When I was sixteen years old, an event took place which had a decisive influence on my whole life. . . .

Army Cadet

The first Danish-German war broke out about this time [1848], and

[1] Hans Mattson, *Reminiscences: The Story of an Emigrant* (St. Paul: D. D. Merrill Company, 1891), pp. 11–13.

I, with many other youths, felt a hearty sympathy for the Danes. The Swedish government resolved to send troops to help their neighbors, and a few regiments marching through our city fanned our youthful enthusiasm into flame. Finally, a detachment of the artillery, quartered in the city, was ordered to leave for the seat of war, and now I could no longer restrain myself, but besieged my parents to let me join that part of the army which was going to the battlefield, and to clinch the argument I was cruel enough to send word to my distressed mother that if she would not consent I would run away from home and join the army anyway. This last argument made her yield, and in the fall of 1849 I became an artillery cadet, being then in my seventeenth year.

But although I won this victory over my mother, whose greatest desire was that I should become a clergyman, she in turn gained a victory over me by persuading the surgeon of the battalion, who was also our family physician, to declare me sick and send me to the hospital, although I had only a slight cold; thus my plan to go with the army to Schleswig-Holstein was frustrated. This did not make much difference, however, as the war was virtually closed before our troops arrived at the place of destination, and my time could now be more profitably employed in learning the duties of a soldier, and in taking a course of mathematics and other practical branches at the regimental school.

I remained in the army a year and a half, during which time I received excellent instruction in gymnastics, fencing and riding, besides the regular military drill. Two winters were thus devoted to conscientious and thorough work at the military school.

No Chance for Advancement

Knowing that the chances for advancement in the Swedish army during times of peace were at this time very slim for young men not favored with titles of nobility, and being also tired of the monotonous garrison life, my friend Eustrom and myself soon resolved to leave the service and try our luck in a country where inherited names and titles were not the necessary conditions of success.

Emigration

At that time America was little known in our part of the country, only a few persons having emigrated from the whole district. But we knew that it was a new country, inhabited by a free and independent people, that it had a liberal government and great natural resources, and these inducements were sufficient for us. My parents readily consented to my emigration, and, having made the necessary preparations, my father took my friend Eustrom and myself down to the coast with his own horses, in the first part of May, 1851. It was a memorable evening, and I shall never forget the last farewell to my home, in driving out from the court into the village street, how I stood up in the wagon, turned towards the dear home and waved my hat with a hopeful hurrah to the "folks I left behind." A couple of days' journey brought us to a little seaport, where we took leave of my father and boarded a small schooner for the city of Gothenburg.

At that time there were no ocean steamers and no emigrant agents; but we soon found a sailing vessel bound for America on which we embarked as passengers, furnishing our own bedding, provisions and other necessaries, which our mothers had supplied in great abundance. About one hundred and fifty emigrants from different parts of Sweden were on board the brig *Ambrosius.* In the middle of May she weighed anchor and glided out of the harbor on her long voyage across the ocean to distant Boston.

We gazed back at the vanishing shores of the dear fatherland with feelings of affection, but did not regret the step we had taken, and our bosoms heaved with boundless hope. At the age of eighteen, the strong, healthy youth takes a bright and hopeful view of life, and so did we. Many and beautiful were the air-castles we built as we stood on deck, with our eyes turned towards the promised land of the nineteenth century. To some of these castles our lives have given reality, others are still floating before us.

4. A Daughter from Ireland[1]

✤ Anonymous

The Carnegies and the Mattsons were poor but not starving. That was not true of the immigrants who fled from the disastrous potato famine that struck Ireland between 1846 and 1851. A

[1] "The Life Story of an Irish Cook," Hamilton Holt, ed., *The Life Stories of Undistinguished Americans as Told by Themselves* (New York: James Pott & Company, 1906), pp. 143–145.

SOME PERSONAL TESTIMONIES: Many who came to America wrote vivid accounts of their lives in the new land. Three of the best were done by Mary Antin (above, left), Jewish refugee from Russia, who won renown as a writer; Carl Schurz (above, right), who fled revolution in Germany and became a successful journalist and statesman; and Andrew Carnegie (below), who left poverty in Scotland and developed an industrial empire in America.

million and a half people died in that awful calamity, and a million others emigrated. Those who came here had been the poorest of the poor in Ireland and remained in that condition for many years in America. Few of them, moreover, had had any formal education. Yet they managed to leave behind a record of their journey. The piece below, for example, is the story of an Irish-American cook whose employer, a writer, took it down in the following form. ■

I don't know why anybody wants to hear my history. Nothing ever happened to me worth the tellin' except when my mother died. Now she was an extraordinary person. The neighbors all respected her, an' the minister. "Go ask Mrs. McNabb," he'd say to the women in the neighborhood here when they come wantin' advice.

But about me — I was born nigh to Limavaddy; it's a pretty town close to Londonderry. We lived in a peat cabin, but it had a good thatched roof. Mother put on that roof. It isn't a woman's work, but she — was able for it.

John, Matthew, and Joseph

There were sivin childher [seven children] of us. John an' Matthew they went to Australia. Mother was layin' by for five year to get their passage money. They went into the bush. We heard twice from them and then no more. Not another word and that is forty year gone now — on account of them not reading and writing. Learning isn't cheap in them old countries as it is here, you see. I suppose they're dead now — John would be ninety now — and in heaven. They were honest men. My mother sent Joseph to Londonderry to larn the weaver's trade.

Field Work and Lace Work

My father he never was a steady worker. He took to the drink early in life. My mother an' me an' Tilly we worked in the field for Squire Varney. Yes, plowin' an' seedin' and diggin' — any farm work he'd give us. We did men's work, but we didn't get men's pay. No, of course not. In winter we did lace work for a merchant in Londonderry. . . . It was pleasanter . . . [than] diggin' after my hands was fit for it. But it took two weeks every year to clean and soften my hands for the needle.

A Daughter from Ireland

Famine Years, Maria Dies

Pay was very small and the twins — that was Maria and Philip — they were too young to work at all. What did we eat? Well, just potatoes. On Sundays, once a month, we'd maybe have a bit of flitch [salt pork]. When the potatoes rotted — that was the hard times. Oh, yes, I . . . [remember] the famine years. An' the cornmeal that the 'Mericans sent. The folks said they'd rather starve . . . [than] eat it. We didn't know how to cook it. Here I eat corn dodgers and fried mush fast enough.

Maria — she was one of the twins — she died the famine year of the typhus and — well, she sickened of the herbs and roots we ate — we had no potatoes.

Tilly Goes to America

Mother said when Maria died, "There's a curse on old green Ireland and we'll get out of it." So we worked an' saved for four year an' then Squire Varney helped a bit an' we sent Tilly to America. She had always more head than me. She came to Philadelphia and got a place for general housework at Mrs. Bent's. Tilly got but two dollars a week, bein' a greenhorn. But she larned hand over hand, and Mrs. Bent kept no other help and laid out to teach her. She larned her to cook and bake and to wash and do up shirts — all American fashion. Then Tilly axed three dollars a week. Mother always said, "Don't ax a penny more than you're worth. But you know your own vally [value] and ax that."

I Follow

She had no expenses and laid by money enough to bring me out before the year was gone. I sailed from Londonderry. The ship was a sailin' vessel, the "Mary Jane." The passage was $12. You brought your own eating, your tea an' meal, an' most had flitch. There was two big stoves that we cooked on. The steerage was a dirty place and we were eight weeks on the voyage — over time three weeks. The food ran scarce, I tell you, but the captain gave some to us, and them that had plenty was kind to the others. I've heard bad stories of things that went on in the steerage in them old times — smallpox and fevers and starvation and worse. But I saw nothing of them in my ship. The folks were decent and the captain was kind.

5. A French-Canadian Farmer[1]
✤ Jacques Ducharme

Most immigrants were farmers or peasants in their native lands. Quite a few of them, particularly in the early periods of American history, were attracted to the United States because of its abundant land. (See Section IV, selection 1.) But after the industrialization of America, which began in the mid-1800's, immigrant farmers were lured by American factories. Below, in the opening pages of an insightfully written historical novel, there is a portrait of a French-Canadian farmer who immigrated to industrial New England after the Civil War. The author, a novelist and newspaperman, was educated at Assumption College, a Franco-American institution located in Worcester, Massachusetts. The hero of his novel was modeled, in all probability, after his own immigrant father. ■

Jean Baptiste Delusson came to Holyoke, Massachusetts, in 1874. It was toward noon of a day in July, and, as he wore a suit of heavy black stuff, it seemed unbearably hot. He alighted from the train and looked about him. He expected to see Nicholas Dulhut, who had induced him to make the long journey from his farm in Saint Valérien, Québec, to this New England town. Long after the other passengers had met friends and gone, Jean Baptiste stood on the station platform and waited.

There was that about him which betrayed the countryman: the stillness of his pose, the large hands, the gaunt frame, and the face worked upon by wind and weather, making the eyes seem very deep-set. Gray eyes they were, and calm, and they looked about with curiosity. Occasionally he would remove his black straw hat and wipe his brow. Other times he would slowly pace to and fro on the platform in front of the station, a man who seemed to have ample leisure to wait.

Two-Day Train Trip from Montreal

His journey had taken him two days. He left Montreal on Tuesday, and it was now Thursday. Tho the trip was a long one to a man who

[1] Jacques Ducharme, *The Delusson Family* (New York: Funk and Wagnalls, 1939), pp. 3–6.

had never been much more than fifty miles from his farm, he had not been wearied by the incessant movement. It had rather stimulated him, and his eyes had been ever on the alert as the scenery of this new country unfolded before him. At first the train rolled along through the flat country of Québec, where the soil was like clay, and where only two hills were to be seen, that of Beloeil, and that of Rougemont. Then they came into Vermont, and the Green Mountains offered him a sense of peace and color, heightened by occasional gleams from Lake Champlain.

He knew vaguely that some years ago there had been civil war in the United States, but the region through which he was now passing had not been touched. Here was a life that he could understand, for it was a country of farms, where little happened to disturb a man's actions or thoughts. The transition into the green hills was a pleasant one for Jean Baptiste, and he felt that he had come into a promised land. Should the fair words of Dulhut be true, and work easily obtainable, then he could return to Canada for his family. In a few years' time, if God were good to them, they would have a farm amid rolling hills, instead of the gray-white house on level ground, which stood about a mile from the village, and which boasted but one shade tree.

A Recruiting Official Meets Jean Baptiste

He had been content to live in Saint Valérien, a small town within ten miles of Saint Ours, on the Rivière Noire, which flowed into the Saint Francis and eventually into the Saint Lawrence. But one day, when he came in from the fields for his noonday meal, he found a man waiting for him. This was Nicholas Dulhut.

Nicholas Dulhut was a descendant of the famous *coureur de bois*[2] of Colonial days, the Sieur de Lhut, and seemed to have inherited some of his ancestor's love of roving. A native of Saint Ours near the Saint Lawrence, he went one day to Montreal where he met a man connected with the paper industry, which was then booming. A talk with this man convinced Dulhut that in the United States there was money to be made. Without further ado Dulhut boarded a train, having written an apologetic note to his wife, promising to return. He returned two years later after his family had joined him in Holyoke.

[2] [**coureur de bois:** a French or French-Indian trapper of North America, especially of Canada.]

His journey to Canada then was for an entirely different purpose. He had been commissioned by his employers as a sort of recruiting officer, to encourage others of his countrymen to emigrate to Holyoke, where work was awaiting them and wages were good. A new word, progress, was current, and the people of that day used to take advantage of it. Dulhut began to visit Canada on an average of once a month, to convince farmers or anyone who would listen to him, that to the south, some three hundred miles away, work and money were to be had by those who would help in the harvest of wealth.

He came down to Massachusetts in 1854 for the first time, when he left Montreal so abruptly. Seventeen years later he called at Jean Baptiste's farm. He had known Jean Baptiste slightly from the day they met at a wedding, with whose principals the Dulhut and the Delusson families were distantly connected.

Their Conversation

The conversation began that noon with the usual banalities. Dulhut asked Jean Baptiste if he expected a good crop that year. There should be a sufficiency of rain, Jean Baptiste thought, which was all that was needed, as the soil was rich and had been little cultivated in this region. The two men sat on the back porch, out of the hot sun, and Jean Baptiste slowly sipped a glass of water drawn from the well. Dulhut had refused refreshment. He had only stopped on his way through to Drummondville, he said, and as he pronounced the name, he did not obviously mince the word, as Canadians do when they speak English. After a while he disclosed the real purpose of his visit:

"Listen, Delusson, I have just come down from the States. I want to find men willing to work in the mills up there. The wages are good, and I will see that you get work. Do you care to come?"

Jean Baptiste did not answer immediately. He had done a long morning's work. He felt pleasantly tired, and it was good to sit down for a while and sip a glass of cool water. He was not in the mood to make a decision, nor indeed was it expected of him. Dulhut merely dropped a seed of thought which would grow, or else die, if Jean Baptiste preferred to live on as he had been living, and as his father had lived. So he waited before replying, and let his eyes follow the expanse of the fields to the horizon, where they rested, while his mind adjusted itself to the question. Then he said:

"How long have you been there, Dulhut?"

"Seventeen years."

"What is it like?"

"I am at Holyoke, which is a very large village. Some ten thousand people. It is on the Connecticut River, and there are mountains all about. It is not at all like this." He motioned with his hand, and his tone held something of distaste, as if he had come to love the new country better than the old.

Wants Better Things for His Children

Jean Baptiste noticed this tone, and the manner in which the names of the village and the river had rolled off Dulhut's tongue. This was a foreigner speaking, and no longer one of them; yet he held out to Jean Baptiste a prospect of riches. It was something that could not be ignored, for he was a married man, and had four children. Farming was a good life and a healthy one, but there was too little profit in it when one worked a new piece of land. Jean Baptiste read a great deal and through the printed page knew something of the outside world. He wanted for his children better things than he had known.

6. A Jewish Girl from Russia[1]

✣ Mary Antin

Jews have lived in America since the seventeenth century and have come here from almost every country. They arrived in largest numbers, however, from czarist Russia after the 1880's. The Russian law of that time compelled Jews to live in a western area of the country known as the Pale. It was there, in the town of Polotzk, that Mary Antin was born in 1881. Her father, first a teacher and then a storekeeper, lost his business after he and his wife got sick. Mary Antin was then ten years old. Shortly thereafter, for reasons she describes below in her moving autobiography, the Antins left for Boston. Mary Antin went on to become a well-known American writer. ■

The next year or so my father spent in a restless and fruitless search for a permanent position. My mother had another serious illness,

[1] Mary Antin, *The Promised Land* (Boston: Houghton Mifflin Company, 1912), pp. 140–141, 148–149, 162.

and his own health remained precarious. What he earned did not more than half pay the bills in the end, though we were living very humbly now. Polotzk seemed to reject him, and no other place invited him.

An Anti-Semitic Outbreak

Just at this time occurred one of the periodic anti-Semitic movements whereby government officials were wont to clear the forbidden cities of Jews, whom, in the intervals of slack administration of the law, they allowed to maintain an illegal residence in places outside the Pale, on payment of enormous bribes and at the cost of nameless risks and indignities.

It was a little before Passover that the cry of the hunted thrilled the Jewish world with the familiar fear. The wholesale expulsion of Jews from Moscow and its surrounding district at cruelly short notice was the name of this latest disaster. Where would the doom strike next? The Jews who lived illegally ... [outside] the Pale turned their possessions into cash and slept in their clothes, ready for immediate flight. Those who lived in the comparative security of the Pale trembled for their brothers and sisters without, and opened wide their doors to afford the fugitives refuge. And hundreds of fugitives, preceded by a wail of distress, flocked into the open district, bringing their trouble where trouble was never absent, mingling their tears with the tears that never dried.

The open cities becoming thus suddenly crowded, every man's chance of making a living was diminished in proportion to the number of additional competitors. Hardship, acute distress, ruin for many: thus spread the disaster, ring beyond ring, from the stone thrown by a despotic official into the ever-full river of Jewish persecution.

A New Meaning for Passover

Passover was celebrated in tears that year. In the story of the Exodus we would have read a chapter of current history, only for us there was no deliverer and no promised land.[2]

But what said some of us at the end of the long service? Not "May we be next year in Jerusalem," but "Next year — in America!" So

[2] [**Exodus:** the story of the escape of the Israelites from bondage in Egypt during the 1200's B.C. and their long migration to Palestine, the "promised land."]

there was our promised land, and many faces were turned towards the West. And if the waters of the Atlantic did not part for them, the wanderers rode its bitter flood by a miracle as great as any the rod of Moses ever wrought.[3]

My father was carried away by the westward movement, glad of his own deliverance, but sore at heart for us whom he left behind. It was the last chance for all of us. We were so far reduced in circumstances that he had to travel with borrowed money to a German port, whence he was forwarded to Boston, with a host of others, at the expense of an emigrant aid society. . . .

Preparing to Join Father

I am sure I made as serious efforts as anybody to prepare myself for life in America on the lines indicated in my father's letters. In America, he wrote, it was no disgrace to work at a trade. Workmen and capitalists were equal. . . . The cobbler and the teacher had the same title, "Mister." And all the children, boys and girls, Jews and Gentiles, went to school! Education would be ours for the asking, and economic independence also, as soon as we were prepared. He wanted Fetchke and me to be taught some trade; so my sister was apprenticed to a dressmaker and I to a milliner. . . .

But I — I had to be taken away from the milliner's after a couple of months. I did try, honestly. With all my eyes I watched my mistress build up a chimney pot of straw and things. I ripped up old bonnets with enthusiasm. I picked up everybody's spools and thimbles, and other far-rolling objects. I did just as I was told, for I was determined to become a famous milliner, since America honored the workman so. But most of the time I was sent away on errands — to the market to buy soup greens, to the corner store to get change, and all over town with bandboxes half as round again as I. It was winter, and I was not very well dressed. I froze; I coughed; my mistress said I was not of much use to her. So my mother kept me at home, and my career as a milliner was blighted.

This was during our last year in Russia, when I was between twelve and thirteen years of age. I was old enough to be ashamed of my failures, but I did not have much time to think about them, because my Uncle Solomon took me with him to Vitebsk. . . .

---

[3] [**rod of Moses:** According to the biblical account of the Exodus, the waters of the Red Sea were divided when Moses stretched out a rod. Thus, the Israelites were able to flee from Egypt.]

Summons to America

And even Vitebsk, for all its peepholes into a Beyond, presently began to shrink in my imagination, as America loomed near. My father's letters warned us to prepare for the summons, and we lived in a quiver of expectation.

Not that my father had grown suddenly rich. He was so far from rich that he was going to borrow every cent of the money for our third-class passage; but he had a business in view which he could carry on all the better for having the family with him; and, besides, we were borrowing right and left anyway, and to no definite purpose. With the children, he argued, every year in Russia was a year lost. They should be spending the precious years in school, in learning English, in becoming Americans. United in America, there were ten chances of our getting to our feet again to one chance in our scattered, aimless state.

So at last I was going to America! Really, really going, at last! The boundaries burst. The arch of heaven soared. A million suns shone out for every star. The winds rushed in from outer space, roaring in my ears, "America! America!"

7. A Jamaican Schoolboy[1]
✛ William Scott

Many immigrants chose to come to America because they regarded it as a land of educational opportunity. Parents wanted their children to have a chance to go to school, but frequently young people immigrated to the United States of their own accord for that reason. One of them, the author of the reading below, was a Negro schoolboy from Jamaica. Like the French-Canadian farmer about whom you have just read, William Scott's decision to immigrate to America was influenced by a successful immigrant from his native land. His story, which he told in an interview thirty years after his decision, is taken from the standard history of the 145,000 black immigrants who arrived in the United States between 1899 and 1937. ■

---

[1] Ira De A. Reid, *The Negro Immigrant, His Background, Characteristics and Social Adjustment, 1899–1937* (New York: Columbia University Press, 1939), pp. 182–183.

A Jamaican Schoolboy

My family was exceedingly poor so when I finished my grade school education at the age of 13 I felt it necessary that I should hunt some sort of job to help out in my maintenance. Class system, which was then and still is one of the depressing evils of the colony, dictated that unless I could secure what I have since learned to classify as a white collar job, I would have been ostracized by my associates.

When I was a youngster my aunt washed, sewed, baked, sold almost everything she could in the house to pay my fees in the private school. The full term was four years, but I could only attend two and one-half years.

Influence of an American Uncle

Just about that time an uncle, now pastoring in California, was attending one of the Negro colleges in the East. He sent me a catalog of the school and when I read of the great work of that institution and how it was possible for ambitious young men who were not afraid or ashamed to work to acquire an education there my heart was set on attending it. I wrote asking my uncle to advance my traveling expenses. He graciously sent me $80.00. My ship-fare was $60.00 and the balance, with what my aunt could scrape together, was used to outfit me for the trip.

In my village was a tailor who styled himself a "First Class American Tailor." As my mind flashes back to that period with its ultimate results I am sure my aunt took me to him largely because of the name "American Tailor" rather than because of his ability. I was a fairly tall youngster for my age and one of the customs of my people is to keep a boy in a boy's place. I was too tall for short pants, and not quite tall enough for long pants so the tailor thought he would compromise. He made me some three-quarter pants that struck me midway between the ankles and the knees. My coat was an abbreviation — just two or three inches below the waistline. To this was added a Bowler Hat, a cross between a derby and a felt hat.

This Promised Land of Opportunity

Then came October 1, 1908, and after the prayers and admonitions of taking good care of myself, being a good boy, making a man of myself, etc. — the kisses, the embraces, the farewells — my aunt placed around my neck a tape with a purse with $10.00 (a gold piece), the last of her possessions. She placed me in charge of the purser of the ship and we set sail for America at noon, October 1, 1908.

8. A Mexican Storekeeper[1]
♣ Pablo Mares

> By the middle of the 19th century, as a result of war, annexation, and purchase, the United States acquired from Mexico a huge territory now occupied by California, Arizona, New Mexico, Texas, Colorado, Utah, and Nevada. Many Mexicans were living in those areas when they passed to the United States, and today their descendants belong to the oldest families in the American Southwest. But not until the 20th century did a significant number of Mexicans immigrate to the United States. (See Section II, selection 5.) Their reasons for doing so were many. Below, a small businessman gives as his reason the disorders of the Mexican Revolution, which began in the 1910's and continued into the next decade. ■

In my youth I worked as a house servant, but as I grew older I wanted to be independent. I was able through great efforts to start a little store in my town. But I had to come to the United States, because it was impossible to live down there with so many revolutions.

A Dislike for Fighting

Once even I was at the point of being killed by some revolutionists. A group of revolutionists had just taken the town and a corporal or one of those who was in command of the soldiers went with a bunch of these to my place and began to ask me for whiskey and other liquors which I had there. But, although I had them, I told them that I didn't sell liquor, but only things to eat and a few other things, but nothing to drink. They didn't let me close the store but stayed there until about midnight. The one in command of the group then went to another little store and there got a couple of bottles of wine. When he had drunk this it went to his head and he came back to my store to bother me by asking for whiskey, and saying that he knew that I had some.

He bothered me so much that we came to words. Then he menaced me with a rifle. He just missed killing me and that was because an-

[1] *The Mexican Immigrant, His Life Story,* Autobiographic Documents, collected by Manuel Gamio (Chicago: The University of Chicago Press, 1931), pp. 2–4.

other soldier hit his arm and the bullet lodged in the roof of the house. Then some others came and took the fellow away and let me close the store.

On the next day, and as soon as I could, I sold everything that I had, keeping only the little house — I don't know in what condition it is today. The Villistas[2] pressed me into the service then, and took me with them as a soldier. But I didn't like that, because I never liked to go about fighting, especially about things that don't make any difference to one. So when we got to Torreon I ran away just as soon as I could. That was about 1915.

From El Paso to Miami

I went from there to Ciudad Juarez and from there to El Paso.

There I put myself under contract to go to work on the tracks. I stayed in that work in various camps until I reached California. I was for a while in Los Angeles working in cement work, which is very hard. From there I went to Kansas, and I was also in Oklahoma and in Texas, always working on the railroads. But the climate in those states didn't agree with me, so I beat it for Arizona. . . .

Some friends told me that I could find a good job here in Miami. I have worked in the mines here, in the King, the Superior and the Globe. In all of them it is more or less alike for the Mexicans. Here in the Miami mine I learned to work the drills and all the mining machinery and I know how to do everything. The work is very heavy, but what is good is that one lives in peace. There is no trouble with revolutions nor difficulties of any kind. Here one is treated according to the way in which one behaves himself and one earns more than in Mexico.

The United States and Mexico Compared

I have gone back to Mexico twice. Once I went as far as Chihuahua and another time to Torreon, but I have come back, for in addition to the fact that work is very scarce there, the wages are too low. One can hardly earn enough to eat. It is true that here it is almost the same, but there are more comforts of life here. One can buy many things cheaper and in payments. I think that as long as we have so many wars, killing each other, we will not progress and we shall always

---

[2] [**Villistas:** followers of Pancho Villa, one of the revolutionary leaders.]

be poor. That is what these *bolillos*[3] want. It is here that the revolutions are made. It is over there that the fools kill each other. It is better for the *bolillos* that we do that, for they want to wipe us out in order to make themselves masters of all that we possess. It is a shame that we live the way we do and if we go on we shall never do anything.

I don't care about political matters. It is the same to me to have Calles as Obregón[4] in the government. In the end neither one of them does anything for me. I live from my work and nothing else. If I don't work I know that I won't eat and if I work I am sure at least that I will eat. So that why should we poor people get mixed up in politics? It doesn't do us any good. Let those who have offices, who get something out of it, get into it. But he who has to work hard, let him live from his work alone.

It is not, as I have already told you, that I like it more here. No one is better off here than in his own country. But to those of us who work, it is better to live here until the revolutions end. When everything is peaceful and one can work as one likes, then it will be better to go back there to see if one can do anything. There are no profits in small businesses. Only the large businesses make money. They sell to the little stores and these just manage to get by. Here in Miami one can live as one wishes without being bothered.

[3] [bolillos: nickname given to the Americans by the Mexican.]
[4] [**Plutarco Elias Calles** and **Alvaro Obregón** were revolutionary generals who joined forces in 1920 against the government of President Venustiano Carranza.]

Part Two

Introduction
IV. Jobs and Housing
V. Community Life
VI. Politics
VII. The Achievement

The Immigrants Adjust to America

Part Two: Introduction

Some immigrants embarked for America thinking that they were going to El Dorado. They "expect God to supply them a paradise here," an Illinois farmer observed of fellow Norwegians in the late 1830's. This expectation continued into the twentieth century and was kept alive by stories of immigrants who had done fabulously well. Andrew Carnegie's autobiography, for example, gave the impression that only in America could a poor boy become a millionaire.

To immigrants who failed to make good, on the other hand, the image of El Dorado was a mirage. In letters home to friends and relatives, they criticized the American people, the American land, American cities, American factories, American weather — in a word, all things American — as harsh, forbidding, and cruel. Many of them returned to the old country in defeat and advised their countrymen to stay where they were. America was a trap, they said.

That America was a paradise for some immigrants but a trap for others is undeniable. Yet, if such extremes were real, they were hardly typical. The vast majority of immigrants did not succeed as millionaire businessmen. But neither did the majority fail and go back embittered to the ancestral village or town. Most immigrants adapted to a strange culture and built a new life for themselves.

Problems of Adjustment to a New Life

We tend to take their achievement for granted. Yet their struggle was so hard that only an act of the imagination can recapture it. Few Americans today move into a new neighborhood without a wrench. Imagine what it would be like to move to a different country! Nothing would be familiar — not the people or their language; not their traditions or their schools; not their sports, food, or the hundreds of other things that a person takes for granted in his own way of life.

If one feels with immigrants the wrench of moving, then one can only marvel that so few of them gave up the struggle and went home. The difficulties of learning English were immense. Even British immigrants had to get used to speech that did not sound quite like their own. Remember, too, that most immigrants were poor, uneducated peasants who rarely had ventured far from their villages until they came to America. Such people do not easily give up their culture for another. Yet they had to change. The problems of adjusting to a new country transformed a man's life and, ultimately, his way of looking at life.

Making a Living

The first problem was to earn a living. A lucky few with capital and skills America needed — artisans, farmers, businessmen, and professional men — did in the New World what they had done in the Old. (*See Section IV, selections 1 and 2.*) Most immigrants, however, took what jobs they could find as unskilled workers. This sometimes involved a loss in status. (*See Section IV, selection 7.*) Depending on when they came, the men built canals, laid railroad track, loaded and unloaded boats, and worked in the mines, factories, and mills. Their work was not only low-paying; it was also dangerous. (*See Section IV, selection 5.*) As late as 1900, around 60 per cent of the workers earned less than 600 dollars a year, the bare minimum to support a family. That is why their children and wives had to work and why child labor was, until fairly recently, commonplace. (*See Section IV, selection 3.*)

Finding a Home

The second problem was housing. Here, too, the immigrants had to get used to the unfamiliar. Most of them had lived in villages or small towns where everyone knew everyone else. Few of them recreated the familiar pattern. The American farmer built his house next to his farm, and that is what immigrant farmers did. Their first house was apt to be a log cabin or, if they settled on the woodless prairies, a sod house. It stood by itself — not, as in the Old World, among other houses in a village community. Small wonder that many immigrant farmers suffered intense loneliness. (*See Section IV, selection 1, and Section V, selection 1.*)

The problems were different in the cities and the mill and mining towns. Immigrants crowded into barracks, tenements, or single-family homes converted into multiple-dwelling units. Housing was so inadequate that it became a major social problem. (*See Section IV, selection 8.*) Rarely did immigrants live among native Americans. They lived in the older, decaying, densely populated neighborhoods that native Americans vacated for homes in "better" parts of the cities or in the suburbs. The same thing is true today for the most recent newcomers to the cities from Puerto Rico and the American South. Similarly, before the Civil War, when the most recent newcomers had emigrated from Ireland and Germany, the slum-dwellers were mostly Irish and German.

Seeking Fellowship

After housing and jobs came community organization. Therein lies a third problem that the immigrants faced in adjusting to America. In the old country, people had enjoyed social lives within inherited institutions. In this country they had to create institutions. Like human beings the world over since the beginning of time, the immigrants turned for fellowship and help to their own kind.

Each immigrant group established its own churches, schools, newspapers, burial societies, insurance companies, clubs, lodges, taverns, and the like. (*See Section* V.) Some native Americans criticized the existence of a Little Italy, a Little Poland, a Little Bohemia, a Little Germany, a little Trinidad, a little Mexico, or some other immigrant community. Yet the newcomers, while striving for the familiar, did not quite reproduce what they had known in the Old World. Many of them, for example, read a newspaper in their own language only after they came to America. Old World newspapers had generally been written for the educated classes. In some parts of Europe, moreover, minority nationalities had not been allowed to have newspapers in their own languages.

Learning American Politics

The fourth and final problem of adjustment had to do with politics. Here, too, immigrants faced a new experience. Millions of them for the first time joined a political party, voted, and learned the meaning of representative government. This was true even of many immigrants from Great Britain, where the vote was denied to workers until the late nineteenth century. In America, naturalized immigrants not only could but were *expected* to vote.

Their political leaders were usually American party managers of immigrant parentage who looked after the newcomers' personal needs in exchange for their votes. Reformers called such leaders "bosses" and accused them of being dishonest and selfish. The bosses defended themselves by saying that they Americanized the immigrants and taught them the power of the ballot. It is still a subject of controversy whether the bosses abused their trust and the immigrants misused their votes. (*See Section VI, selections 1–3.*) Over the years, however, the immigrants and their leaders enlarged their view of politics. Men like Alfred E. Smith and Fiorello H. La Guardia, for example, stood for progressive reform. (*See Section VI, selection 4.*)

There is still another controversy. Immigrants believed that they had a right as American citizens to take an interest in the fate of the countries from which they had come. This, however, seemed to impinge on American foreign policy, and such critics as Theodore Roosevelt condemned "double loyalties." Who was right, the immigrants or their critics? (*See Section VI, selection 5, and Section IX, selection 3.*)

Contributing to American Life

The last section in Part Two calls attention to the contribution of immigration to America. It is easy enough to cite prominent immigrants who enriched this society in the arts, the sciences, the professions, business, and other areas of American life. Yet influence flowed not only from the top down but also from the bottom up. Ordinary people contributed to America's economic expansion, its westward movement, its fluid class structure, and its culture. If one includes the children and the grandchildren of the immigrants, the contribution of immigration to this country is incalculable.

Common Problems of Adjustment

One final introductory remark is in order. Some textbooks still make a distinction between "old immigrants" from northern Europe and "new immigrants" from southern and eastern Europe. In contrast to the "new immigrants," according to this view, the "old immigrants" adjusted so easily to America that they rapidly disappeared into the "mainstream." Evidence fails to support this claim. As late as the 1920's, to cite a single example, the largest number of foreign-language newspapers in America were the newspapers of "old immigrants." (*See Section V, selection 5.*)

This is not to say that all immigrants and all immigrant groups were identical. Differences existed, but they were not the prejudiced distinctions invented by bigots. This much the record tells us. Regardless of birthplace and time of arrival in America, tens of millions of newcomers to this country made painful adjustments and developed patterns of group life to satisfy their particular needs. The best way to understand this phenomenon is to put yourself in the place of the immigrants. Relive, in the following selections, what they lived through in putting down roots in a strange land. ■

IV. Jobs and Housing

Farmer, merchant, manufacturer, banker, millhand, artist, printer, journalist, coal miner, servant, house painter, steel worker — there was no end to the ways in which immigrants earned a living. Most of them, however, started out at the lower end of the economic scale. This section of the book barely suggests the range of occupations on that or any other level. More important, because they are in the words of the immigrants themselves, the documents speak to us in human terms about what it meant to support one's self and put a roof over one's head in alien surroundings. ∎

1. Farming in Missouri[1]
♣ Anonymous

It fell to the British, Germans, and Scandinavians to form the backbone of the American farming population. That was because they happened to come to this country when it was primarily agricultural and needed farmers. By the end of the nineteenth century, as a result of the industrial revolution and the closing of the frontier, immigrant manpower flowed largely into the cities.

There can be no question but that the immigrant who had been a farmer in his native country was fortunate in being able to re-establish himself on the land when he came to America. Nevertheless, he encountered much that was strange and hard. In the following letter, translated from the original Norwegian, a newcomer describes his initial reactions to settling in rural Missouri in the 1830's. ∎

[1] From a settler in Missouri to a friend, October 15, 1838, in Theodore C. Blegen, ed., *Land of Their Choice, The Immigrants Write Home* (Minneapolis: University of Minnesota Press, 1955), pp. 46–48. © Copyright 1955 by the University of Minnesota.

Farming in Missouri   **85**

We finally arrived in New York after having been at sea for eight weeks, less two days. There were about seventy passengers on the ship, all Germans, except my fellow travelers from Norway and me. Our accommodation on board the ship was insufficient, and as a result the air was very close and unhealthful. But nobody died, though there was some illness.

From New York to Missouri

We stayed six days in New York until we got our money problems and other affairs settled. Here we met several Norwegians and Danes, among whom was a Norwegian named Cleng Peerson, who has lived in America for about twenty years and knows the country very well, as he has traveled about in almost all of the United States and speaks English fairly well. He advised us to go to Missouri, where he and several Norwegians from the district of Stavanger have made their homes. As he was on his way home, he accompanied us on the long trip across this country, . . . and this was a great help to us in many respects. In Rochester our group was increased by the family of Ole Reiersen and several other Norwegians.

The trip was very long and difficult . . . ; because of the unusual drought, the water in the rivers, especially in Ohio, had become so low that the ship ran aground every day or stuck in the sand banks. Then it would take much time and work to get loose again. After much trouble and expense, on October 4 we finally arrived at this place, an area almost entirely uninhabited. A couple of miles farther west the land is completely desolate, until you get to where the Indians live, about a hundred miles from here. We are staying with the nine or ten Norwegians who have made their homes here. None of them has bought the land he has claimed, and most of them do not have any money to redeem it with, so that very soon the land will come up for public sale. . . .

Strange Land, Strange Climate

Here are large grass-covered plains with bigger or smaller patches of woods in between, so that one may select a piece that has both. It is true that the land here is good, but for a Norwegian or any other foreigner to come this far into the country involves a great many difficulties and privations. . . . All the Norwegians I have talked to agree with this. If they had known beforehand what they would have to go through, they would not have undertaken the journey. They have sent many letters to Norway describing the glories of the country, but they never mention a word about the hardships they find here and the difficulties of the journey, about which they now have much to say in conversation.

I, too, have acquired some experience. I shall not go into detail about it, but I think it is my duty to say something. The change in climate causes much illness. During the daytime there is heat here to which we are not accustomed, and the nights are very cool, often with heavy fogs that cause many colds and attacks of ague. Often there is a sudden change from hot to very cold air.

Everybody Builds a Log Cabin

To these tribulations must be added the open log cabins, which have chimneys of wood and clay. Only the immediate vicinity of the fire gets warmed up, since there is a draught through the whole house, or rather hut. And yet you have to be thankful if you have such a hut to seek shelter in, in a land that is almost uninhabited. You might think that we would not have to live in such poor houses or travel this far into the country. But only those who have enough money can avoid this, for all land, even in Illinois, has been bought up and can only be had at second hand at prices ranging from $5 to $20 an acre. And as far as building is concerned, it would be very expensive to hire workers. Everybody builds his own log cabin as well as he can, simply with an ax, and for the most part the cabins are without windows. Because of all this, and other matters, I consider it precarious for everyone to go to America. . . .

Come by Way of New Orleans

The shortest and cheapest way to get here is via New Orleans and up the Mississippi. From New Orleans it is about 1800 miles to this place, and this distance is covered on steamboats in ten or fourteen days. But from New York we had a distance of about 2500 miles, which it took us almost eight weeks to travel, mainly because the route was so difficult. It is a great advantage to bring all kinds of iron tools if you come here. A carpenter's ax, for instance, costs from $3 to $5, and everything else in proportion to this. The transportation is not expensive, since usually you can get your baggage shipped free of charge on the steamboats.

2. A Skilled Artisan in New York City[1]
✤ Samuel Gompers

Samuel Gompers, president of the American Federation of Labor for almost forty years, came as a boy with his family to America in 1863. He had served a three-year apprenticeship, starting at the age of ten, as a cigarmaker in his native London. Like immigrant farmers who settled on the land, the young artisan was able to continue his trade in this country. In the following selection, taken from his autobiography, Gompers describes his early years in New York City. ∎

On the first day, we found a home in Houston and Attorney Streets. Those four rooms signified progress from the little London home. Our neighbors were chiefly American, English, and Holland Dutch. I was then thirteen years, six months, and two days old.

Father began making cigars at home and I helped him. Our house was just opposite a slaughter house. All day long we could see the animals being driven into the slaughter-pens and could hear the turmoil and the cries of the animals. The neighborhood was filled with the penetrating, sickening odor. The suffering of the animals and the nauseating odor made it physically impossible for me to eat meat for many months — after we had moved to another neighborhood. . . .

New York City in the 1860's

New York in those days had no skyscrapers. Horse tram cars ran across town. The buildings were generally small and unpretentious. Then, as now,[2] the East Side was the home of the latest immigrants who settled in colonies making the Irish, the German, the English and Dutch, and the Ghetto districts. The thousands from eastern Europe had not then begun their great immigration. . . .

---

[1] From the book *Seventy Years of Life and Labor* by Samuel Gompers (New York: Dutton, 1925, 2 vols.), Vol. I, pp. 24–25, 33–34, 44–45. Copyright, 1925, by E. P. Dutton & Co., Inc. Renewal, 1953, by Gertrude Gleaves Gompers. Reprinted by permission of the publishers.

[2] [Gompers was writing in the 1920's.]

Jobs and Housing

Gompers Joins a Trade Union and Looks for a Job

In 1864 I joined the Cigarmakers' Local Union No. 15 which was the English-speaking union of New York City. This organization was not strong. There was also Union No. 90 of German-speaking cigarmakers which was affiliated to the German Labor Union that met in the Tenth Ward Hotel. All my life I had been accustomed to the labor movement and accepted as a matter of course that every wage-earner should belong to the union of his trade. I did not yet have a conscious appreciation of the labor movement. My awakening was to come later. However, I attended union meetings and observed union regulations.

For the first year and a half after we came to New York I worked with my father at home. Father paid a deposit for materials and worked at his bench at home instead of in a shop. At that time home work was not exploited as it was later under the tenement-house system.[3] When I determined to find work outside, I had the self-confidence that goes with mastery of a trade. In hunting for a job, I chanced to fall in with another cigarmaker much older than I. Together we went from shop to shop until we found work. With a bit of nervousness but with sure, quick skill I made my first two cigars which the boss accepted and I became a permanent workman in the shop....

The Cigar Shop

Any kind of an old loft served as a cigar shop. If there were enough windows, we had sufficient light for our work; if not, it was apparently no concern of the management. There was an entirely different conception of sanitation both in the shop and in the home of those days from now. The toilet facilities were a water-closet and a sink for washing purposes, usually located by the closet. In most cigar shops our towels were the bagging that came around the bales of Havana and other high grades of tobacco. Cigar shops were always dusty from the tobacco stems and powdered leaves. Benches and work tables were not designed to enable the workmen to adjust bodies and arms comfortably to work surface. Each workman supplied his own cutting board . . . and knife blade.

---

[3] [See the next selection, pages 89–92.]

The Shop as Classroom

The tobacco leaf was prepared by strippers who drew the leaves from the heavy stem and put them in pads of about fifty. The leaves had to be handled carefully to prevent tearing. The craftsmanship of the cigarmaker was shown in his ability to utilize wrappers to the best advantage, to shave off the unusable to a hairbreadth, to roll so as to cover holes in the leaf, and to use both hands so as to make a perfectly shaped and rolled product. These things a good cigarmaker learned to do more or less mechanically, which left us free to think, talk, listen, or sing.

I loved the freedom of that work, for I had earned the mindfreedom that accompanied skill as a craftsman. I was eager to learn from discussion and reading or to pour out my feeling in song. Often we chose someone to read to us who was a particularly good reader, and in payment the rest of us gave him sufficient of our cigars so he was not the loser. The reading was always followed by discussion, so we learned to know each other pretty thoroughly. We learned who could take a joke in good spirit, who could marshall his thoughts in an orderly way, who could distinguish clever sophistry from sound reasoning. The fellowship that grew between congenial shopmates was something that lasted a lifetime.

3. Tenement Factories[1]
✤ Jacob A. Riis

Some twenty-five years after Samuel Gompers arrived in New York City, the introduction of machinery in cigarmaking led to the displacement of skilled artisans and the hiring of unskilled workers. The trade was also revolutionized when the tenement house replaced the loft as the place where cigars were made. Home and factory, in other words, became one and the same thing. The long hours, low pay, wretched conditions, and child labor led to the writing of an exposé, of which part is reprinted here. It was written by a Danish-born newspaperman, Jacob A. Riis, whose books and articles did much to awaken the social conscience of New Yorkers some 60 to 80 years ago. ■

[1] Jacob A. Riis, *How the Other Half Lives, Studies Among the Tenements of New York* (New York: Charles Scribner's Sons, 1906), pp. 137–142.

Fifty-fourth and Seventy-third Streets . . . are the centers of populous Bohemian settlements. The location of the cigar factories, upon which he [the Bohemian immigrant] depends for a living, determines his choice of home, though there is less choice about it than with any other class in the community, save perhaps the colored people.

Tenement Factories

Probably more than half of all the Bohemians in this city are cigarmakers, and it is the herding of these in great numbers in the so-called tenement factories, where the cheapest grade of work is done at the lowest wages, that constitutes at once their greatest hardship and the chief grudge of other workmen against them. The manufacturer who owns, say, from three or four to a dozen or more tenements contiguous to his shop fills them up with these people, charging them outrageous rents, and demanding often even a preliminary deposit of five dollars "key money"; deals them out tobacco by the week, and devotes the rest of his energies to the paring down of wages to within a peg or two of the point where the tenant rebels in desperation. When he does rebel, he is given the alternative of submission, or eviction with entire loss of employment. His needs determine the issue. Usually he is not in a position to hesitate long. . . .

The Whole Family Works

Men, women, and children work together seven days in the week in these cheerless tenements to make a living for the family, from the break of day till far into the night. Often the wife is the original cigarmaker from the old home, the husband having adopted her trade here as a matter of necessity, because, knowing no word of English, he could get no other work. As they state the cause of the bitter hostility of the trades unions, she was the primary bone of contention in the day of the early Bohemian immigration. The unions refused to admit the women, and, as the support of the family depended upon her to a large extent, such terms as were offered had to be accepted. The manufacturer has ever since industriously fanned the antagonism between the unions and his hands, for his own advantage. The victory rests with him, since the Court of Appeals decided that the law, passed a few years ago, to prohibit cigarmaking in tenements was unconstitutional, and thus put an end to the struggle. . . .

Three Examples

Take a row of houses in East Tenth Street as an instance. They contained thirty-five families of cigarmakers, with probably not half a dozen persons in the whole lot of them, outside of the children, who could speak a word of English, though many had been in the country half a lifetime. This room with two windows giving on the street, and a rear attachment without windows, called a bedroom by courtesy, is rented at $12.25 a month. In the front room man and wife work at the bench from six in the morning till nine at night. They make a team, stripping the tobacco leaves together; then he makes the filler, and she rolls the wrapper on and finishes the cigar. For a thousand they receive $3.75, and can turn out together three thousand cigars a week. The point has been reached where the rebellion comes in, and the workers in these tenements are just now on a strike, demanding $5.00 and $5.50 for their work. The manufacturer having refused, they are expecting hourly to be served with notice to quit their homes, and the going of a stranger among them excites their resentment, until his errand is explained. While we are in the house, the ultimatum of the "boss" is received. He will give $3.75 a thousand, not another cent. Our host is a man of seeming intelligence, yet he has been nine years in New York and knows neither English nor German. Three bright little children play about the floor.

His neighbor on the same floor has been here fifteen years, but shakes his head when asked if he can speak English. He answers in a few broken syllables when addressed in German. With $11.75 rent to pay for like accommodation, he has the advantage of his oldest boy's work besides his wife's at the bench. Three properly make a team, and these three can turn out four thousand cigars a week, at $3.75 [a thousand]. This Bohemian has a large family; there are four children, too small to work, to be cared for....

Here is a suite of three rooms, two dark, three flights up. The ceiling is partly down in one of the rooms. "It is three months since we asked the landlord to fix it," says the oldest son, a very intelligent lad who has learned English in the evening school. His father has not had that advantage, and has sat at his bench, deaf and dumb to the world about him except for his own, for six years. He has improved his time and become an expert at his trade. Father, mother and son together, a full team, make from fifteen to sixteen dollars a week.

A man with venerable beard and keen eyes answers our questions through an interpreter, in the next house. Very few brighter faces would be met in a day's walk among American mechanics, yet he has in nine years learned no syllable of English. German he probably does not want to learn. His story supplies the explanation, as did the stories of the others. In all that time he has been at work grubbing to earn bread. Wife and he by constant labor make three thousand cigars a week, earning $11.25 when there is no lack of material; when in winter they receive from the manufacturer tobacco for only two thousand, the rent of $10 for two rooms, practically one with a dark alcove, has nevertheless to be paid in full, and six mouths to be fed. He was a blacksmith in the old country, but cannot work at his trade because he does not understand "Engliska." If he could, he says, with a bright look, he could do better work than he sees done here. It would seem happiness to him to knock off at 6 o'clock instead of working, as he now often has to do, till midnight.

But how? He knows of no Bohemian blacksmith who can understand him; he should starve. Here, with his wife, he can make a living at least. "Aye," says she, turning, from listening, to her household duties, "it would be nice for sure to have father work at his trade." Then what a home she could make for them, and how happy they would be. Here is an unattainable ideal, indeed, of a workman in the most prosperous city in the world! There is genuine, if unspoken, pathos in the soft tap she gives her husband's hand as she goes about her work with a half-suppressed little sigh.

4. Pick and Shovel[1]

✤ Constantine M. Panunzio

> Constantine M. Panunzio had been a sailor in Italy before he arrived in America as an orphan boy at the turn of this century. Interested Americans eventually steered him to college, and Panunzio went on to become a professor and a writer. During his early days in this country, however, he drifted into hard, low-paying jobs for which he had no training. That was true in general of unskilled immigrants. In the following piece, taken from his autobiography, Panunzio describes not only his first experiences in Boston but also how the "padrone" system recruited cheap pick-and-shovel labor. ■

[1] Constantine M. Panunzio, *The Soul of an Immigrant* (New York: The Macmillan Company, 1921), pp. 75–80.

On the fifth day, by mere chance, I ran across a French sailor on the recreation pier. We immediately became friends. His name was Louis. Just to look at Louis would make you laugh. He was over six feet tall, lank, queer-shaped, freckle-faced, with small eyes and a crooked nose. I have sometimes thought that perhaps he was the "missing link" for which the scientist had been looking. Louis could not speak Italian; he had a smattering of what he called "italien," but I could not see it his way. On the other hand, I kept imposing upon his good nature by giving a nasal twang to Italian words and insisting on calling it "francese." We had much merriment. Two facts, however, made possible a mutual understanding. Both had been sailors and had traveled over very much the same world; this made a bond between us. Then too, we had . . . a strange capacity for gesticulation and facial contortion, which was always our last "hope" in making each other understood.

A Lodging House in the North End

Not far from the recreation pier on which we met is located the Italian colony of "North End," Boston. To this Louis and I made our way, and to an Italian boarding house. How we happened to find it and to get in I do not now recall. It was a "three-room apartment" and the landlady informed us that she was already "full," but since we had no place to go, she would take us in. Added to the host that was already gathered there, our coming made fourteen people. At night the floor of the kitchen and the dining table were turned into beds. Louis and I were put to sleep in one of the beds with two other men, two facing north and two south. As I had slept all my life in a bed or bunk by myself, this quadrupling did not appeal to me especially. But we could not complain. We had been taken in on trust, and the filth, the smells and the crowding together were a part of the trust.

"Peek and Shuvle"

We began to make inquiries about jobs and were promptly informed that there was plenty of work at "pick and shovel." We were also given to understand by our fellow-boarders that "pick and shovel" was practically the only work available to Italians. Now these were the first two English words I had heard and they possessed great charm. Moreover, if I were to earn money to return home and this was the only work available for Italians, they were weighty words for me, and I must master them as soon as well as possible and then set out to find their hidden meaning. I practiced for a day or two until I could say "peek" and "shuvle" to perfection.

Then I asked a fellow-boarder to take me to see what the work was like. He did. He led me to Washington Street, not far from the colony, where some excavation work was going on, and there I did see, with my own eyes, what the "peek" and "shuvle" were about. My heart sank within me, for I had thought it some form of office work; but I was game and since this was the only work available for Italians, and since I must have money to return home, I would take it up. After all, it was only a means to an end, and would last but a few days.

Italians and Excavation Work

It may be in place here to say a word relative to the reason why this idea was prevalent among Italians at the time, and why so many Italians on coming to America find their way to what I had called "peek and shuvle." It is a matter of common knowledge, at least among students of immigration, that a very large percentage of Italian immigrants were *contadini* or farm laborers in Italy. American people often ask the question, "Why do they not go to the farms in this country?" This query is based upon the idea that the *contadini* were farmers in the sense in which we apply that word to the American farmer.

The facts in the case are that the *contadini* were not farmers in that sense at all, but simply farm-laborers, more nearly serfs, working on landed estates and seldom owning their own land. Moreover, they are not in any way acquainted with the implements of modern American farming. Their farming tools consisted generally of a *zappa* (a sort of wide mattock), an ax, and the wooden plow of biblical times. When they come to America, the work which comes nearest to that which they did in Italy is not farming, or even farm labor, but excavation work. This fact, together with the isolation which inevitably would be theirs on an American farm, explains, in a large measure, why so few Italians go to the farm and why so many go into excavation work. . . .

Now, though Louis and I had never done such work, because we were Italians we must needs adapt ourselves to it and go to work with "peek and shuvle." (I should have stated that Louis, desiring to be like the Romans while living with them, for the time being passed for an Italian.) . . .

EARNING A LIVING: Immigration provided the labor needed by the expanding American economy. But for the individual immigrant untrained in special skills this usually meant a life of toil. Pick-and-shovel workers like the man above built the railroads, factories, and cities of modern America. On New York's Lower East Side, factory and home were one for many immigrant families. Top, a tenement family making garters, about 1910. While most Chinese laborers settled in the West, some were hired by a Massachusetts shoe factory (left).

The "Padrone"

One morning we were standing in front of one of those infernal institutions which in America are permitted to bear the name of "immigrant banks," when we saw a fat man coming toward us. "*Buon giorno* [Good morning], *padrone*," said one of the men. "*Padrone?*" said I to myself. Now the word *padrone* in Italy is applied to a proprietor, generally a respectable man, at least one whose dress and appearance distinguish him as a man of means. This man not only showed no signs of good breeding in his face, but he was unshaven and dirty and his clothes were shabby. I could not quite understand how he could be called *padrone*. However, I said nothing, first because I wanted to get back home, and second because I wanted to be polite when I was in *American* society!

The *padrone* came up to our group and began to wax eloquent and to gesticulate (both in Sicilian dialect) about the advantages of a certain job. I remember very clearly the points which he emphasized: "It is not very far, only twelve miles from Boston. For a few cents you can come back any time you wish, to see *i parenti e gli amici*, your relatives and friends. The company has a 'shantee' in which you can sleep, and a 'storo' where you can buy your 'grosserie' all very cheap. 'Buono paga' (Good pay)," he continued, "$1.25 per day, and you only have to pay me fifty cents a week for having gotten you this 'gooda jobba.' I only do it to help you and because you are my countrymen. If you come back here at six o'clock to-night with your bundles, I myself will take you out."

The magnanimity of this man impressed Louis and me very profoundly; we looked at each other and said, "Wonderful!" We decided we would go; so at the appointed hour we returned to the very spot. About twenty men finally gathered there and we were led to North Station. There we took a train to some suburban place, the name of which I have never been able to learn.

First Job in America

On reaching our destination we were taken to the "shantee" where we were introduced to two long open bunks filled with straw. These were to be our beds. The "storo" of which we had been told was at one end of the shanty. The next morning we were taken out to work. It was a sultry autumn day. The "peek" seemed to grow heavier at every stroke and the "shuvle" wider and larger in its capacity to hold the gravel. The second day was no better than the first, and the third was worse than the second. The work was heavy and monotonous to Louis and myself especially, who had never been *contadini* like the rest. The *padrone* whose magnanimity had so stirred us was little better than a brute. We began to do some simple figuring and discovered that when we had paid for our groceries at the "storo," for the privilege of sleeping in the shanty, and the fifty cents to the *padrone* for having been so condescending as to employ us, we would have nothing left but sore arms and backs. So on the afternoon of the third day Louis and I held a solemn conclave and decided to part company with "peek and shuvle" — for ever. We left, without receiving a cent of pay, of course.

5. Killed in a Foundry[1]
✣ Antoni Butkowski

By 1900 many American coal miners and steel workers were former peasants from Poland, Russia, the Ukraine, Ruthenia, Slovakia, Lithuania, and other parts of Slavic Europe. Their migrations took place when American heavy industry, expanding at a fantastic rate, needed abundant labor. The wages were low, the hours long, and the dangers appalling. It is estimated that, in the early 1900's, around 40,000 men died in industrial accidents every year. In the following letter, translated from the original Polish, the writer informed his family in the old country of the death of his brother in a foundry. The letter was dated April 26, 1903. ■

Now I inform you, dearest parents, and you, my brothers, that Konstanty, your son, dearest parents, and your brother and mine, my brothers, is no more alive. It killed him in the foundry, it tore him in eight parts, it tore his head away and crushed his chest to a mass and broke his arms. But I beg you, dear parents, don't weep and

---

[1] William I. Thomas and Florian Znaniecki, *The Polish Peasant in Europe and America* (Chicago: University of Chicago Press, 1918, 5 vols.), Vol. II, pp. 263–264.

don't grieve. God willed it so and did it so. It killed him on April 20, in the morning, and he was buried on April 22.

He was buried beautifully. His funeral cost $225, the casket $60. Now when we win some [money] by law from the company, we will buy a place and transfer him that he may lie quietly, we will surround him with a fence and put a cross, stone, or iron upon his grave. This will cost some $150. For his work, let him at least lie quietly in his own place. It is so, dear parents: Perhaps we shall receive from the [insurance] society $1000, and from the company we don't know how much, perhaps 2000, perhaps 3000, and perhaps 1000.... Whatever we receive, after paying all the expenses I will send you the rest, dear parents, and I will come myself to my country....

Once more I tell you, dear parents, don't listen to anybody, to any letters which anybody will write to you, but listen to me, your son. I cannot close the door myself before lawyers. Some advise well, others still better, but I have a wise man. And now I tell you, dear parents, read this note, which is cut out of a paper; you will know who is guilty of his death. But nothing can be done, dear parents. Don't weep, for you won't raise him any more. For if you had looked upon him, I don't know what would have become of you....

6. A Servant Girl[1]

♣ Aleksandra Rembieńska

Except in the South, most maids in this country until recently were unmarried immigrant girls. These girls did better economically in America than in the old country. Yet they worked long days at little pay in households where often they did not know the language. The letter below, written originally in Polish, captures the hardship and loneliness that an immigrant girl went through in 1912. ◼

O Dear Auntie: I received your letter on February 20 and I write you on February 25. Dear auntie, you wrote 3 letters and I know

---

[1] Thomas and Znaniecki, *The Polish Peasant in Europe and America* (Chicago: University of Chicago Press, 1918, 5 vols.), Vol. II, pp. 254–255.

nothing about them; I receive only this one. O dear auntie, you write to me that I either don't wish to write or that I have forgotten [you]. O dear auntie, I will not forget until my death. I write letters, one to auntie and the other to my parents. Perhaps somebody has intercepted those letters at the post-office and does not give them to you. Now, dear auntie, I inform you that I am in good health, thanks to our Lord God, which I wish also to you, dear auntie. May God help you the best; may I always hear that you are doing well; I shall be very glad then.

And now, dear auntie, I inform you that I am in the same place in service with an English [-speaking] master and mistress who don't know a word of Polish, and I don't know English; so we communicate with gestures and I know what to do, that's all. I know the work and therefore I don't mind much about the language. But, dear auntie, I went intentionally into an English household in order that I may learn to speak English, because it is necessary, in America, as the English language reigns. I am in good health, only I am a little ill with my feet, I don't know what it is, whether rheumatism or something else. I walk very much, because from 6 o'clock in the morning till 10 o'clock in the evening I have work and I receive $22 a month, and I have 7 persons, and 16 rooms to clean, and I cook; everything is on my head.

And now, dear auntie, please don't be angry with me for not answering directly, for I have no time, neither in the day nor the evening. I am always busy. And now, dear auntie, I thank you very much for the news, for now I know everything. You ask about that young man, what happened. Nothing happened, only it is so that I did not wish to marry him, because I don't wish to marry at all; I will live alone through this my life to the end. He is a good fellow, nothing can be said, his name is Thomas Zylowski. He wants it to be in summer, after Easter, but I don't think about marrying, I will suffer alone to the end in this world.

O dear auntie, I write you that I have nothing to write, only I ask you for a quick answer. And now I beg you, auntie, write me what happened with [two illegible names of boy and girl]. I wish you a merry holiday of Easter time. O dear God, why cannot I be with auntie and divide the egg together with parents and brothers and sisters! When I recall all this, I would not be sorry if I had to die right now.

7. Loss in Status[1]

♣ An Anonymous Black Teacher

The anonymous author of the following selection, a black schoolmaster from the British West Indies, was forced to enter the American working force as a day laborer. Imagine how you would feel if you had a to take a job inferior to the one for which you had been trained. The loss in status would be painful. Immigrants from white-collar backgrounds were particularly susceptible to that kind of hurt. Few were as fortunate as our author, who, as he tells us, eventually managed to return to a profession. His story is taken from a study of black immigrants who came to America in the first four decades of this century. ■

I was inducted into American labor one fine Sabbath morning while on my way to apply for an elevator boy's job I had seen in the newspaper want column. While passing through a side street in the lower section of Manhattan I watched and silently criticized the ungodliness of men working on a building construction on the Lord's Day. While musing, a foreman of the laborers' gang came up to me and in his native Irish accent said, "Want to work?" "Yes," was my reply. "Well, god damn it, take that collar and tie off and pitch in." Without stopping to think, I obeyed.

Loading Bricks

I left my coat collar and tie in the basement, got hold of a wheelbarrow and soon found myself loading it with bricks which I transported to the bricklayers. There were about two dozen of us in the labor gang. It was apparent that these workers were of all races and nationalities. After three or four hours I was shifted to the concrete gang, i e., to transport concrete. How I did welcome that whistle at mid-day! I was so tired and my hands were so painful that I stretched myself out on a plank to rest. One fellow said to me, "Don't worry, you will break in." I bought some lunch and went back to work. At five o'clock my day's work was done.

[1] Ira De A. Reid, *The Negro Immigrant, His Background, Characteristics and Social Adjustment, 1899–1937* (New York: Columbia University Press, 1939), pp. 196–198.

Psychic Loss, Economic Gain

. . . I went home, washed up and rested. My roommate, whom I saw once or twice per week — he was working on two jobs — asked me once during that week if I was working. "Yes," was my reply. That's all he wanted to know so I said nothing else. But when I had time to reflect I felt rather badly. I wondered at times if I was the same person who but lately had been a very successful schoolmaster with hundreds of children and their parents looking up to me as their idol, with someone to do every form of menial work that I required at my least bidding, and here I was, transformed into a day laborer, trucking bricks and concrete.

I decided to quit, so I completed that week and got a porter's job in a hotel at $18 per week and meals. After being on the job for about four weeks I was fired for being too slow and inexperienced. One thing resulting from this in my favor, however, was that I decided to turn in the time checks from the first job. To my surprise I was paid $37.50 for that week's work of seven days, time-and-a-half for Sunday. It took me almost two months to earn a like sum in my home country. That amount for one week's work was a financial shock to me.

Happy Ending

I landed a job in a wholesale firm through a young lady who worked for one of the bosses. This boss was a German. He invited me to his house and along with his wife entertained me royally. I was a kind of novelty on that job then. To see a colored man with a pencil behind his ears checking goods, receiving and shipping thousands of dollars' worth of merchandise each week without making the slightest error, was something extraordinary to all the colored help and white clerks in that establishment.

My salary was stepped up to $35.00 per week, and pretty soon I was entirely in charge of the place on Sundays, taking the keys home with me. I was even given the combination for the safe. One Sunday while there in some part of the building hoodlums stole thirteen bags of sugar from a lower floor. There was quite a furore by the police and some of the bosses. But I was not even scared of losing my job for my honesty was above reproach. When I finally resigned from the job to enter medical school I was given a fine send-off, and I still keep my reference from the Head of that concern.

8. Tenement House Evils[1]

✢ Robert DeForest and Lawrence Veiller

Enough has been said thus far — about the log cabin, the four rooms opposite a slaughterhouse, the cigar factory, the lodging house — to indicate the kind of housing that was available to immigrants on arrival. The worst housing was the slum tenement. Families that did well moved to better lodgings, but still more recent newcomers filled the rooms they vacated. That is one reason why America has had a persistent slum problem for more than a century. Below, in a selection taken from a study of New York City in the early 1900's, the housekeeper of a typical tenement describes the evils of that kind of dwelling. ■

The housekeeper of one of the old-style tenements, on the lower East Side, a building five rooms deep, the three inner ones with no outside windows, who has lived in East Side tenements for twenty years, said in answer to questions that the worst things about the old tenements were the water-closets and sinks in the halls, both of which could be remedied.

Plumbing

. . . The Board of Health inspector tells her that according to the law, at the time when they were built, they are all right, but she says they "stink horribly" and in other tenements are just as bad.

Four families have to use one toilet, men, women, and children, "so," she says, "we use it as little as possible. I have the children go to the toilet at school, for I am afraid of sickness. It is so horrid for my daughter that she waits to use the toilet where she works. She hasn't been inside of one here for four or five months."

The toilets are in the yard. The families take turns in keeping them clean, and they are supposed to be scrubbed once a week, but are often left for two weeks, and it is always done at irregular intervals.

The worst of the sinks is that people wash at the sinks in the public halls; big girls, without their waists and barefooted, come out and wash there. The halls are never clean on account of the sinks;

[1] Robert W. DeForest and Lawrence Veiller, *The Tenement House Problem* (New York: The Macmillan Company, 1903, 2 vols.), Vol. I, pp. 385–386.

people come out and wash their dishes in them, and wash their meat in the sinks. They spill the water around the sinks, and when the halls are cold in winter the water freezes and makes the floors slippery. She thinks it wouldn't cost the landlords very much to put water in the rooms.

Dark Halls

The landlord turns out the gas in the halls when they [the tenants] light it, even if the inspector has ordered it to be lighted. Sometimes when an inspector has a grudge against a landlord he comes very often; then the landlords gives him a tip, $2, $6, or even $10, and everything is all right.

Fire-escapes

Fire-escapes ought to be kept clear. Her husband goes up and down those on their house once a week and throws away any rubbish on them; ... [he] makes the people take in anything they value, so that the fire-escapes are kept clear. On the receipt blanks there is a footnote, which says, among other things, that the fire-escapes must be kept clear. She thinks the housekeeper and landlord can do it if they want to. She said, "I tell you when the landlord and housekeeper keep together they can do more than the tenement house inspector."

Boarders

In regard to boarders she is very strict. When people keep three or four, men and women together, she puts the tenant out, or when there are two families in one room. She says there are twenty-three boarders in the house across the street.

Bathtubs

Wouldn't care for bathtubs if two or three families must use them, on account of contagion. Shower-baths for men would be nice....

She says in conclusion that she would be perfectly contented if she could only have her own water-closet and water in her room.

V. Community Life

Many of us become especially aware of ourselves in the presence of people different from ourselves. That has been the experience, for example, of American business and military families who live abroad. A foreign environment intensifies their consciousness that they have their own language, sports, religion, foods, schools, clubs, music, entertainment, newspapers, books, and so on. Such Americans, whether they live in Paris, Tokyo, or Saigon, create their own communities. That fact should help us to understand how immigrants to this country ordered their social lives. Each group established a community life of its own. Nevertheless, in doing so, they entered American society, whose essence was, and still is, the voluntary association. ■

1. The Lack of Community[1]
✛ E. V. Smalley

> Some Americans criticized immigrants for settling among their own kind and thus forming "colonies." Yet the immigrants who had the hardest time in adjusting to America were usually those who failed to re-create familiar patterns of community life. This was particularly true of newcomers on the sparsely populated plains and prairies. The article below, by a sympathetic journalist, captures the terrible loneliness of homesteaders in the Dakotas and Nebraska three-quarters of a century ago. ■

In no civilized country have the cultivators of the soil adapted their home life so badly to the conditions of nature as have the people of our great northwestern prairies. This is a strong statement, but I am led to the conclusion by ten years of observation in our plains region.

[1] E. V. Smalley, "The Isolation of Life of Prairie Farmers," *Atlantic Monthly*, LXXII (September, 1893), pp. 378–380.

The European Village

The European farmer lives in a village, where considerable social enjoyment is possible. The women gossip at the village well, and visit frequently at one another's houses; the children find playmates close at hand; there is a school, and, if the village be not a very small one, a church. The post wagon, with its uniformed postilion merrily blowing his horn, rattles through the street every day, and makes an event that draws people to the doors and windows. The old men gather of summer evenings to smoke their pipes and talk of the crops; the young men pitch quoits and play ball on the village green. Now and then a detachment of soldiers from some garrison town halts to rest. A peddler makes his rounds. A black-frocked priest tarries to join in the chat of the elder people, and to ask after the health of the children. In a word, something takes place to break the monotony of daily life. The dwellings, if small and meagerly furnished, have thick walls of brick or stone that keep out the summer's heat and the winter's chill.

The American Homestead

Now contrast this life of the European peasant, to which there is a joyous side that lightens labor and privation, with the life of a poor settler on a homestead claim in one of the Dakotas or Nebraska. Every homesteader must live upon his claim for five years to perfect his title and get his patent[2]; so that [even] if there were not the universal American custom of isolated farm life to stand in the way, no farm villages would be possible in the first occupancy of a new region in the West without a change in our land laws. If the country were so thickly settled that every quarter-section of land (160 acres) had a family upon it, each family would be half a mile from any neighbor, supposing the houses to stand in the center of the farms; and in any case the average distance between them could not be less. But many settlers own 320 acres, and a few have a square mile of land, 640 acres. Then there are school sections, belonging to the state, and not occupied at all, and everywhere you find vacant tracts owned by eastern speculators or by mortgage companies, to which former settlers have abandoned their claims, going to newer regions, and leaving their debts and their land behind. Thus the average space

[2] [**patent:** document attesting to the land-grant.]

separating the farmsteads is, in fact, always more than half a mile, and many settlers must go a mile or two to reach a neighbor's house. This condition obtains not on the frontiers alone, but in fairly well-peopled agricultural districts. . . .

Each Family to Itself

In such a region, you would expect the dwellings to be of substantial construction, but they are not. The new settler is too poor to build of brick or stone. He hauls a few loads of lumber from the nearest railway station, and puts up a frail little house of two, three, or four rooms that looks as though the prairie winds would blow it away. Were it not for the invention of tarred building-paper, the flimsy walls would not keep out the wind and snow. With this paper the walls are sheathed under the weather-boards. The barn is often a nondescript affair of sod walls and straw roof. Lumber is much too dear to be used for dooryard fences, and there is no inclosure about the house. A barbed-wire fence surrounds the barnyard. Rarely are there any trees, for on the prairies trees grow very slowly, and must be nursed with care to get a start. There is a saying that you must first get the Indian out of the soil before a tree will grow at all; which means that some savage quality must be taken from the ground by cultivation.

In this cramped abode, from the windows of which there is nothing more cheerful in sight than the distant houses of other settlers, just as ugly and lonely, and stacks of straw and unthreshed grain, the farmer's family must live. In the summer there is a school for the children, one, two, or three miles away; but in winter the distances across the snow-covered plains are too great for them to travel in severe weather; the schoolhouse is closed, and there is nothing for them to do but to house themselves and long for spring. Each family must live mainly to itself, and life, shut up in the little wooden farmhouses, cannot well be very cheerful.

Temporary Diversion

A drive to the nearest town is almost the only diversion. There the farmers and their wives gather in the stores and manage to enjoy a little sociability. The big coal stove gives out a grateful warmth, and there is a pleasant odor of dried codfish, groceries, and ready-made clothing. The women look at the display of thick cloths and garments, and wish the crop had been better, so that they could buy some of the things of which they are badly in need. The men smoke corncob pipes and talk politics. It is a cold drive home across the wind-swept prairies, but at least they have had a glimpse of a little broader and more comfortable life than that of the isolated farm.

Little Social Life

There are few social events in the life of these prairie farmers to enliven the monotony of the long winter evenings; no singing-schools, spelling-schools, debating clubs, or church gatherings. Neighborly calls are infrequent, because of the long distances which separate the farmhouses, and because, too, of the lack of homogeneity of the people. They have no common past to talk about. They were strangers to one another when they arrived in this new land, and their work and ways have not thrown them much together. Often the strangeness is intensified by differences of national origin. There are Swedes, Norwegians, Germans, French Canadians, and perhaps even ... Finns and Icelanders, among the settlers, and the Americans come from many different states. It is hard to establish any social bond in such a mixed population, yet one and all need social intercourse, as the thing most essential to pleasant living, after food, fuel, shelter, and clothing.

Insanity

An alarming amount of insanity occurs in the new prairie states among farmers and their wives. In proportion to their numbers, the Scandinavian settlers furnish the largest contingent to the asylums. The reason is not far to seek. These people came from cheery little farm villages. Life in the fatherland was hard and toilsome, but it was not lonesome. Think for a moment how great the change must be from the white-walled, red-roofed village on a Norway fiord, with its church and schoolhouse, its fishing-boats on the blue inlet, and its green mountain walls towering aloft to snow fields, to an isolated cabin on a Dakota prairie, and say if it is any wonder that so many Scandinavians lose their mental balance.

There is but one remedy for the dreariness of farm life on the prairies: the isolated farmhouse must be abandoned, and the people must draw together in villages.

2. Sociability in East Harlem[1]
✣ *Edward Corsi*

Contrast the loneliness you have just read about with the sociability described below. The setting is New York City's East Harlem. Yet the place itself is not important; for there were many other urban neighborhoods where immigrants enjoyed an equally rich social life among people of their own kind. The author of the following piece, born in Italy, was a social worker in the 1920's. During the great depression of the next decade, he served as President Hoover's commissioner of immigration and naturalization and then entered the cabinet of New York Mayor Fiorello H. La Guardia (page 135) as relief administrator. The article was published in 1925. ■

My neighborhood is on the East Side. Two hundred thousand men and women in a territory less than one square mile in size. . . . Nowhere in America is congestion with its inevitable poverty, disease, and crime more pronounced, nor life with its interminable ebbs and flows more strenuous. The lower East Side (we are on the upper East Side) questions our claim to greatest congestion. Perhaps it is right. . . . But the lower East Side will concede us, we hope, one honor at least — that of having the most populated block in the city, in the country. Of this we are proud. Five thousand human beings in one city street; as many as fifteen to a four-room flat; two, three, and even four hundred to a tenement intended for fifty! . . .

The Neighborhood Changes

When William Kieft was Governor of Nieuw Amsterdam,[2] a few years before Peter Stuyvesant came on the scene, old Dr. Johannes de la Montagne, founder of Nieuw Haarlem, wrote to a friend overseas that his village, now my neighborhood, had no less than "thirty male residents, mostly heads of families and freeholders." That was quite a number for those days! Later on, when the dignified Washington made love to pretty Marie Philipse (here in my neighborhood) and

[1] Edward Corsi, "My Neighborhood," *Outlook*, CXLI (September 16, 1925), pp. 90–92.
[2] [1637–1645.]

Nieuw Amsterdam had become New York, the modest village had grown to a fair-sized town. It remained as such until America's gates, in the decades following the Civil War, were thrown open to the breadwinners of the Old World. Then the change came. The newcomers not only dispossessed the old stock, but transformed the quiet-living American community into a noisy miniature Europe of their own....

Twenty-seven Nationalities

There are twenty-seven nationalities in the neighborhood, including, of course, the Chinese laundrymen, the gypsy phrenologists, the Greek and Syrian storekeepers. East, along the banks of the East River, ... are the Italians; on Pleasant Avenue are the Poles, Austrians, and Hungarians. West ... are the Jews, sons of many lands; near them are the Turks and Spaniards. North ... are the Negroes, gradually moving down.... South, resisting the merciless invasion of the Jews and Italians, are the Germans and Irish, remnants of a stock that once ruled this part of town. Scattered throughout the neighborhood, with limits well defined, are lesser groups — Finns, Russians, French, Swedes, Danes, Rumanians, and Jugoslavs. Here and there, like refugees in exile, are a few Americans of old stock....

The cosmopolitan character of the neighborhood is evidenced, not only in the signs of many languages, the chop suey, rotisseries, and spaghetti houses, the synagogues and Catholic temples, the flags of many colors, the foreign papers on every news-stand, but in the types one meets on the streets — tall blond Nordics, olive-skinned, dark-haired Mediterraneans, long-bearded Semites and Slavs, massive Africans, East Indians, gypsies, Japanese, and Chinese....

Little Italy

"Little Italy," with its picturesque markets, tenor-voiced vendors, Vesuvio restaurants, candle-shops, statuette dealers, religious and patriotic societies, dark-eyed *signorine* and buoyant men, is but a reproduction of Bella Napoli.[3] The feast of Our lady of Mount Carmel, one of many feasts throughout the year, with its processions of barefoot devotees winding through the decorated and lighted streets, is a dramatic event....

[3] [**Bella Napoli:** beautiful Naples.]

The Neighborhood in General

What is true of the Italian is true, more or less, of others in the neighborhood, of the neighborhood in general. The life of the Old World is re-enacted here. Were it not for the "flappers" and the "cake-eaters" of the younger generation, "Americans" to the core, the illusion would be complete. They "Americanize" the picture, but do not destroy it. Paris is not more interesting nor Vienna gayer than this miniature Europe which is Paris, Vienna, and Naples combined. To be sure, we have not the imposing opera houses, theaters, and hotels of those cities. . . . We are a community of workers, and our life is proletarian. But we have our cafés, rathskellers, spaghetti houses, cabarets, dance-halls, and, since the Volstead Act, our "speak-easies" for the "regulars." We have Yiddish theaters and Italian marionette shows, not to mention the movie and vaudeville houses. Our second-hand book-shops are as good as those of Paris. So are our music stores.

3. The Church[1]
✤ Robert E. Park and Herbert A. Miller

> *The most treasured immigrant institution was the church or synagogue. But in the Old World a person was born into a parish or congregation where the buildings already existed. Here, on the other hand, the immigrants had to organize themselves into a religious body, find a pastor, raise money without government help, and erect a house of worship. Over the years, moreover, the church or synagogue took on functions deriving from the American experience. This process of adjusting to America is outlined below in the brief history of a Catholic parish in an industrial town in Connecticut between 1889 and 1920. It was written by the priest of the parish.* ■

The first Pole who came to New Britain [Connecticut] was Mr. Thomasz Ostrowski. After him others began to arrive and in September, 1889, a mutual-help society under the patronage of St. Michael

[1] From Robert E. Park and Herbert A. Miller, *Old World Traits Transplanted* (New York: Harper & Brothers, 1921), pp. 217–219.

the Archangel was established. . . . In 1894 Priest Dr. Misicki, rector of the parish in Meriden, Connecticut, came every Sunday to celebrate the holy mass in New Britain in the old Irish church on Myrtle Street, at a yearly salary of $500. Then the society, together with other noble-minded Poles, began to think about establishing a Polish parish, which was organized under the patronage of St. Kazimierz. . . .

St. Kazimierz Founded

In September, 1895, Rev. Lucyan Bójnowski . . . was appointed rector of the parish . . . and a wooden church was built under the patronage of the Sweetest Heart of Jesus. . . . First of all Priest Bójnowski made efforts to turn the people from drink, from getting married in court, from indecent dress, from holding balls on Saturdays and nightly revelries, from playing cards, loafing in saloons, fighting in their homes, immoral life, conjugal infidelity, theft, bad education of children, indecent behavior on the street, and disorderly conduct at weddings and christenings. Instead, he encouraged them to go to confession and communion, to participate in various divine services, to belong to fraternities, etc. . . .[2]

A Quarter Century Later

(1) The old church now [1921] contains schoolrooms and the rectorate. It is worth $25,000. (2) The new church (the largest in New Britain) cost $150,000 when built, and is now worth $300,000. (3) The new school was built in 1904 at the cost of $150,000. It is now worth twice as much. (4) A house for the teaching nuns is worth $15,000. (5) The parish has a cemetery worth $25,000. There are no debts on all of these buildings and lots.

(6) In 1889 a co-operative bakery was established with an original capital of $6000 contributed by 5 associations. At present its property is worth $60,000. (7) In 1904 a Polish orphanage was founded. It owns now 4 houses, 146 acres within the limits of the town, 107 acres outside the limits, 30 head of cattle, 7 horses, 70 hogs, 500 hens; total value over $200,000. No debts. (8) There is a parochial printing office. The lot, the building, and the machinery are worth $35,000. There is a debt of $5000.

(9) The Polish Loan and Industrial Corporation, founded in 1915, has a capitalization of $50,000, and owns $45,000 worth of houses.

[2] From a history of the parish of New Britain, written by Priest Bójnowski, and published in 1902. [Footnote in original.]

112 Community Life

(10) The Polish Investment and Loan Corporation, founded in 1915, has a capitalization of $75,000 and real estate worth $10,000. (11) The People's Savings Bank, founded in December, 1916, has $496,000 deposited. (12) The New Britain Clothing Corporation, founded in 1919, capitalized at $50,000, has merchandise worth $100,000 and real estate worth $140,000. (13) The White Eagle Factory, established in 1919, capitalized at $25,000, produces cutlery. All of the above are co-operative organizations.

(14) We gave 750 soldiers to the American army and 301 to the Polish army [in Word War I]. (15) We have contributed to the Polish Relief Fund and to the Polish Army Fund, up to this moment, $110,672.36. (16) The parish counts now nearly 9000 souls, including children. In 1894 there were only 700, counting Lithuanians, Slovaks, and Poles. (17) The parochial school has 35 teachers and an attendance of 1736 children.[3]

[3] Letter of Priest Bójnowski to Florian Znaniecki. We know from other sources that most of the institutions of the parish are due to the initiative of Priest Bójnowski himself. [Footnote in original.]

4. Mutual Aid Societies[1]
♣ Robert E. Park and Herbert A. Miller

The immigrants arrived not only with religious needs but also with a need to cope with sickness, accidents, unemployment, and death. They had an understandable fear — even terror — of being disabled or dying in a strange land without a proper burial. Therein lies the reason for founding what were called mutual-aid, or mutual-benefit, societies. Each immigrant group established its own societies. The following piece, published in 1921, concerns the mutual-aid societies of only three groups, but they were representative of others. ■

Slovenians

The Slovenians have many fraternal organizations. The most important are: the Carniolian Slovenian Catholic Union, organized in Joliet, Illinois, April 2, 1894. It has 17,000 members, capital to the

[1] Park and Miller, *Old World Traits Transplanted* (New York: Harper & Brothers, 1921), pp. 128–130.

WHERE THEY LIVED: Immigrants who had no money for further travel settled in the port cities where they arrived. Jacob Riis's camera recorded scenes from the crowded New York tenements that served as first homes for many eastern Europeans (left and below). Other immigrants headed farther west. German-speaking Mennonites from Russia settled in Kansas, where they built earth-hugging homes (above) like those they had left on the Russian steppes. With precious seeds of winter wheat brought from the old country, these hard-working farmers transformed the Kansas plains into rich fields of grain.

amount of $650,000, and has paid out $1,376,135.32 in benefits. The Slovenian National Benefit Society was organized in 1904, and has its headquarters at Chicago. Its capital is $525,000; it has over 18,000 members and has paid out in benefits $1,029,081. It has 341 branches, distributed in 27 states, and one in Canada. The Slovenian Workingmen's Benefit Association was founded August 16, 1908, in Johnstown, Pennsylvania. Its assets on June 30, 1918, were $158,096.93, of which $45,000 was invested in Liberty Bonds. It has 146 branches, which include 7299 adult members and 4500 junior members. It has paid out in benefits $1,000,000. In Cleveland there are 5 branches with a total of 605 members.

Italians

The Italians of Chicago have 110 mutual-aid societies, representing a population of about 150,000. As the names suggest, the membership is generally from the same Italian province and frequently from the same village. . . . The most popular . . . , the *Unione Siciliana*, has 28 lodges. Sick benefits in this order range from $8 to $12 per week, and a death benefit of $1000 is paid. The monthly fees of these societies run from 30 to 60 cents. There is also, in all societies, a death assessment, making the average cost of membership from $12 to $15 per year. . . . Funeral expenses ranging from $50 to $90 are paid, and every member makes a contribution of $2 to the family of the dead member. During the sickness of a member all other members are obliged to visit and assist him if he lacks a family. . . . All members are obliged to attend the funeral, under penalty for absence. A band of musicians is always provided.

Jews

. . . The Jewish [fraternal] orders constitute a valuable and important factor in our commercial life. The interests of about a million Jews are involved in their existence and welfare. . . . An important phase is that the recipient of benefits from the lodge or order does not lose his self-respect, nor his standing in the organization, as is often the case of recipients of public charity. . . .

The lodges of the various orders have been and still are the most valuable schools through which our immigrated Jews pass. Many have learned their English at their lodge meetings. Others have acquired there their knowledge of parliamentary procedure and decorum at public meetings. Many of our best-known public men and speakers have begun their careers modestly, in filling an office in their lodge or joining the debates at the meetings. In fact most of our people gain their connection with and knowledge of American Jewish activities, and take an interest in the same, through their affiliation with the Jewish fraternal orders. . . . For organizing, molding and interesting large masses of Jews in the large Jewish problems, they have been found the best means.

5. The Press[1]
✦ Winifred Rauschenbusch

> By 1920 over a thousand newspapers in more than thirty foreign languages were being published in the United States. Along with the church and fraternal organizations, the press was crucial in keeping alive native languages. That, in turn, strengthened the cohesiveness of immigrant communities. Yet, as the following piece shows, the press reported more activities in America than in the old countries. Paradoxical as it may seem, the foreign-language newspaper was an important agency of Americanization. ■

As a type of the foreign-language paper modeled on the American newspaper, the Milwaukee *Herold* is one of the most interesting German papers.

The owners of the *Herold* are connected with the tanning and brewery interests of Milwaukee and as such are an integral part of Milwaukee's commercial and political life. The *Herold* is not an isolated newspaper; it is the morning paper of the Germania Corporation, the largest German newspaper corporation in the United States.

Instead of pointing out what is American about the paper, it is really necessary to point out what is German. The sensational content of the general news, the diversity of the "ads," the features, such as market reports, women's patterns, and sporting columns, characteristic of American papers, and the amount of sensational news dealing with the breakdown of family relations, all mark the paper as American.

[1] Winifred Rauschenbusch, in Robert E. Park, *The Immigrant Press and Its Control* (New York: Harper & Brothers, 1922), pp. 353–354.

116   Community Life

The paper is, of course, entirely commercial, and as such caters both to the German-born who have assimilated American ways and those who have not. For the latter the paper retains its serial story and a page of organization notices with the brief headlines and neatly topical arrangement characteristic of a European newspaper. This page, which might be supposed to reflect the life of the German colony of Milwaukee, is amusingly penetrated with American customs and content. The St. Aloysius Sodality of St. Michael's Catholic Church presents on Sunday a play called "A Man from Denver." The Humboldt Verein No. 6, G. U. G. Germania, at a special session to be addressed by the Headquarters Agitation Committee, promises to have the G. U. G. Germania Booster Club there to make things lively. A Lutheran church, whose members are scattering, presents its pastor with an auto, so that the German church will not be forced to disintegrate.

6. Conflict Between Generations

The ancient Greek and Hebrew writers believed that the conflict between parents and children is universal. It probably is, but in America immigration gave a special twist to the generation gap. Immigrant parents grew up in one kind of society, and their native American children in still another. Roles of authority were frequently reversed when a child questioned his father's and mother's loyalties, customs, expectations, and language. ∎

A. BOHEMIANS IN CHICAGO[1]

✣ Mary E. McDowell

When Mary E. McDowell wrote the following article early in this century, the majority of the population in northern industrial cities consisted of immigrants and their American-born children. As a social worker who lived among immigrants in Chicago, Miss McDowell was particularly sensitive to the generational struggle in their families. The story she tells about one Bohemian-Amer-

[1] Mary E. McDowell, "The Struggle in the Family Life," *Charities,* XIII (December 3, 1904), pp. 196–197.

ican family was true of many other families all over America. In reading her account try to relive the tensions and hostilities on both sides of the generation gap. They were a fall-out in the painful process of Americanization. ■

It is said that the criminals of the cities come from the ranks of the children of the immigrants, not from the immigrants themselves. Those who live near these transplanted people tell us of the struggle in the family life between the standards of the old country father and mother and those of the children who have learned the language and caught the spirit of the new country. . . .

Gap Between Children and Parents

The child stands between the new life and its strange customs; he is the interpreter; he often is the first breadwinner; he becomes the authority in the family.

The parents are displaced because they are helpless and must trust the children. This superficial, though very practical, superiority forces the children and parents into a false position with relation to each other and towards the outside world. The parents have religious and social ideals and an impassioned faith that in America is to be found liberty and independence. The children's ideals are formed by the teachers, the politicians, and often the saloonkeepers. The parents' ideals are discredited; they are old-fashioned. In some way the children enter into their parents' vague desire for freedom, but it becomes to them such freedom as is hurriedly realized in a do-as-you-please philosophy. They have lost the restraints of an old community feeling that surrounded the parents in their old home and have not yet become rooted in the new restraints by the public opinion of a neighborhood they do not know. The parents' values are belittled and their loyalties scorned.

"Shut up talking about Bohemia," said a boy to his mother who was shedding homesick tears as she spoke of the beauties of her old home. "We are going to live in America, not in Bohemia." She had the vision of beauty, while she was living in the sordid ugliness of the stockyard district of Chicago, and her boy could never have her vision.

The children are determined to drop the mother tongue, and they very soon learn English, while the parents are past the age when it is easy to acquire a new language. One often hears of children refusing to answer in the language of the family. Everything seems to be done to develop and educate the children, forgetting that this cannot be done for the child independently of the family or the community. The school, the church, the social settlement all emphasize the child's importance. The parents are ignored, left behind, and the breach between the new and the old in the family is not spanned as yet by any of the agencies in the community.

How to Bridge the Gap

. . . How shall this breach be bridged? What is done will be experimental, but something must be done, for the situation is serious and often tragic. The public school lectures given in the foreign tongues to adults are suggestive, and lead one to ask why not enlarge the usefulness of the schoolhouse to meet the need of foreign families.

To begin the bridge from the child's side: cannot the parents, their home country, its beauties, its heroes, legends, stories, history, songs, be made of interest to the children? Will it not place the parents in an atmosphere of poetry of idealization and make them an important factor to the children? Admiration is a strong element in education. Win back the parental authority by admiring all that is admirable in their past. Create a historic perspective that will give self-respect to the new citizenship and will lead to respect for authority in the home and the state.

Start the bridge from the side of the parent by giving to them in their native tongue, American history, constitutional history, old country songs, old country scenes, art, etc., with that of the new country.

Let the parents and children *together* have a special life in the schoolhouse, bring them together in social relation with English-speaking teachers and friends, let them sing together the national songs of America and of the old lands.

Instilling Reverence for Old and New

Patriotic Americans may think this dangerous and say the English language is the only one that must be used in the schools, forgetting that this closes all avenues of culture to the adult foreigners. It is more dangerous not to supply this great need of the hungry hearts of the homesick old country parents who are losing their grip on their children. The too early developed young Americans must gain reverence for their parents and for authority in the home, or we shall have an increase of lawlessness. Open the schools for the foreign parents who, with their children, may learn what true freedom is and what American hospitality is. What the new patriotic societies are doing for Americans, we can do for the foreigners; recall the best of their past, recognize their heroes and start an impulse of admiration for all that is noble in the old and the new.

B. CUBANS IN MIAMI[1]

✤ The New York Times

Almost 70 years have passed since Miss McDowell wrote the magazine article you have just read, and yet little seems to have changed. One of the most recent immigrant groups in America, Miami's large Cuban population, is currently troubled by a generation gap similar to that of Chicago's Bohemians seven decades ago. It is aggravated, however, by the cultural upheaval that has been shaking America as a whole since the mid-1960's. That is a major conclusion of the following selection, which was written for The New York Times. ■

MIAMI, April 15, 1971 — Puffs of clouds sail across the Miami evening sky and a buttermilk moon casts a soft half-light on the roofs of the sprawling Cuban district. Under one roof, Ada Merritt Junior High School, America's newest immigrants sing a chorus of their first English words: ". . . four, five, six . . ." Rolando Amador, a handsome teacher with dark curly hair, stands beneath a giant banyan tree in the courtyard and listens to the sing-song count of his countrymen echoing from an upstairs classroom window.

Successful Immigrants

"There are many people in Miami who still resent Cubans settling here," he says, "but for the most part we have been the most successful immigrants in American history. Americans find it hard to look down their nose at us because we arrived here loaded with American characteristics. We are just too outgoing and enterprising and hardworking for them to stay mad with us."

[1] "Cuban Exiles, Too, Are Troubled by Generation Gap," *The New York Times*, April 16, 1971.

Ten years ago, on April 17, 1961, Cuban exiles suffered a bitter defeat at the Bay of Pigs, an event the people of Little Havana, the southwest section of this city, will commemorate this Saturday by dedicating a memorial. That defeat marked the end of the exiles' serious hopes for a swift return to their homeland. Since then, the population of Little Havana has swelled to 300,000 Cubans, about half the number of refugees who have entered this country since Fidel Castro seized power in 1959.

It's Dumb to Be Raised Like My Parents

In recent years, as more and more Cubans accepted permanent exile, they have turned their energies away from chimerical anti-Castro talk to doing combat with the American way of life.

Mr. Amador, a lawyer in pre-Castro Cuba who now heads his school's community program for adults and children, shows a visitor around the school, which recalls a turn-of-the-century settlement house in New York City. Next to the classroom where Cuban adults struggle with English, children study the Spanish language. Down the hall, men who were airline pilots in Cuba learn the intricacies of Federal air control operations, while in the auditorium boys from the neighborhood hold band practice.

"I still can't believe they are Cuban children when I see this long hair and bell-bottom trousers," Mr. Amador says with a smile. "Their parents go crazy with them. Do you know what it means for a Cuban father to see his son grow a beard like Castro? And the older generation thinks the peace symbol their children wear is diabolic — a twisted cross. I know of families where fathers and sons have fist fights over these things."

In the school cafeteria a rehearsal is under way for a Quince, a traditional celebration of a girl's 15th birthday that signals her symbolic entry into womanhood. In the middle of the floor a dance master instructs 14 teen-age couples in the ritualized performance as Gloria Beltran, the girl who will be honored, watches from the sidelines near a group of middle-age women chaperones.

Gloria, whose long brown hair gives a heart-shaped frame to her face, says that she does not feel as free in this country as she did in Cuba, which she left three years ago, because her parents are concerned about drugs and crime in Miami and are very strict with her. After her party next month, she will be allowed to date, but only in the company of a chaperone, presumably her mother, who speaks no

English, a custom that Gloria says she will accept until her marriage.

However, one of her friends, Graciela Balanzategin, a pretty 13-year-old who left Cuba when she was 4 years old and only dimly remembers life on the island, expresses her distaste with Cuban tradition that builds a wall around a young woman until her wedding day.

"I don't want to be raised like my parents were," she insists in a voice free of accent. "I think it's dumb."

Another girl who is older described her fights with her family over dating. "They finally realized that to get along they would have to let me out of the house more often. I told them it was either that or else I was moving out," she said.

Two months ago Mr. Amador started a weekly group therapy session at the school called El Club. A psychiatric caseworker meets with neighborhood teen-agers who are experiencing serious problems with their parents.

The Price of Success

Employment is high in the Cuban community and the glow of prosperity is visible in the auto showrooms and the miles of shops with Spanish names that line S.W. Eighth Street, the heart of Little Havana, where in the late evening the clubs and cafes are alive with people enjoying la vida buena.

The price of success has been costly. Conversion to American styles of living (fast food, traffic jams, uprooted families) has confounded and frightened those who seek protection and comfort inside Little Havana as more of their sons and daughters move away to the suburbs (crab grass, supermarkets, car pools). The upheaval has threatened to disrupt the traditional strong Cuban family unit, built around cousins, aunts and grandparents, and divorce, suicide, and mental illness have risen sharply.

Generation Gap Compounded

Part of the problem rests with a period of immigration that coincided with a decade of upheaval in the host country. The initial cultural shock was compounded by the dizzying social changes under way in this country that perplexed most Americans. The generation gap that was splitting native families, for instance, was creating unbridgeable chasms for Cuban fathers and sons who had to contend with additional problems of language and culture.

Bernardo Benes, a community leader with bright blue eyes and vivid red hair, worries that the older generation is neglecting these mounting problems, just as he says they allowed social conditions in pre-Castro Cuba to deteriorate until it was too late.

"Part of our downfall in Cuba was the fact that we had no national conscience," remarks Mr. Benes as he sits in a popular cafe called Badia's and sips dark, aromatic Cuban coffee that is heavily laced with sugar. "Here the people are more selfish than ever.

"The generation gap among Cubans is far worse than the Americans," he says, "and Cubans better start facing up to it and finding solutions instead of just sitting around waving the anti-Castro flag. That way we will be more effective anti-Communists."

For the present, he says, the exiles must prepare for an indefinite stay in the United States, and he concedes that as many as 50 per cent or more of the Cubans would never leave their adopted country even if given the chance to return to Cuba. "Despite the fact that the Cuban exiles have been the most privileged political exiles in history, it has been a long and sad 10 years for us," he says, and finishes drinking his coffee.

7. Black Immigrant Communities[1]
✤ Ira De A. Reid

To many American whites, black immigrants were indistinguishable from native Negroes with roots deep in the American past. But in Harlem, and other communities like it, the immigrants were very distinguishable indeed. Like white immigrants from different parts of the world, they differed from each other, and from native Americans as well, with regard to language, religion, national loyalties, customs and habits. (See Section II, selection 6.)

Understandably, each immigrant group created a community life of its own. Also, each of them ran into a generational problem. The cultural adjustment of black immigrants can serve as a summary of the themes presented in this section of the book.

[1] Ira De A. Reid, *The Negro Immigrant, His Background, Characteristics and Social Adjustment, 1899–1937* (New York: Columbia University Press, 1939), pp. 124, 126, 128–129, 131–133, 144–145, 156–157.

Black Immigrant Communities

The following selection, which is about Harlem, was written by an Atlanta University professor of sociology on the eve of World War II. ■

The native Negro is relatively homogeneous in his religious activity, being first a Baptist and then a Methodist. The foreign-born Negro, however, is found, for the most part, in the Lutheran, Christian, Moravian, Wesleyan, Protestant Episcopal, Baptist (Jamaican) and Catholic churches — and "not averse to having a white pastor," since he had been accustomed to one in the islands whence he has come. The Census of Religious Bodies for 1926 listed the number of churches among Negroes in congregations with which foreign-born Negroes usually affiliate as follows:

African Orthodox Church	13
African Orthodox Church of New York	3
Christian Church	1,044
Lutheran Congregations (United Lutheran)	3,650
Wesleyan Methodist	619
Moravians	127
Episcopals (Protestant and Reformed)	7,368
Roman Catholic	16,940
Seventh Day Adventists	1,981

Religion and the church are the last bulwark of the Negro immigrants' traditional system. Religious attitudes remain strong even in the second generation of immigrants and are manifest in the degree to which children are sent to Sunday School, the influence of the rector or the priest, and the importance attached to such customs as are part of their parents' religious practices. The most modern church in Harlem is the Community Church (later affiliated with the Unitarian denomination) organized, pastored and, to a great extent, attended by foreign-born Negroes. But at the same time the majority of the churches keep alive the tradition of the homeland. An excellent example is provided by this announcement of a Coronation Ball, in which the values of the homeland are combined with interests in the current setting. Even the subscription price is given in English monetary values.

More than 5,000 persons attended this coronation ball honoring the new king and queen — George VI and Elizabeth. The Union Jack and colonial flags were flown with the Stars and Stripes, and the singing of "God Save the King" preceded that of "The Star Spangled Banner" in what was called "a highlight in international amity." The affair was attended by Sir Gerald Campbell, British Consul-General to New York, and eighteen members of his staff. . . .

The church more so than any other institution has tended to keep alive homeland values, frequently taking as its responsibility the fostering of extra-religious functions that would otherwise increase the visibility of the immigrant group. Thus, the mourning attending the death of George V was widely observed in Harlem churches. The *affaires de coeur* of Edward VIII were widely condemned by the ecclesiastical leaders. Special coronation services for George VI were held at one of the Baptist churches and a coronation tea was poured at the Wesleyan Methodist Church. Through such activity the church becomes a conserver of the culture as well as an organization for facilitating the immigrants' adjustment and preventing complete personal disorganization. . . .

Funerals and Wakes

The wake of the West Indies is perpetuated in the United States. There friends sit up all night with the relations of the dead, praying, feasting and socializing. In some islands the "wake" is an occasion for much merriment for the younger groups, ranging in type from the simple telling of Anansi stories to dancing and drinking parties. No body is kept in the home longer than three days. Celebrations may continue for the whole period prior to the funeral. After the burial services friends and relatives return to the home of the deceased and are served food and drink as befits the class of the family. In New York City the "wake" continues to be a period of celebration for some islanders, although the corpse is now embalmed and kept in an undertaking establishment. Friends are still served at the home after the funeral. The element of merrymaking is determined by the moral standards and religious beliefs of the decedent's family. The occasion is always the perfect setting for reunions and reminiscences. . . .

Marriage

Customs of marriage undergo only slight revision in the foreign-born family of culture, particularly if both parents are foreign-born. There must be a wedding. The old customs of courtship in which the young native upon becoming interested in a young lady "addressed" himself to her parents, stating his intentions before being permitted to call, have passed. But, perhaps, no event is more solemnly and more glamorously staged than the romantic customs of the wedding. All of the formal traditions of the church wedding, followed by only the wealthy in the United States, are included in the nuptial ceremony. As one writer has expressed it, "The big question in West Indian circles is not whom you marry but how you marry." . . . An ordinary American marriage might mean only the girl and boy's dropping two nickels in the subway and slipping downtown and becoming Mr. and Mrs. But your true Jamaican marriage, your true Barbadian marriage, your true Virgin Island or Trinidadian marriage means prosperity for everybody. . . . The florist, the dressmaker, the shoe salesman, the caterer, the jeweler, the tailor, the butcher, the baker and the candlestick maker all get their share when the bride of island lineage is given in marriage." Receptions are attended by from two to five hundred guests, and, to a much greater extent than is true among the native-born Negroes, the strict regulations of formal attire and etiquette are observed. . . .

Other Groups

Since 1925 the major group life of the immigrants who wish to maintain ethnic contacts has been through the various beneficial, social and cultural societies they have organized. These institutions have, in the main, been the direct outgrowth of circumstances and need. Thus one finds approximately 30 benevolent associations and mutual aid societies organized by immigrant groups from Anguilla, Antigua, Guiana, Dominica, Grenada, Montserrat, British Jamaica, St. Lucia, Turks Caicos Island, Trinidad, and the British Virgin Islands.

Numerous social clubs organized on the basis of color-class plus status in the United States; literary clubs, particularly among the British West Indians; cricket clubs and tennis associations. In addition, there are such politically centered groups as the Afro-American Voters Coalition, to foster naturalization and political participation; Utilities D'Haiti to promote the sale of Haitian products; Caribbean Fisheries to foster the development of commerce and trade in sea foods; several Virgin Island societies to promote the civic, political, economic and social welfare of the Virgin Islands and their people whether at home or abroad; the Consolidated Tenant's League to promote the housing interests of Negro residents; the West Indies Communities' Development League to encourage colonization in

British Guiana; The Council on West Indian Affairs; the Jamaica Progressive League; and The United Aid for Persons of African Descent....

The Second Generation

The second generation of Negro immigrants now numbers over eighty thousand persons. Except among the Spanish and Portuguese-speaking groups these children of immigrants have lost most of the social characteristics of their parents, reacting more favorably to the traditions and institutions of the Negro community. They react against the standards, interests and attitudes of the foreign group, promoting thereby conflicts between the two generations as well as between the two cultures. In the main, the conflicts are those of mental attitudes rather than of physical behavior. This is partly due to the fact that the vast majority of foreign-born persons come from English-speaking countries, bringing with them family and culture traditions which if not exactly identical with American customs, are certainly not incompatible with the tenets of the social *milieu* in which their children grow up....

Though the children of Negro immigrants quickly lose their identity as immigrant offspring, they frequently find themselves amid conflicting situations. Many of them, oppressed by feelings of inferiority in such areas as New York and Boston, break away from the homes of their parents and eventually repudiate their origins.

Assimilation in both its economic and cultural aspects does not differ greatly for the immigrant children and those of the second generation. The older generation may encounter psychological friction in endeavoring to change its habits, but education and experience quickly modify habits, customs and traditions for the younger group. Frequently the clashes between the older and younger immigrants of a family group occur when the parents have not been able to secure the economic footing that would permit a ready and facile adjustment to the demands of the new environment. But they, as do the youth of the second generation, learn to sing "America," and pointedly state the shortcomings of the United States much more quickly than their forebears.

VI. Politics

The function of American government, according to James Madison, is to mediate conflicting interests. This view of democracy assumes that society is composed of many groups and, what is equally important, that those groups have a right to satisfy legitimate needs through politics. Newcomers to America had such needs but came from societies where politically most of them had counted for nothing. The extent to which immigrants learned the meaning of representative government was, therefore, a form of Americanization. ■

1. Ward Politics[1]
✤ George Washington Plunkitt

The ward boss was the local, or neighborhood, leader of a political party. Usually the native American child of foreign-born parents, he stood as a bridge between the Old and the New Worlds. The immigrants looked up to him as friend, adviser, and benefactor, and gave him their votes in exchange for his favors. No one has described how the system worked better than George Washington Plunkitt, who broke into politics in the 1850's through Tammany Hall, the Democratic party machine in New York City. In the following talk recorded by a newspaperman early in the 1900's, Plunkitt sums up half a century's experience in ward politics. ■

---

[1] From the book *Plunkitt of Tammany Hall* by William L. Riordon. Dutton Paperback Edition (1963), pp. 25–28. Reprinted by permission of E. P. Dutton & Co., Inc.

There's only one way to hold a district: you must study human nature and act accordin'. You can't study human nature in books. Books is a hindrance more than anything else. If you have been to college, so much the worse for you. You'll have to unlearn all you learned before you can get right down to human nature, and unlearnin' takes a lot of time. Some men can never forget what they learned at college. Such men may get to be district leaders by a fluke, but they never last.

To learn real human nature you have to go among the people, see them and be seen. I know every man, woman, and child in the Fifteenth District, except them that's been born this summer — and I know some of them, too. I know what they like and what they don't like, what they are strong at and what they are weak in, and I reach them by approachin' at the right side.

Young People

For instance, here's how I gather in the young men. I hear of a young feller that's proud of his voice, thinks that he can sing fine. I ask him to come around to Washington Hall and join our Glee Club. He comes and sings, and he's a follower of Plunkitt for life. Another young feller gains a reputation as a baseball player in a vacant lot. I bring him into our baseball club. That fixes him. You'll find him workin' for my ticket at the polls next election day. Then there's the feller that likes rowin' on the river, the young feller that makes a name as a waltzer on his block; the young feller that's handy with his dukes — I rope them all in by givin' them opportunities to show themselves off. I don't trouble them with political arguments. I just study human nature and act accordin'. . . .

Older Voters

As to the older voters, I reach them, too. No, I don't send them campaign literature. That's rot. People can get all the political stuff they want to read — and a good deal more, too — in the papers. Who reads speeches, nowadays, anyhow? It's bad enough to listen to them. You ain't goin' to gain any votes by stuffin' the letter boxes with campaign documents. Like as not you'll lose votes, for there's nothin' a man hates more than to hear the letter carrier ring his bell and go to the letter box expectin' to find a letter he was lookin' for, and find only a lot of printed politics. I met a man this very mornin' who told me he voted the Democratic state ticket last year just because the Republicans kept crammin' his letter box with campaign documents.

Ward Charity

What tells in holdin' your grip on your district is to go right down among the poor families and help them in the different ways they need help. I've got a regular system for this. If there's a fire in Ninth, Tenth, or Eleventh Avenue, for example, any hour of the day or night, I'm usually there with some of my election district captains as soon as the fire engines. If a family is burned out, I don't ask whether they are Republicans or Democrats, and I don't refer them to the Charity Organization Society, which would investigate their case in a month or two and decide they are worthy of help about the time they are dead from starvation. I just get quarters for them, buy clothes for them if their clothes were burned up, and fix them up till they get things runnin' again. It's philanthropy, but it's politics, too — mighty good politics. Who can tell how many votes one of these fires brings me? The poor are the most grateful people in the world, and, let me tell you, they have more friends in their neighborhoods than the rich have in theirs.

If there's a family in my district in want, I know it before the charitable societies do, and me and my men are first on the ground. I have a special corps to look up such cases. The consequence is that the poor look up to George W. Plunkitt as a father, come to him in trouble — and don't forget him on election day.

Another thing, I can always get a job for a deservin' man. I make it a point to keep on the track of jobs, and it seldom happens that I don't have a few up my sleeve ready for use. I know every big employer in the district and in the whole city, for that matter, and they ain't in the habit of sayin' no to me when I ask them for a job.

Never Forget the Children

And the children — the little roses of the district! Do I forget them? Oh, no! They know me, every one of them, and they know that a sight of Uncle George and candy means the same thing. Some of them are the best kind of vote-getters. I'll tell you a case. Last year a little Eleventh Avenue rosebud, whose father is a Republican, caught hold of his whiskers on election day and said she wouldn't let go till he'd promise to vote for me. And she didn't.

2. Tammany Attacked[1]
♣ Lincoln Steffens

The history of boss politics is, in part, a story of corruption, incompetence, graft, and stealing. Even Plunkitt said: "I seen my opportunities and I took 'em," though he defended himself by claiming that he practiced "honest graft." Periodically, therefore, reformers have attacked organizations like Tammany Hall. At the turn of this century, the journalist Lincoln Steffens made a reputation for himself by exposing abuses in municipal government in more than half a dozen major cities. The following selection contains the substance of Steffens' criticism of the Tammany leaders and the people who supported them. ■

Tammany is corruption with consent; it is bad government founded on the suffrages of the people. The Philadelphia [political] machine is more powerful. It rules Philadelphia by fraud and force and does not require the votes of the people. The Philadelphians do not vote for their machine; their machine votes for them. Tammany used to stuff the ballot boxes and intimidate voters; today there is practically none of that. Tammany rules, when it rules, by right of the votes of the people of New York. . . .

Democratic Corruption

Tammany's democratic corruption rests upon the corruption of the people, the plain people, and there lies its great significance; its grafting system is one in which more individuals share than any I have studied. The people themselves get very little; they come cheap, but they are interested. Divided into districts, the organization subdivides them into precincts or neighborhoods, and their sovereign power, in the form of votes, is bought up by kindness and petty privileges.

They are forced to a surrender, when necessary, by intimidation, but the leader and his captains have their hold because they take care of their own. They speak pleasant words, smile friendly smiles, notice

[1] Lincoln Steffens, *The Shame of the Cities* (New York: McClure, Phillips & Co., 1904), pp. 290–293, 295–296, 302.

the baby, give picnics . . . or a slap on the back; find jobs, most of them at the city's expense, but they have also news-stands, peddling privileges, railroad and other business places to dispense; they permit violations of the law, and if a man has broken the law without permission, see him through the court. Though a blow in the face is as readily given as a shake of the hand, Tammany kindness is real kindness, and will go far, remember long, and take infinite trouble for a friend.

The power that is gathered up thus cheaply, like garbage, in the districts is concentrated in the district leader, who in turn passes it on through a general committee to the boss. This is a form of living government, extra-legal, but very actual, and though the beginnings of it are purely democratic, it develops at each stage into an autocracy. . . .

The Leaders Are All Rich

No wonder the leaders are all rich; no wonder so many more Tammany men are rich than are the leaders in any other town; no wonder Tammany is liberal in its division of the graft. Croker[2] took the best and safest of it, and he accepted shares in others. He was "in on the Wall Street end," and the Tammany clique of financiers have knocked down and bought up at low prices Manhattan Railway stock by threats of the city's power over the road; they have been let in on Metropolitan deals and on the Third Avenue Railroad grab; the Ice trust is a Tammany trust; they have banks and trust companies, and through the New York Realty Company are forcing alliances with such financial groups as that of the Standard Oil Company.

Croker shared in these deals and business. He sold judgeships, taking his pay in the form of contributions to the Tammany campaign fund, of which he was treasurer, and he had the judges take from the regular real estate exchange all the enormous real estate business that passed through the courts, and give it to an exchange connected with the real estate business of his firm, Peter F. Meyer & Co. This alone would maintain a ducal estate in England. But his real estate business was greater than that. It had extraordinary legal facilities, the free advertising of abuse, the prestige of political privilege, all of which brought in trade; and it had advance information and followed, with profitable deals, great public improvements. . . .

[2] [**Richard Croker:** Tammany boss, 1886–1894 and 1897–1901.]

Selling Out Their Own People

Tammany leaders are usually the natural leaders of the people in these districts, and they are originally good-natured, kindly men. No one has a more sincere liking than I for some of those common but generous fellows; their charity is real, at first. But they sell out their own people. They do give them coal and help them in their private troubles, but, as they grow rich and powerful, the kindness goes out of the charity and they not only collect at their saloons or in rents — cash for their "goodness"; they not only ruin fathers and sons and cause the troubles they relieve; they sacrifice the children in the schools; let the Health Department neglect the tenements and, worst of all, plant vice in the neighborhood and in the homes of the poor.

3. Tammany Defended[1]
♣ William T. Stead

> *No one has yet refuted Lincoln Steffens' charges. Yet there is more to the story than he told. Below is a defense of Tammany by Richard Croker, the Tammany boss referred to in Steffens' account. Croker argues that his organization strengthened democracy by teaching immigrants how to be citizens. He expressed this idea in an interview that he gave to William T. Stead, a British journalist, while they were aboard a passenger liner crossing to England. Stead, at first skeptical, ended by agreeing with Croker.* ■

"Think what New York is and what the people of New York are [Croker said to me]. One half, more than one half, are of foreign birth. We have thousands upon thousands of men who are alien

---

[1] William T. Stead, "Mr. Richard Croker and Greater New York," *Review of Reviews*, XVI (October, 1897), pp. 345–346.

born, who have no ties connecting them with the city or the state. They do not speak our language, they do not know our laws, they are the raw material with which we have to build up the state. How are you to do it on mugwump[2] methods? I tell you it cannot be done."

Tammany's Service to the State

We were silent for a time. Mr. Croker took a turn or two, and then resumed:

"People abuse Tammany for this and for that. But they forget what they owe to Tammany. There is no denying the service which Tammany has rendered to the Republic. There is no such organization for taking hold of the untrained friendless man and converting him into a citizen. Who else would do it if we did not? Think of the hundreds of thousands of foreigners dumped into our city. They are too old to go to school. There is not a mugwump in the city who would shake hands with them. They are alone, ignorant strangers, a prey to all manner of anarchical and wild notions. Except to their employer they have no value to any one until they get a vote."

"And then they are of value to Tammany?" I said, laughing.

"Yes," said Mr. Croker, imperturbably; "and then they are of value to Tammany. And Tammany looks after them for the sake of their vote, grafts them upon the Republic, makes citizens of them in short; and although you may not like our motives or our methods, what other agency is there by which so long a row could have been hoed so quickly or so well? If we go down into the gutter it is because there are men in the gutter, and you have got to go down where they are if you are to do anything with them."

A Great Digestive Apparatus

"And so," I said, "Tammany is a great digestive apparatus, fed with all manner of coarse, indigestible food, that would give a finer stomach sudden death. But Tammany's stomach is strong; nothing is too rough for Tammany's gastric juice, and so you build up the body politic out of material —"

"That but for us [Croker broke in] would have remained undigested and indigestible — a menace to the state, a peril to society. You

---

[2] [**mugwump:** a political independent; one who seeks reforms in government without participating in party politics.]

may carp at our motives and criticize our methods — we do not complain. All that we say is we have done the work, and we deserve more recognition for that than we have yet received. . . ."

Distinctively American

"Tammany," said Mr. Croker, "is everywhere spoken against because it is said to be a foreign organization. Tammany, on the contrary, is a distinctively American organization founded on much more thorough-going American principles than those which find favor with the framers of the Charter of Greater New York, for instance. It makes me tired to hear their talk about foreigners. Where would America be today without foreigners?"

Mr. Croker's question this time admitted of an easy answer. It would have been in the hands of the Red Indians. From the *Mayflower* downwards the white people of the United States have all been foreigners at first.

Mr. Croker went on: "This discrimination against citizens because of the place of their birth seems to me un-American and unjust. Do not these men pay taxes, found homes, build up states, and do a great deal more in the government of the city than our assailants? They may have been born under another flag. But they forswear their own nationality, they swear allegiance to our flag; they filled the ranks of our armies in the great war;[3] everywhere they fulfill the duties and accept all the burdens of the citizen, and yet we are told they are foreigners.

"Sir," said Mr. Croker, speaking with more earnestness than was usual with him, "in Tammany Hall there is no discrimination against citizens on account of race or religion. We meet on the common ground of one common citizenship. We know no difference of Catholic or Protestant, of Irishman, German, or American. Every one is welcome amongst us who is true to the city and true to the party. To me the old sectarian quarrels are absolutely inconceivable. Priests have no voice in the management of Tammany Hall. It is of the people, created for the people, controlled by the people — the purest and strongest outcome of the working of democratic government under modern conditions."

[3] [great war: the Civil War.]

POLITICS: Lincoln Steffens (below), noted journalist, exposed the corruption of city governments controlled by political bosses who traded small favors in return for the votes of poor and uninformed immigrants. The cartoon below, drawn by Thomas Nast, depicts the leaders of Tammany Hall lining their pockets at the expense of the unfortunate poor. Fiorello H. La Guardia (left), son of immigrant parents and long-time mayor of New York City, fought for reform in city government and what he called "a new school of politics."

4. Issue Politics[1]
✤ Fiorello H. La Guardia

The most serious criticism of the bosses and their constituents is that they blocked efforts to reform evils in society. By World War I, however, a new generation was showing that immigrants and their political leaders could take a larger view of politics than did the old ward bosses. This new generation included men like Fiorello La Guardia and Alfred E. Smith (page 167). La Guardia was the American-born son of a Jewish mother and Italian father who had come to this country in 1880. He achieved fame first as a World War I hero, then as a seven-term Republican congressman, and finally as a three-term (1934–1945) mayor of New York City. Below, in a piece written just before he entered Congress from East Harlem, La Guardia called for "a new school of politics." ■

The new school of politics requires the carrying on of reform where necessary — the enactment of proper welfare legislation and putting into practice the guarantee in the great American Charter [the Constitution] that each citizen is entitled to happiness along with the protection of life and property. This new school is interested more in principles and policies than in the personal ambition of men to hold office. That is why followers of this new school of politics . . . are more interested in policies than candidates. . . .

Labor

But it has so happened, in all ages of the world, that some have labored, and others have without labor enjoyed a large proportion of the fruits. This is wrong, and should not continue. To secure to each laborer the whole product of his labor, or as nearly as possible, is a worthy object of any good government.

Please reread the last paragraph and then read it again. Who do you suppose wrote it? A great humanitarian, a great American, a

---

[1] Fiorello H. La Guardia, "The New School of Politics," Numbers 1, 3, 9 (mss., 1922), F. H. La Guardia Papers, Municipal Archives and Records Center, New York City.

great President, our own Abraham Lincoln, and he had in mind existing economic conditions of his time with a vision of economic conditions as they would exist fifty years from then. Surely no one will deny the Americanism of Abraham Lincoln. No partisan can question the Republicanism of Abraham Lincoln, but it so happens today that some men who claim to be exponents of Republican principles know as much about the teachings of Abraham Lincoln as Henry Ford knows about the Talmud.[2] ...

Make New York the City Beautiful

What could a sympathetic governor, with the aid of the state legislature, willing to co-operate with the City of New York, be able to do for New York City?

They could make *New York the city beautiful — the home of happiness*. There should not be a hungry child or woman within the confines of the Great City. This is all possible. An enlightened people should be willing to invest in the health and happiness of the great masses, rather than a few be permitted to thrive on their misery and poverty. Let us make it the city beautiful — the home of happiness. ...

A Program for New York

Proper nourishment for all children by means of nutritious luncheons at school.

A bit of green wherever there is a vacant space.

The demolition of all old-type congested tenements and construction of cheerful up-to-date sanitary apartments.

A window for each room — a bit of sunshine for each window.

Taxing into usefulness all idle land within the city limits.

Increased number of baby health stations.

Proper distribution of certified milk for infants.

More playgrounds and more parks with good music — open-air concerts in season. ...

Terminal and retail markets with daily data of crop conditions and prices paid to the farmers.

All underground rapid transit. Taking away all elevated structures from the streets.

---

[2] [**Talmud:** a collection of traditional Jewish laws and literature. At this time Ford, the automobile manufacturer, was publishing anti-Semitic material.]

Light, heat and power by electricity generated by the water power all over the state — God's gift to the people of New York. . . .

Streets to be kept thoroughly clean and cheerful.

Lower East Side to be as well cared for as upper West Side.

Establish proposed . . . great musical and art center.

Timely aid and assistance given without embarrassment and humiliation to residents in temporary distress, thereby preventing them from becoming permanent public charges.

Parks, driveways, municipal farms, stadiums, boulevards, memorials, bridges, tunnels and all works of embellishment and construction should be provided for so as to absorb unemployment when same occurs and to be postponed when industry and seasonal occupations require labor.

This would permit the building of greater structures than the Tower of Babylon or the Temple of Solomon or the Pyramids at small cost and at the same time establish the best insurance against unemployment.

Practical Measures, Not Dreams

The above are not dreams — they are practical suggestions. It may seem costly, but they will pay for themselves in the next twenty years. . . .

Is it not strange that a country will spend a thousand dollars on a high explosive shell and manufacture them by the thousands to put in a costly cannon to shoot and kill, but will count twelve pennies to furnish an infant a quart of certified milk? Why is it that in times of war a shipping board will have thousands of ships bringing munitions and implements of destruction, carry men to kill and die at a cost of hundreds of millions, and in time of peace these same ships are permitted to rust and rot at anchor instead of carrying food, clothes and supplies to the needy and the hungry? Think!

I am not at all discouraged. I am very hopeful. The time is so rapidly approaching when these changes will be brought about. What today is accepted as necessary and proper, but a few years ago was frowned upon and considered radical. We are moving forward more rapidly than some of the smug reactionaries realize. Let's get together and make New York the city beautiful — the Home of Happiness.

5. Foreign Affairs [1]
✣ *Survey*

Most immigrants before coming to America used the word "country" for the village, province, county, or town where they lived. Someone living in Naples, for example, thought of himself as a Neapolitan, not as an Italian. The American experience changed that kind of identity. As immigrants speaking the same language drew together, they founded organizations to promote the welfare of Italy, Ireland, Germany, Hungary, Czechoslovakia, Yugoslavia, Greece, Lithuania, or whatever country they came from.

These nationalistic interests came to a head during World War I, when they received support from President Wilson in his crusade for self-determination in Europe. The following article reports a conference of Polish-Americans held in 1918, not long before the war ended. Similar conferences were held by many other ethnic groups in America at the time. ■

"There should be a united, independent and autonomous Poland — Woodrow Wilson." These words, embossed upon their badges, were worn above the hearts of all delegates to the first national convention representing all the Polish elements in the United States, held . . . in Detroit. The significance of the convention was two-fold; it had great international and strategic importance politically and it furnished a unique exhibition of human values.

Political Importance

Its political importance was seen in the initial interchange of telegrams between the convention and President Wilson. It was seen in the daily cabling to Europe of the proceedings of the convention. It was seen in the message of the convention, sent through the State Department, encouraging the Poles of Prussia, Austria, and Russia to

---

[1] "The Spirit of Poles in America," *Survey*, XL (September 28, 1918), pp. 720–721.

resist the seductive promises of the Central Powers and to [have faith] . . . in the ultimate victory of the Allies, through whom alone Poland can realize her hopes.[2] It was seen in the presence of Roman Dmowski, president of the Polish National Committee, recognized by the Allies as exercising the functions of a *de facto* government.

News from Abroad

Mr. Dmowski is a man a little past middle age, somewhat grey, of strong face and figure, with the Lincoln type of physiognomy, deeply chiseled with thought and suffering. He has been a member of the Russian Duma[3] and a pleader for Poland in the chancelleries of Europe. Having left Paris only ten days since, he brings to the convention direct testimony to the effectiveness of American military support. But his chief concern is lest, by lying promises now or diplomatic chicanery later, Poland will be cheated of her dues. A plausible German suggestion has been that of a plebiscite [vote] of Polish peoples as to their future governmental status. Mr. Dmowski declares that the investigations of the Paris Committee have revealed the fact that during the war eight millions of Poles in the several Polish lands have perished. This includes the women and children who died of starvation and disease, as well as those who have been compelled to take up arms against their brother Poles of other lands. In addition, there are 700,000 men who have been . . . dragged away to forced service behind the German lines. In these conditions no normal plebiscite can be taken.

Women Delegates Prominent

About one hundred of the delegates are women; and the third vice-president, Miss Napieralska of Chicago, sometimes called the Polish Joan of Arc, is a prominent figure on the platform, as is Madame Paderewski. The Poles are loyal to their women, and intend to give them the ballot in the coming republic of Poland.

---

[2] [Poland as a nation had not existed since 1795, when it was partitioned among Russia, Prussia, and Austria. In 1915, during World War I, German forces drove the Russians out of much of Poland. The Central Powers (Germany and Austria) then attempted to set up a Polish government which would be under their control. But in November, 1918, soon after the convention described in this article, the Poles declared an independent republic of Poland.]

[3] [**Duma**: the representative assembly in czarist Russia.]

A Famous Pianist Speaks

The most dramatic figure of the convention is Ignace Jan Paderewski.[4] Years ago he replied to the Russian emperor, who had congratulated that country on having produced so eminent a musician — "Your Majesty, I am a Pole." That speech cost him the fortune he might have won by a concert tour in Russia. The same spirit today has led him to turn the entire stream of his genius into the channel of patriotic devotion. He has vowed that he will never play again till Poland is free. He is great as an orator, as he is great as a musician. He made the keynote address in English on the opening day, and on Wednesday night he spoke over two hours and a half in Polish to an audience whose enthusiasm grew with every word, and who rose to their feet at its close with uplifted hands and glowing faces, to swear their devotion to the holy cause of Poland's freedom. Said Paderewski:

> The Poles in America do not need any Americanization. It is superfluous to explain to them what are the ideals of America. They know them well, for they have been theirs for a thousand years. In 1180 the first Polish parliament granted to every individual, both rich and poor, the right of freedom and possession. In 1413, by her free union with Lithuania, she established the form of government of united states. In the sixteenth century, when religious persecution was at its height throughout Europe, the Roman Catholic Church of Poland declared for complete religious liberty.
> The Poles of America are hard-working people; poor, not rich. Among four millions there is not one millionaire. But in a certain American city the native-born population, including a good sprinkling of millionaires, made a per capita contribution to the Red Cross of $12.50, while the Poles, with no millionaires, averaged $23.

Measures to Win the War

The enthusiasm of the convention [delegates] found practical expression in their vote to support the Polish White Cross, the child of Madame Paderewski's devoted heart, whose object is to minister to the Polish soldiers in France; and [in their] vote to raise ten million dollars and half a million men to win the war and to rebuild Poland.

Hardheaded business men are back of this effort. The president of the permanent organization is John F. Smulski, a Chicago banker and former state treasurer of Illinois. On Thursday afternoon $20,000

---

[4] [Ignace Jan Paderewski: a renowned Polish pianist (1860–1941). In 1919 he served for ten months as premier of the new Polish republic.]

was raised in half an hour, and the effort was suspended merely because of the pressure of more important business. One man pledged $5000, practically his all. A widow who had worked eighteen years to buy a home gave its value, $7500, and will begin anew.

The objective of the convention was enunciated by Chairman Smulski in the opening address: "We are assembled here to make certain that every ounce of strength of the entire Polish immigration in America is back of President Wilson and the Stars and Stripes." The tasks of the convention he declared to be: providing moral support to 215,000 Polish boys in the American army; furnishing a moral barrage for the Polish army in France, whose loyalty has been commended by Secretary [of War] Baker; sending a word of cheer to the Polish boys in the American navy; and sending a wave message through the German lines into Poland, warning them against the alluring but perfidious advances of Austrian and Prussian politicians, and cheering them with our confidence in the final victory of the Allied nations.

The noble spirit of the final resolutions is shown in that they renounced any freedom for Poland apart from her "sister Lithuania" and all other oppressed nations. "Poland," they declared, "desires liberty and consolidation for the Czechs and Slovaks, for the Jugoslavs, for wronged Rumania — with whom Poland will live in harmony and love."

A Permanent and Unified Organization

The principal achievement of the convention was the formation of a permanent and unified organization, superior to any preceding it and embracing in its scope all the activities necessary not only to win the war but [also necessary] to the reconstruction that must follow. It is, in short, the germ of the Polish republic to be. It is backed by all the spiritual and material resources of American Poles, four million strong — more in number than the Swedes in Sweden, the Swiss in Switzerland, the Bulgars in Bulgaria, or the Serbs in Serbia.

VII. The Achievement

One way of measuring the achievement of the immigrants is to ask what they contributed to America. To answer that question would require a very fat book indeed. The outstanding historian of the subject begins his chief work in these words: "Once I thought to write a history of the immigrants in America. Then I discovered that the immigrants were American history."[1] Their significance in this country's development has already been the subject of a number of selections in this book. The following section calls specific attention to the importance of immigration in America's economy, culture, and wars. ■

1. An Expanding Economy[2]
✣ President's Commission on Immigration and Naturalization

> To list all the celebrated people of "foreign stock," as the Census Bureau calls first- and second-generation Americans, would be tedious. They have been included by the thousands in the many editions of Who's Who in America. More than a few of them signed the Declaration of Independence, drafted the Constitution, and emerged as heroes in every war this country has fought.
>
> The following excerpt, from a volume prepared by a commission appointed by President Harry S. Truman, can only suggest the debt that America owes to citizens of foreign birth who distinguished themselves in one occupation or another. But America owes no less a debt to millions of ordinary immigrants who enriched the economy as workers, farmers, and consumers. That contribution, too, President Truman's committee acknowledged. ■

[1] Oscar Handlin, *The Uprooted* (Boston: Atlantic-Little, Brown and Company, 1951), p. 3.
[2] The President's Commission on Immigration and Naturalization, *Whom We Shall Welcome* (Washington, D.C.: Government Printing Office, 1953), pp. 24, 26.

Influence from the Top Down

No roster of leading Americans in business, science, arts, and the professions could be complete without the names of many immigrants. In our history the following aliens may be mentioned, among many, who became outstanding industrialists: Andrew Carnegie (Scot), in the steel industry; John Jacob Astor (German), in the fur trade; Michael Cudahy (Irish), of the meat-packing industry; the DuPonts (French) of the munitions and chemical industry; Charles L. Fleischmann (Hungarian), of the yeast business; David Sarnoff (Russian), of the radio industry; and William S. Knudsen (Danish), of the automobile industry.

Immigrant scientists and inventors are likewise too numerous to list in detail. Among those whose genius has benefited the United States are Albert Einstein (German), in physics; Michael Pupin (Serbian), in electricity; Enrico Fermi (Italian), in atomic research; John Ericsson (Swedish), who invented the ironclad ship and the screw propeller; Giuseppe Bellanca (Italian) and Igor Sikorsky (Russian), who made outstanding contributions to airplane development; John A. Udden (Swedish), who was responsible for opening the Texas oil fields; Lucas P. Kyrides (Greek), industrial chemistry; David Thomas (Welsh), who invented the hot blast furnace; Alexander Graham Bell (Scot), who invented the telephone; Conrad Huber (Russian), who invented the flashlight; and Otto Mergenthaler (German), who invented the linotype machine. . . .

From the Bottom Up

In the 145 years of unrestricted immigration into the United States, from 1776 to 1921, immigrants generally came when and where they were needed. There is no evidence that their arrival caused either unemployment or impoverishment. The contrary view was generally held by the founding fathers. James Madison, at the Constitutional Convention of 1787, said: "That part of America which has encouraged them [the foreigners] has advanced most rapidly in population, agriculture, and the 'arts.'"

Whether immigration was cause or effect, it is true to-day, as it was in Revolutionary times, that the richest regions are those with the highest proportion of recent immigrants. The Commission found a striking correspondence between per capita income and per cent of population foreign-born. . . . The per capita incomes are highest in regions with a high percentage of recent foreign stock, lowest where immigrants are few. Immigrants went to the regions where there was demand for labor as expressed in high wages. In turn their industry, their skills and their enterprise were major factors in the economic development that has made these regions prosperous.

2. Culture[1]

✣ Ernst Frederick Philblad

Everyone knows the name of the Italian-born Arturo Toscanini and his great contribution to music in America. Still other immigrant conductors, and composers and painters and architects as well, have enriched this nation's cultural life. Less famous performers, too, have left a mark on the arts in America. Out of the Yiddish-language theater, for example, came several Broadway and Hollywood stars. The following article, by a Swedish-American, describes how his ethnic group contributed to musical life in Kansas early in the century. ■

... In the heart of the agricultural district, about two hundred miles west of Kansas City, lies the little town of Lindsborg, a hamlet of scarcely two thousand souls, which is the musical center of the Southwest. . . . the community is made up almost entirely of immigrants from Sweden and their children. . . . Lindsborg is the center of a Swedish colony of about forty square miles in extent. Its only boast above the neighboring towns is the presence of Bethany College and the annual musical events at Easter time.

Concerts a Home Affair

Each Easter week its people perform Handel's "Messiah," with a chorus of five hundred voices and an orchestra of forty pieces. With the exception of the soloists, who now are stars of the first magnitude on the artistic firmament, it is entirely a home affair. The membership of the organization is made up of the merchants, artisans, farmers, and housewives of the town and surrounding countryside, together with the students of the college. The chorus is more than thirty years old and has given Handel's "Messiah" eighty-seven times.

[1] Ernst Frederick Philblad, "A Swedish Bayreuth in Kansas," *American-Scandinavian Review*, I (May, 1913), pp. 9–13.

Among its members there are those who participated in the first performance, and it is no uncommon thing for three generations of the same family to be represented. From the bass section more than one grandfather hears the voices of his daughter and granddaughter singing among the sopranos and altos....

Widespread Attraction

The Messiah is given three times each season — Palm Sunday, Good Friday and Easter Sunday. Each afternoon and evening of the week are given over to musical entertainment by visiting artists or members of the faculty. Every available room in the public hostelries, as well as in private homes, is in demand. On the Messiah days the railroads furnish special train service. A single one of these special trains brought in over twelve hundred visitors for the concerts on the opening day of the season this spring. During the hours these strangers are in the city Lindsborg finds its population increased threefold....

Setting

The whole undertaking has about it something of the old-world atmosphere of simplicity bordering on the severely primitive. The concerts are given in a large wooden structure, octagonal in shape and furnished with wooden benches. The women in the chorus are attired in white and the men in conventional black. As the five hundred singers arise at the signal of the director, the effect is overwhelming. There is no applause during the program, which lasts about three hours, and the atmosphere is rather that of a religious service than of the concert hall.

History

Lindsborg was founded by a colony of Swedish immigrants, who ... came over in 1868 and 1869. The spiritual leader of the little band was Rev. Olof Olsson, a man distinguished for his intellectual attainments, artistic temperament and religious devotion. He was accustomed to gather the sturdy pioneers and their buxom wives in some sod house on the storm-swept prairie to dispel the oppressive solitude of the long winter nights by teaching them the rudiments of choral singing. It was merely a matter of the singing-school, common in rural districts a generation ago.

The credit for the existence of the Bethany Oratorio Society, however, is due Dr. Carl Swensson, who in 1879 came to Lindsborg, fresh from college, to be pastor of the church. In 1881 he founded Bethany Academy, which has since grown into a college, with a student body of nine hundred and a teaching staff of forty. It was to raise funds for Bethany College that the Lindsborg Chorus was established. Handel's "Messiah," which he had found particularly inspiring, was made the repertoire of the chorus. His wife, Mrs. Alma Swensson, who served the church as organist, added to her duties those of choral director. After spending the winter months in study the chorus was ready for its first public appearance in the spring of 1882. After the concert at home Swensson took his singers to the neighboring parishes of Salina, McPherson, Fremont, and Salemsborg, realizing a net profit of $200 on the undertaking. A man of great vision, he was quickly alert to the moral and esthetic advantages of the Oratorio Society. While it brought beauty into the dull routine of pioneer life, it justified itself by . . . [raising funds for] the support of the infant college.

Role in the Community

Bethany Oratorio Society has demonstrated its usefulness, as well as its artistic value. Through its efforts the little Swedish hamlet on the broad prairies of Kansas has been made one of the musical centers of the country. It has brought into the materialistic life of a new state — where in the nature of things the butter and bread question is uppermost — something of the softening influence of old-world culture, and has gained for the Swedish immigrant a distinction beyond that of "a hewer of wood and a drawer of water." The Messiah at Lindsborg has proved a tangible contribution to that new seething life which is springing out of the prairies of the great Southwest.

3. Wartime Loyalty[1]
✢ Josephine Roche

War put the loyalty of immigrants to a severe test. Would they support their adopted country even if it fought against their ancestral land? The decisive answer to that question came when, in 1917, the United States entered World War I against the Central Powers — Germany and Austria-Hungary. To mobilize

[1] *Complete Report of the Chairman of the U.S. Committee on Public Information* (Washington, D.C.: Government Printing Office, 1920), pp. 80–81, 95–99, 102–103.

> *American opinion, the government established a Committee on Public Information, with a special division devoted to the foreign-born. The division, headed by Josephine Roche, concentrated on the fourteen largest ethnic groups of the immigrant population. Miss Roche describes below the success of her staff and the importance of immigrants in prosecuting the struggle against the Central Powers.* ■

It was realized that the work could receive unreserved confidence and support from the foreign-born only if conducted on a thoroughly democratic plan. Therefore, co-operation and suggestions of their leaders of the foreign language press and organizations were sought. Representatives were appointed from the foreign language groups to act as managers of the Foreign Language Bureaus of the division. They were given the responsibility for the development of this work among their people; for sending them official information in their language through their press [and] their organizations, and through wide correspondence and personal work; for endeavoring to rectify wrong conditions affecting the foreign-born; and for making available to the native-born important facts about their groups. . . .

Press Work

For these fourteen foreign language groups there are approximately 865 foreign language newspapers. About 745 of this number are issued regularly and were received by the bureaus. . . . [These bureaus] . . . sent out an approximate total of 2318 news releases to the 745 foreign language newspapers. Only 32 papers did not use the material, all but three of these being small papers of a highly specialized character; 96 per cent of the papers availed themselves extensively of the material. Very many papers used all but a few releases. It was a frequent occurrence to have foreign language papers come in carrying on their front page two or three columns of the bureaus' material. These 2318 releases were based on material from . . . government sources. . . . The Departments of Labor, War, Internal Revenue, and Agriculture are those whose material was most extensively used and most desired. . . .

Work with Organizations

National and local organizations, fraternal, educational, religious, beneficial, and social in type, are a powerful factor among the foreign-

HE EFFORTS AND TAL-
NTS OF MANY PEO-
LE: America is the achieve-
ent of people from many
nds. A war bond poster
om World War I (below)
onored soldiers with typical
ames. A half century later
mes on American service
sters still show a variety of
ational origins.

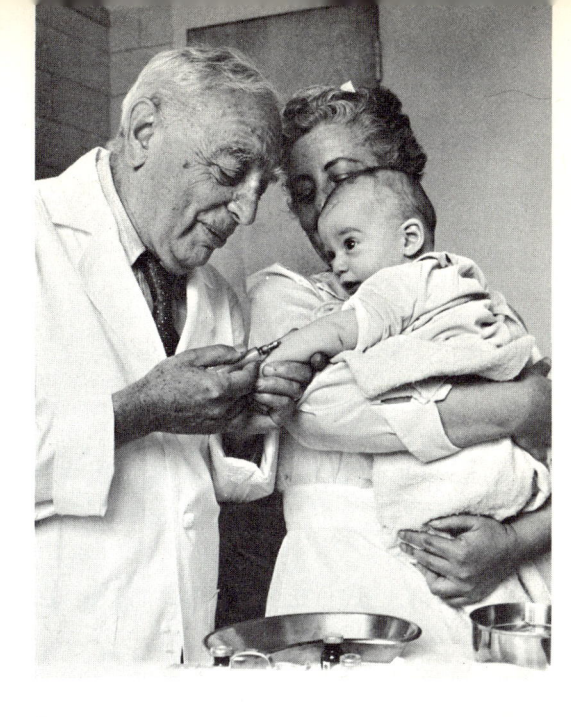

Immigrants have made especially notable contributions in science and music. Above, Bela Schick (1877–1967), world-famous doctor, scientist, and teacher, came to this country from Hungary. He is shown here administering the Schick test for diphtheria immunity to a small patient. Below, Erich Leinsdorf, a native of Austria, is eminent among the many foreign-born musicians and conductors who have enriched American cultural life.

speaking groups. Their conventions bring together hundreds of delegates from all the various centers of the foreign-language groups, and their activities and influence are far-reaching.

The information on government activities prepared in the form of bulletins or circular letters by the bureaus and sent these organizations was insured a complete hearing by their members. Draft and registration circulars, regulations issued by the Passport Control Division of the Department of State, [and] income-tax provisions were carefully and thoroughly distributed by them. They also gave most valuable and suggestive advice as to the needs and desires of their groups for instruction and understanding. . . .

Immigrant Loyalty

Of equal importance with this work of reaching the foreign-speaking groups with information as described has been what this work has revealed about these groups. The war gave a chance for a dramatic and striking manifestation of their services and loyalty to the country. After the armistice their interest and devotion was just as great in helping in the difficult transition and reconstruction problems. The same unreserved spirit with which they had enlisted in the army, and in the Liberty loan and war-savings stamp campaigns, marked their efforts in peace [and] in encouraging all their people to become citizens, to learn English, [and] to carry out any suggestions coming from government sources. Numerous printing concerns have offered to print and distribute among their people books on American history, civics, and the Constitution. Editors of several groups have been running serials on citizenship and wish to carry translations of the best American stories in their papers. They have asked us to suggest these and to get translation rights for them. . . .

Telling America About the Immigrants

To bring to the attention of the public some of these significant facts, we started in August, 1918, the Foreign Information Service, directed by Mr. Donald Breed, until November, and after that by Mr. Barett Clark. To quote from Mr. Clark's report:

> It has been the policy of this service to encourage the foreign-language groups of America by releasing stories telling of their co-operation with the government in such matters as the Liberty loan, the Red Cross, etc., and to assist the foreign-language press not only in securing

prompt and efficient co-operation with the government departments, but by informing the American people through the native-language press of the work that had been done and was now being done by the foreign-language press in helping the foreigner to become a better American.

Over 50 such stories were released to 3300 American papers and . . . clippings kept until the first of the year showed a wide and interested use. Typical among them are: "The Jugo-Slav Club," "Greek-American Boys Are Genuine Patriots," "Lithuanians Support Fourth Liberty Loan," "The Czecho-Slovaks in America," "Ukrainians in America Eager for Education," and "Russian-Americans Aid America in Bond Sales." . . .

Americanization a Two-Way Process

For years national unity and progress have demanded the release of the neglected potentialities of our millions of new Americans into a fuller participation in our country's life. For this there is necessary a mutual process of education of native and foreign born. Full information on American life, opportunities, customs, and laws must reach the men and women coming here from foreign lands immediately upon their arrival. Necessarily it must be in their own language. The more they learn in this way of our fundamental democracy and the possibilities for them and their children in this country, the keener become their desire and efforts to learn "America's language." To withhold this information or delay it until, according to theoretic calculation, these immigrants have had time to acquire English is to deliberately create a period of cruel bewilderment and false impressions for them which dampens whatever enthusiasm they had originally to study English. The numerous un-American conditions and injustices to which so many immigrants have fallen victims must be wiped out. Explanations and instruction about America given to the fullest extent carry little weight when individuals have been wronged.

The ignorance of many native-born Americans about European peoples and their contemptuous attitude toward persons with different customs from their own are just as serious obstacles to assimilation and unity as the tendency of some immigrants to cling to Old World ways; understanding must come, on our part, of the heritages of these newcomers, their suffering and struggles in Europe, and the contributions they bring us if we will only receive them.

Part Three

        Introduction
VIII. Cycles of Bigotry
  IX. Concepts of Americanism and Americanization
   X. Immigration Policy

America Adjusts to the Immigrants

Part Three: Introduction

We have just seen how the immigrants adjusted to America. Now, in this final part of the book, we must turn the problem around. How did America respond to the immigrants? At stake for our country was whether the massive ingathering of people from all over the world would result in harmony or discord.

Bigotry Fluctuates According to Fear

It would be easy to conclude that discord was the rule. The anti-Catholic Know-Nothing Party of the 1850's; the California riots against the Chinese in the 1870's; the anti-German hysteria of World War I; the Ku Klux Klan crusade for Anglo-Saxon supremacy in the 1920's; the internment of Japanese-Americans during World War II — these and other outbreaks of bigotry mar American history. (*See Section VIII.*) But they were not the rule. Organized hate erupted only in periods of fear and disappeared with the return of confidence. These outbreaks of discord were, therefore, temporary and short-lived. The American norm has been "live and let live."

The Decision to Welcome Unlimited Numbers

Here it is necessary to emphasize the fact that the character of nations frequently stems from decisions they make at turning points in their history. In 1776, for example, Revolutionary leaders decided to break away from England, despite indifference and opposition to the cause of independence on the part of many colonists. A new nation thus came into being. Again, in 1787 and 1788, a debate took place over the kind of government that would best meet the needs of the young nation. The states settled the issue by ratifying the new plan of government outlined in the Constitution. That document is still the living law of the land.

With regard to immigration, America in the eighteenth century made still another decision of monumental consequence. It adopted, over the warnings of a minority, a policy of unrestricted immigration. Had America chosen otherwise, it might very well have developed like Canada and Australia. Ungenerous throughout most of their histories in admitting foreigners, those two vast countries have remained underpopulated.

The decision reached in the eighteenth century remained in force for more than a hundred years. During that time, a minority of bigots to the contrary, Americans believed in immigration as a positive good. It increased the population, expanded the economy, and hastened the rounding out of the nation's continental boundaries. What is equally important, America had confidence in its ability to absorb people of almost any ancestry, religion, or economic status. The only provision was that immigrants link their individual futures to the future of the New World.

Melting Pot or Symphony Orchestra?

Therein lies the significance of the *melting pot*. This figure of speech, expressed for the first time in the eighteenth century, was echoed over the next two centuries. (*See Section I, selection 6, and Section IX, selections 1A and 1B.*) Its central proposition was that America was a nation in the making. Out of the energies and talents of newcomers and people already here, it was hoped, a new man and a distinctive culture would emerge.

Many people, on the other hand, have argued that America should encourage immigrants and their children to retain their distinctiveness. (*See Section IX, selection 2.*) This doctrine, known as *cultural pluralism*, has become particularly popular since the early 1900's. Pluralists hold that America, instead of being called a melting pot, should be compared to a symphony orchestra, whose many different players constitute an intricate but harmonious whole. What America ought to be, of course, is a matter of personal preference. As a matter of record, however, America has been *both* a melting pot and a symphony orchestra.

The Rejection of Unlimited Immigration

Both metaphors were rejected in the 1920's. In that decade, a high point in bigotry, many nativists (people who felt antagonistic to the foreign-born) insisted that only Anglo-Saxons could be Americans. That view was reflected in the Johnson-Reed Act of 1924. (*See Section X, selection 3.*) This law not only limited the amount of immigration in general; it also placed severe restrictions on "non-Anglo-Saxon" immigration. Reasserted in the McCarran-Walter Act of

1952, the decision of the 1920's rejected a historic policy that had made America what it was. (*See Section X, selection 4.*)

How can we account for so momentous a reversal? Those who favored the restriction of immigration argued that America had always been an Anglo-Saxon nation. Yet that was not so. Besides, when the term "Anglo-Saxon" was used early in American history, it was applied to a people who were said to have a remarkable capacity to absorb other peoples. By the 1920's, as several readings in this book reveal, the advocates of Anglo-Saxon supremacy preached a doctrine of exclusiveness. (*See Section VIII, selection 3, and Section X, selection 3.*)

That doctrine originated around the 1880's in the writings of certain historians, sociologists, anthropologists, economists, biologists, and statisticians who classified mankind into inferior and superior "races." They placed Anglo-Saxons (also called "Nordics" and "Aryans") at the top of the white classification and southern and eastern Europeans at the bottom. Such writers argued that intellectual and moral characteristics were inherited — they claimed, in other words, that heredity counted for everything and environment for nothing. That is why, according to this view, some nations moved ahead while others fell behind. Few scholars or scientists today accept this biological view.

But some Americans found in these ideas an explanation for what was wrong with their country. If America suffered from slums, poverty, juvenile delinquency, drunkenness, violence, and crime, it was, they said, because of "inferior" immigrants from southern and eastern Europe. The advocates of Anglo-Saxon supremacy further argued that America had not suffered from any major social problems when the country's immigrants had been northern Europeans. Such arguments led to the conclusion that only through restriction could America save itself from degeneration.

Not until the 1920's, however, did Congress enact legislation reflecting this conclusion. Why in that decade? Fear is the key to the reversal of 1924. By that time, having rejected the League of Nations after World War I, America feared foreign entanglements. It feared still other things — communism, changes in moral standards, the decline of old-time religion, the violence growing out of the failure of Prohibition — all of which it blamed on foreigners. As American self-confidence had supported the policy of unrestricted immigration, so loss of confidence led to its rejection.

Reaction to Anti-Foreignism

But periods of anti-foreignism, as we have noted, have come and gone like waves. During the Great Depression of the 1930's and World War II, few Americans considered immigration an important issue. More vital concerns at that time were economic recovery and the defeat of the Axis Powers. After the passage of the McCarran-Walter Act in 1952, however, a nationwide demand arose to remove the racism that marred the statute books.

This demand reflected important changes that had taken place since the 1920's. A new generation of scholars had proved that there was no factual basis for the doctrine of Anglo-Saxon supremacy. No longer isolationist, moreover, America had to show an unprejudiced face to the world. Above all, Nazi Germany had demonstrated the appalling consequences of racism; for it was in the name of "Aryan supremacy" that Hitler had sought to exterminate what he called "inferior" peoples.

All of these considerations led Congress in 1965 to repeal the discriminatory legislation by adopting a new immigration law. (*See Section X, selection 5.*) Now, as during most of its history, America does not ask immigrants where they come from but what they can do. Our immigration policy has traveled full cycle.

Yet the foreign-born are unlikely ever again to constitute a substantial proportion of the American people. Our population has reached continental size, and that is why the 1965 law limits immigration to a few hundred thousand people a year. Harmony or discord now depends on how *native* Americans of various religious and ethnic groups, including blacks, choose to get on with each other. The lesson of immigration is that men do not have to be identical to share a common humanity. ■

VIII. Cycles of Bigotry

The absorption of over 45 million immigrants testifies to the tolerance of a nation. But in moments of insecurity and fear Americans sometimes made a scapegoat of the foreign-born. Such moments were likely to occur during economic depressions or just before, during, and right after a war. People hate most easily when they feel threatened. The readings in this section will cover several periods in our country's history when fear enabled bigotry to take hold. ■

1. Know-Nothing Prejudice in the 1850's[1]
✣ "One of 'Em"

Founded in 1854 to curb the growing political power of the foreign-born, the American Party was commonly called the Know-Nothing Party because it had emerged from a secret society. It raised a cry against immigrant candidates for office and proposed that the vote be denied to the foreign-born until they had lived in this country for 21 years. After winning a number of local and state elections, the party finally outraged public opinion with its bigotry. In the 1856 presidential election, Millard Fillmore, the Know-Nothing candidate, received a mere 3 per cent of the electoral vote. Soon torn apart by the slavery issue, which it had tried to avoid by focusing attention on the immigrant, the American Party disintegrated as quickly as it had formed. Below is a sample of its anti-Catholic and anti-foreign sentiments. Note that the editor of the volume from which the selection is taken remained anonymous. ■

America for the Americans, we say. And why not? Didn't they plant it, and battle for it through bloody revolution — and haven't

[1] "One of 'Em," ed., *The Wide-Awake Gift: A Know-Nothing Token* (New York: J. C. Derby, 1855), pp. 40–43.

they developed it, as only Americans could, into a nation of a century, and yet mightier than the oldest empire on earth? Why shouldn't they shape and rule the destinies of their own land — the land of their birth, their love, their altars, and their graves; the land red and rich with the blood and ashes, and hallowed by the memories of their fathers? Why not rule their own, particularly when the alien betrays the trust that should never have been given him, and the liberties of the land are thereby imperiled?

Alien Plague

Lacks the American numbers, that he may not rule by the right of majority, to which is constitutionally given the political sovereignty of this land? Did he not, at the last numbering of the people, count seventeen and a half millions, native to the soil, against less than two and a half millions of actually foreign born, and those born of foreigners coming among us for the last three quarters of a century? Has he not tried the mixed rule, with a tolerance unexampled, until it has plagued him worse than the lice and locust plagued the Egyptian? Has he not shared the trust of office and council, until foreign-born pauperism, vice, and crime stain the whole land — until a sheltered alien fraction have become rampant in their ingratitude and insolence? Has he not suffered burdens of tax, and reproach and shame, by his ill-bestowed division of political power?

America for the Americans! That is the watchword that should ring through the length and breadth of the land, from the lips of the whole people. America for the Americans — to shape and to govern; to make great, and to keep great, strong and free, from home foes and foreign demagogues. . . . In the hour of Revolutionary peril, Washington said, "Put none but Americans on guard to-night." At a later time, Jefferson wished "an ocean of fire rolled between the Old World and the New." To their children, the American people, the father and builders of the Republic bequeathed it. "Eternal vigilance is the price of liberty!" — let the American be vigilant that the alien seize not his birthright.

Root Out Foreign Communities

America for the Americans! Shelter and welcome let them give to the emigrant and the exile, and make them citizens in so far as civil privileges are concerned. But let it be looked to that paupers and criminals are no longer shipped on us by foreign states. Let it be looked to that foreign nationalities in our midst are rooted out; that foreign regiments and battalions are disarmed; that the public laws and schools of the country are printed and taught in the language of the land; that no more charters for foreign ... associations — benevolent, social or other — are granted by our legislatures; that all national and state support given to education have not the shadow of sectarianism about it. There is work for Americans to do. They have slept on guard — if, indeed, they have been on guard — and the enemy have grown strong and riotous in their midst.

America for the Americans! We have had enough of "Young Irelands," "Young Germanys," and "Young Italys." We have had enough of insolent alien threat to suppress our "Puritan Sabbath" and amend our Constitution. We have been ... patient.... But the time is come to right the wrong; the occasion is ripe for reform in whatever we have failed.

The politico-religious foe [Catholicism] is fully discovered — he must be squarely met, and put down. We want in this free land none of this political dictation. We want none of his religious mummeries — let him keep ... [them] in those lands that have been desolated with persecution, and repeopled with serfs and lazzaroni [beggars] by the hierarchy to which he owes supreme religious and temporal obedience. Our feeling is earnest, not bitter. The matters of which we have written are great and grave ones, and we shall not be silent until we have aided in wholly securing America for the Americans!

2. World War I Persecutions of German-Americans[1]
✣ Gerald L. Wendt

The American Protective Association of the 1880's and 1890's tried to revive anti-Catholicism but had even less success than the Know-Nothing Party. Significantly, World War I provided the next setting for widespread nativist fears of European immigrants. Since Germany was the enemy, super-patriots saw in

---

[1] Gerald L. Wendt, "A Plea for Tolerance," *The New Republic*, XIV (April 20, 1918), p. 356. Reprinted by Permission of *The New Republic*, © 1918, Harrison-Blaine of New Jersey, Inc.

German-Americans potential, if not actual, spies, traitors, and saboteurs. Everything German — food, language, music, literature — was suppressed. Sauerkraut, for example, was renamed "liberty cabbage." It is against that background that you should read the following letter to a liberal magazine. ∎

Sir: I am an American of German descent. Both my grandfathers received the Iron Cross from the King of Prussia — and one at once came to America to avoid repetition of the ordeal. My father served his years of military service under the Prussian system — and at once emigrated to the land of freedom. I learned my German at home, my English at school. I learned to love the heritage of beauty [and] of science . . . that came from the Fatherland. But I also learned, . . . in Germany, to understand the meaning of militarism, to dread the menace of imperial politics. When the coming of war found me studying in Paris, I . . . [obeyed] the injunction of . . . President [Wilson] . . . to return home to an impossible neutrality and a futile peace.[2] . . . What salvation to humanity that we all now are coming to understand and are doing our duty! I am in earnest; and thousands of "German-Americans" such as I are more fervently in the war to the end than are those who do the shouting.

A Folk Song Is Treason

. . . It is hard to . . . [fight against relatives and friends in Germany. But] there is now no other way. . . . Far more painful, because so cruelly unjust and unnecessary, is the wanton murder of all that is beautiful and precious in the German heritage. To speak the familiar tongue is sedition. To sing an ancient folk-song is treason. The music, the philosophy, the architecture, the literature of our fathers is rankest poison. We are liable to be "reported" by any moron and subjected to inquisitions by federal agents at every turn. These "heart-to-heart talks," as they are styled, when there is not the least evidence for other action, officially counsel hate toward everything German, vilify our origin and our traditions, and, coming from the government itself, implant a rancor that does not heal. Can one wonder at the numerous suicides among German-Americans? Is it

[2] [When World War I began in Europe in 1914, President Woodrow Wilson urged the American people to be "neutral in fact as well as in name." It was not until April, 1917, that the United States entered the war.]

surprising that it becomes unbearable and that the weaker ones turn truly pro-German, convinced that Prussianism at its worst never sent an agent into their homes to inspect at will, to shout down all their intimate values and to demand vociferous lies against themselves? . . .

Watch Out for a German Accent

A movie theater urges its patrons to listen to the conversation of their neighbors and to report anything suspicious, which may range from a German accent to some impatience with the stupid but perhaps excusable excesses of the war films. A prominent newspaper writes editorially, "If some of these aliens who still imagine they have the same liberty of speech they enjoyed before the war were to wake up some fine morning to find steps had been taken to sequestrate [seize] their property and otherwise deal with their malicious activities, they would get exactly what they deserve." . . . [This] is true of hostile enemy aliens, but . . . is generally applied to hundred per cent Americans who may be singing the innocent songs of their childhood or be speaking to a beloved mother in the only language she can well use.

It is this that causes distraction. . . . Our President does not sympathize. He is making every effort to win the friendship of the German people in Germany. But his own petty officials and the vast majority of his fellow-citizens are making his task impossible and are jeopardizing much of the great good that the war should accomplish by this cruel and purposeless malice. This is the "German-American problem."

3. The Ku Klux Klan in the 1920's[1]

✤ *Hiram Wesley Evans*

The Knights of the Ku Klux Klan, a secret society pledged to keep America "Nordic," was founded in Georgia in 1915.[2] Ten years later, the Klan claimed a membership of five million. Its greatest strength by then was not only in the South but also in

[1] Hiram Wesley Evans, "The Klan's Fight for Americanism," *North American Review*, CCXXIII (March, 1926), pp. 49, 52–55, 63.
[2] The Ku Klux Klan of post-Civil War days had died out by the 1880's. Unlike the old organization, the new Klan did not confine its activities to the South. Later, in the 1950's, the KKK was revived once again.

the Southwest and the North Central states of Ohio, Indiana, and Illinois. Like the Know-Nothings before them, however, the hooded Knights turned out to be a passing aberration. By 1930 fewer than 10,000 members remained. The Klan disgraced itself through its bigotry and such acts of violence as floggings, tar-and-featherings, and even murder. Below you will find a statement of the Klan's beliefs written by its head, whose title was Imperial Wizard of the Invisible Empire. ■

The Ku Klux Klan . . . is an organization which gives expression, direction and purpose to the most vital instincts, hopes and resentments of the old-stock Americans, provides them with leadership, and is enlisting and preparing them for militant, constructive action toward fulfilling their racial and national destiny. . . .

A Movement of Plain People

We are a movement of the plain people, very weak in the matter of culture, intellectual support, and trained leadership. We are demanding, and we expect to win, a return of power into the hands of the everyday, not highly cultured, not overly intellectualized, but entirely unspoiled and not de-Americanized, average citizen of the old stock. Our members and leaders are all of this class; the opposition of the intellectuals and liberals who held the leadership [and] betrayed Americanism, and from whom we expect to wrest control, is almost automatic. . . .

Based on Three "Racial Instincts"

. . . The Klan goes back to the American racial instincts, and to the common sense which is their first product, as the basis of its beliefs and methods. The fundamentals of our thought are convictions, not mere opinions. . . . We know that we are right in the same sense that a good Christian knows that he has been saved and that Christ lives — a thing which the intellectual can never understand. These convictions are no more to be argued about than is our love for our children; we are merely willing to state them for the enlightenment . . . of others.

There are three of these great racial instincts, vital elements in both the historic and the present attempts to build an America which shall fulfill the aspirations and justify the heroism of the men who made the nation. These are the instincts of loyalty to the white race, to the traditions of America, and to the spirit of Protestantism, which has been an essential part of Americanism ever since the days of Roanoke and Plymouth Rock. They are condensed into the Klan slogan: "Native, white, Protestant supremacy."

Racial "Integrity"

First in the Klansman's mind is patriotism — America for Americans. He believes religiously that a betrayal of Americanism or the American race is treason to the most sacred of trusts, a trust from his fathers and a trust from God. He believes, too, that Americanism can only be achieved if the pioneer stock is kept pure. There is more than race pride in this. Mongrelization has been proven bad. It is only between closely related stocks of the same race that interbreeding has improved men; the kind of interbreeding that went on in the early days of America between English, Dutch, German, Huguenot, Irish and Scotch.

Racial integrity is a very definite thing to the Klansman. It means even more than good citizenship, for a man may be in all ways a good citizen and yet a poor American, unless he has racial understanding of Americanism, and instinctive loyalty to it. It is in no way a reflection on any man to say that he is un-American; it is merely a statement that he is not one of us. It is often not even wise to try to make an American of the best of aliens. What he is may be spoiled without his becoming American. The races and stocks of men are as distinct as breeds of animals, and every boy knows that if one tries to train a bulldog to herd sheep, he has in the end neither a good bulldog nor a good collie.

Americanism, to the Klansman, is a thing of the spirit, a purpose and a point of view, that can only come through instinctive racial understanding. It has, to be sure, certain defined principles, but he does not believe that many aliens understand those principles, even when they use our words in talking about them. Democracy is one, fair-dealing, impartial justice, equal opportunity, religious liberty, independence, self-reliance, courage, endurance, acceptance of individual responsibility as well as individual rewards for effort, willingness to sacrifice for the good of his family, his nation and his race before anything else but God, dependence on enlightened conscience for guidance, the right to unhampered development — these are fundamental. But within the bounds they fix there must be the utmost freedom, tolerance, liberalism. In short, the Klansman believes in the greatest possible diversity and individualism within the limits of the American spirit. But he believes also that few aliens can understand that spirit, that fewer try to, and that there must be resistance, intolerance even, toward anything that threatens it, or the fundamental national unity based upon it.

White Supremacy

The second word in the Klansman's trilogy is "white." The white race must be supreme, not only in America but in the world. This is equally undebatable, except on the ground that the races might live together, each with full regard for the rights and interests of others, and that those rights and interests would never conflict. Such an idea, of course, is absurd; the colored races today, such as Japan, are clamoring not for equality but for their supremacy. The whole history of the world, on its broader lines, has been one of race conflicts, wars, subjugation or extinction.... The world has been so made that each race must fight for its life, must conquer, accept slavery or die. The Klansman believes that the whites will not become slaves, and he does not intend to die before his time.

Moreover, the future of progress and civilization depends on the continued supremacy of the white race. The forward movement of the world for centuries has come entirely from it.... Until the whites falter, or some colored civilization has a miracle of awakening, there is not a single colored stock that can claim even equality with the white; much less supremacy.

Protestant Rule

The third of the Klan principles is that Protestantism must be supreme; that Rome[3] shall not rule America. The Klansman believes ... [that] Protestantism is an essential part of Americanism; without it America could never have been created and without it she cannot go forward. Roman rule would kill it.

Protestantism ... has been a distinctly Nordic religion, and it has been through this religion that the Nordics have found strength to take leadership of all whites and the supremacy of the earth. Its destruction is the deepest purpose of all other peoples, as that would mean the end of Nordic rule.

[3] [**Rome:** the Roman Catholic Church.]

A COLD WELCOME: Some immigrants encountered unfriendly faces — or worse — on arriving in America. Top, a magazine cartoon from the late 1800's chided successful Americans who "would close to the newcomer the bridge that carried them and their fathers over." Fear of unemployment made some Americans hostile to low-paid Chinese workers in California (above right, an anti-Chinese mass meeting in 1880), but racial prejudice helped secure legislation barring further Chinese immigration (page 156). The Ku Klux Klan (above left, marching in Washington, D.C., in the 1920's) is probably most notorious of the "hate" groups that periodically appear in American history. KKK targets include immigrants, Negroes, Catholics, and Jews.

It is the only religion that permits the unhampered individual development and the unhampered conscience and action which were necessary in the settling of America. Our pioneers were all Protestants, except for an occasional Irishman — Protestants by nature if not by religion — for though French and Spanish dared and explored and showed great heroism, they made little of the land their own. America was Protestant from birth.

She must remain Protestant, if the Nordic stock is to finish its destiny. We of the old stock Americans could not work . . . if the record of the past proves anything — if we become priest-ridden, if we had to submit our consciences and admit our activities and suppress our thoughts at the command of any man, much less of a man . . . thousands of miles away. This we will not permit. Rome shall not rule us. Protestantism must be supreme.

Let it be clear what is meant by "supremacy." It is nothing more than power of control, under just laws. It is not imperialism, far less is it autocracy or even aristocracy of a race or stock of men. What it does mean is that we insist on our inherited right to insure our own safety, individually and as a race, to secure the future of our children, to maintain and develop our racial heritage in our own, white, Protestant, American way, without interference.

The Klan's Program Not Yet Organized

Just how we of the Klan will accomplish this we do not yet know. Our first task has been to organize and this is not yet quite accomplished. But already we are beginning our second stage, which is to meet, stop and remove the invader and leave ourselves free once more. In the strict sense we have no program. We are not ready for one and have not put our minds to it. No such popular movement ever springs full-panoplied from the head of any man or group. For some time we must be opportunists, meeting the enemy wherever he attacks and attacking where we can. This course, so far, has accomplished much more than could have been done by a hard and fast program. We expect to continue it. . . .

The future of the Klan we believe in, though it is still in the hands of God and of our own abilities and consecration as individuals and as a race. Previous movements of the kind have been short-lived, killed by internal jealousies and personal ambitions, and partly, too, by partial accomplishment of their purposes. If the Klan falls away from its mission, or fails in it, perhaps even if it succeeds — certainly whenever the time comes that it is not doing needed work — it will become a mere derelict, without purpose or force. If it fulfills its mission, its future power and service are beyond calculation so long as America has any part of her destiny unfulfilled. Meantime, we of the Klan will continue, as best we know and as best we can, the crusade for Americanism to which we have been providentially called.

4. An American Catholic Answers Back [1]
✢ Alfred E. Smith

The Klan was proud to play a role in the defeat of Al Smith for President in 1928. Of Irish background, Smith had made his way up through New York politics. As a presidential candidate, he could point to an outstanding record as a four-term governor of that state. Smith was not only hurt but bewildered by frequent charges that his being a Catholic disqualified him for the White House. In the following article, written a year before he received the Democratic nomination, Smith summarized his creed as an American Catholic. It is similar to a speech that John Fitzgerald Kennedy, also a Catholic, would deliver when he ran for President in 1960. ■

I summarize my creed as an American Catholic. I believe in the worship of God according to the faith and practice of the Roman Catholic Church. I recognize no power in the institutions of my Church to interfere with the operations of the Constitution of the United States or the enforcement of the law of the land. I believe in absolute freedom of conscience for all men and in equality of all churches, all sects, and all beliefs before the law as a matter of right and not as a matter of favor. I believe in the absolute separation of Church and State and in the strict enforcement of the provisions of the Constitution that Congress shall make no law respecting an establishment of religion or prohibiting the free exercise thereof. I believe that no tribunal of any church has any power to make any decree of any force in the law of the land, other than to establish the status of its own communicants within its own church.

[1] Alfred E. Smith, "Catholic and Patriot: Governor Smith Replies," *Atlantic Monthly*, CXXXIX (May, 1927), p. 728. Copyright © by The Atlantic Monthly Company, Boston, Mass. 02116. Reprinted with permission.

I believe in the support of the public school as one of the cornerstones of American liberty. I believe in the right of every parent to choose whether his child shall be educated in the public school or in a religious school supported by those of his own faith. I believe in the principle of noninterference by this country in the internal affairs of other nations and that we should stand steadfastly against any such interference by whomsoever it may be urged. And I believe in the common brotherhood of man under the common fatherhood of God.

In this spirit I join with fellow Americans of all creeds in a fervent prayer that never again in this land will any public servant be challenged because of the faith in which he has tried to walk humbly with his God.

5. Japanese-Americans Interned During World War II[1]
✤ Ted Nakashima

Widespread misery caused by the Great Depression of the 1930's provided a new breeding ground for hate groups. But none of them succeeded in creating a major movement; once again it took a war to bring about a serious reaction against immigrants and their children. This time Japanese-Americans were the target. More than 100,000 of them were living in the Pacific West when Japan attacked Pearl Harbor on December 7, 1941. A few months later the United States government "relocated" these Japanese-Americans in "resettlement centers" farther inland. In the selection below a young American objected to being expelled from his home, interned, and called a "Jap." Men like him received permission to form special units in the United States army, under whose colors they fought with unusual distinction. ■

Unfortunately in this land of liberty, I was born of Japanese parents; born in Seattle of a mother and father who have been in this

---

[1] Ted Nakashima, "Concentration Camp: U.S. Style," *The New Republic*, CVI (June 15, 1942), pp. 822–823. Reprinted by Permission of *The New Republic*, © 1942, Harrison-Blaine of New Jersey, Inc.

country since 1901. Fine parents, who brought up their children in the best American way of life. My mother served with the Volunteer Red Cross Service in the last war — my father, an editor, has spoken and written Americanism for forty years.

The Nakashimas

Our family is almost typical of the other unfortunates here at the camp. The oldest son, a licensed architect, was educated at the University of Washington, has a master's degree from the Massachusetts Institute of Technology, and is a scholarship graduate of the American School of Fine Arts in Fontainebleau, France. He is now in camp in Oregon with his wife and three-months-old child. He had just completed designing a much-needed defense housing project at Vancouver, Washington.

The second son is an M.D. He served his internship in a New York hospital, is married, and has two fine sons. The folks banked on him, because he was the smartest of us three boys. The army took him a month after he opened his office. He is now a lieutenant in the Medical Corps, somewhere in the South.

I am the third son, the dumbest of the lot, but still smart enough to hold down a job as an architectural draftsman. I have just finished building a new home and had lived in it three weeks. My desk was just cleared of work done for the Army Engineers, another stack of 391 defense houses was waiting (a rush job), when the order came to pack up and leave for this resettlement center called "Camp Harmony."

Mary, the only girl in the family, and her year-old son, "Butch," are with our parents — interned in the stables of the Livestock Exposition Buildings in Portland.

A Resettlement Center

Now that you can picture our thoroughly American background, let me describe our new home.

The resettlement center is actually a penitentiary — armed guards in towers with spotlights and deadly tommy guns, fifteen feet of barbed-wire fences, everyone confined to quarters at nine, lights out at ten o'clock. The guards are ordered to shoot anyone who approaches within twenty feet of the fences. No one is allowed to take the two-block-long hike to the latrines after nine, under any circumstances.

The apartments, as the army calls them, are two-block-long stables, with windows on one side. Floors are . . . two-by-fours laid directly on the mud, which is everywhere. The stalls are about eighteen by twenty-one feet; some contain families of six or seven persons. Partitions are seven feet high, leaving a four-foot opening above. The rooms aren't too bad, almost fit to live in for a short while.

The food and sanitation problems are the worst. We have had absolutely no fresh meat, vegetables or butter since we came here. Mealtime queues extend for blocks; standing in a rainswept line, feet in the mud, waiting for the scant portions of canned wieners and boiled potatoes, hash for breakfast or canned wieners and beans for dinner. Milk only for the kids. Coffee or tea dosed with saltpeter and stale bread are the adults' staples. Dirty, unwiped dishes, greasy silver, a starchy diet, no butter, no milk, bawling kids, mud, wet mud that stinks when it dries, no vegetables — a sad thing for the people who raised them in such abundance. Memories of a crisp head of lettuce with our special olive oil, vinegar, garlic and cheese dressing.

Today one of the surface sewage-disposal pipes broke and the sewage flowed down the streets. Kids play in the water. Shower baths without hot water. Stinking mud and slops everywhere.

Can this be the same America we left a few weeks ago?

Why Won't America Let Us Be Americans?

As I write, I can remember our little bathroom — light coral walls. My wife painting them, and the spilled paint in her hair. The open towel shelving and the pretty shower curtains which we put up the day before we left. How sanitary and clean we left it for the airlines pilot and his young wife who are now enjoying the fruits of our labor.

It all seems so futile, struggling, trying to live our old lives under this useless, regimented life. The senselessness of all the inactive manpower. Electricians, plumbers, draftsmen, mechanics, carpenters, painters, farmers — every trade — men who are able and willing to do all they can to lick the Axis. Thousands of men and women in these camps, energetic, quick, alert, eager for hard, constructive work, waiting for the army to do something for us, an army that won't give us butter.

I can't take it! I have 391 defense houses to be drawn. I left a fine American home which we built with our own hands. I left . . . good friends, friends who would swear by us. I don't have enough of that

Japanese heritage *ga-man* — a code of silent suffering and ability to stand pain.

Oddly enough I still have a bit of faith in army promises of good treatment and Mrs. Roosevelt's pledge of a future worthy of good American citizens. I'm banking another $67 of income tax on the future. Sometimes I want to spend the money I have set aside for income tax on a bit of butter or ice cream or something good that I might have smuggled through the gates, but I can't do it when I think that every dollar I can put into "the fight to lick the Japs," the sooner I will be home again. I must forget my stomach.

What really hurts most is the constant reference to us evacués as "Japs." "Japs" are the guys we are fighting. We're on this side and we want to help.

Why won't America let us?

IX. Concepts of Americanism and Americanization

Why is it that Americans seem always to be asking who they are? One reason is that, since the beginning of its history, the United States has regarded itself as a nation still in the making. Another is that, for more than three centuries, immigration has been continually changing the ethnic origins of America's people. Understandably, these people continue to ask: What does it mean to be — and to become — an American? ■

1. The Melting Pot

You will remember that in 1782 Crèvecoeur wrote: "Here individuals of all nations are melted into a new race of men . . ." (page 31). This idea derived not only from Crèvecoeur's observations of what was actually going on but, what is equally important, from his hope that the intermarriage of people of different national backgrounds would eventually result in an American type. Other writers were to express this view down to our day. Now as in the past, moreover, many Americans of mixed ancestry can testify to the reality of the melting pot. ■

A. A NINETEENTH CENTURY VIEW[1]

✤ Ralph Waldo Emerson

Ralph Waldo Emerson, a New Englander of colonial stock, was one of the most influential intellectuals of the last century.

[1] Edward Waldo Emerson and Waldo Emerson Forbes, eds., *Journals of Ralph Waldo Emerson* (Boston: Houghton Mifflin Company, 1909–1914, 10 vols.), Vol. VII, pp. 115–116.

> A former Unitarian minister with an immense faith in democracy, he believed that America was still a nation in the process of becoming. During the 1850's, when the anti-immigrant and anti-Catholic Know-Nothing Party came into being, Emerson made the following plea for, as he called it, a "smelting pot." ■

I hate the narrowness of the Native American Party.[2] It is the dog in the manger. It is precisely opposite to all the dictates of love and magnanimity, and therefore, of course, opposite to true wisdom. . . .

Man is the most composite of all creatures. . . . As in the old burning of the Temple at Corinth, by the melting and intermixture of silver and gold and other metals a new compound more precious than any, called the Corinthian brass, was formed; so in this continent, — asylum of all nations — the energy of Irish, Germans, Swedes, Poles, and Cossacks, and all the European tribes — of the Africans, and of the Polynesians — will construct a new race, a new religion, a new state, a new literature, which will be as vigorous as the new Europe which came out of the smelting-pot of the Dark Ages, or that which earlier emerged from . . . barbarism. *La Nature aime les croisements.*[3]

B. A TWENTIETH CENTURY VIEW[4]

✣ Israel Zangwill

> *Israel Zangwill, a British journalist, novelist, short-story writer, and playwright, knew this country as a frequent traveler. One of his plays, produced in America early this century, was set in New York City. In the following scene from* The Melting Pot, *the characters are three immigrants from Russia. Zangwill expresses through David, an idealistic young composer, his faith in the "American crucible." The play was well received in a number of American cities because, according to the critics, it was a "play of the people."* ■

---

[2] [The Know-Nothing Party.]
[3] ["Nature loves cross-breeds."]
[4] Israel Zangwill, *The Melting-Pot, A Drama in Four Acts* (New York: The Macmillan Company, 1909), pp. 36–38.

DAVID

But Miss [Vera] Revendal asked — and I want to explain to her what America means to me.

MENDEL

You can explain it in your American symphony.

VERA

(*Eagerly. To* DAVID.)

You compose?

DAVID

(*Embarrassed.*)

Oh, uncle, why did you talk of — ? uncle always — my music is so thin and tinkling. When I am *writing* my American symphony, it seems like thunder crashing through a forest full of bird songs. But next day — oh, next day!

(*He laughs dolefully and turns away.*)

VERA

So your music finds inspiration in America?

DAVID

Yes — in the seething of the Crucible.

VERA

The Crucible? I don't understand!

DAVID

Not understand! You, the Spirit of the Settlement![5]

(*He rises and crosses to her and leans over the table, facing her.*)
Not understand that America is God's Crucible, the great Melting Pot where all the races of Europe are melting and re-forming! Here you stand, good folk, think I, when I see them at Ellis Island, here you stand

(*Graphically illustrating it on the table.*)
in your fifty groups, with your fifty languages and histories, and your fifty blood hatreds and rivalries. But you won't be long like that, brothers, for these are the fires of God you've come to — these are the fires of God. A fig for your feuds and vendettas! Germans and

---

[5] [Vera was a settlement house worker and so came into frequent contact with immigrants.]

Frenchmen, Irishmen and Englishmen, Jews and Russians — into the Crucible with you all! God is making the American.

MENDEL

I should have thought the American was made already — eighty millions of him.

DAVID

Eighty millions!

(*He smiles toward* VERA *in good-humored derision.*)

Eighty millions! Over a continent! Why, that cockleshell of a Britain has forty millions! No, uncle, the real American has not yet arrived. He is only in the Crucible, I tell you — he will be the fusion of all races, the coming superman. Ah, what a glorious Finale for my symphony — if I can only write it.

2. Cultural Pluralism[1]
♣ Emily Greene Balch

The concept of cultural pluralism has appealed as much to some Americans as the idea of the melting pot has to others. The following selection shows that the former view has not been limited to immigrants. It was written early in the century by a Wellesley College professor of New England Yankee stock who became a specialist in immigration from Slavic Europe. Although not going as far as the priest whose remarks she recorded, Miss Balch agreed on the need to preserve ancestral differences that men revere. ■

One comes sometimes with a sense of shock to a realization of points of view strange to one's own. Take, for instance, a conversation that I once had with a Polish-American priest. I had said something about "Americans," that they were not apt to be interested in Polish history, or something of the sort. Instantly he was on fire.

[1] Emily Greene Balch, *Our Slavic Fellow Citizens* (New York: Charities Publication Committee, 1910), pp. 398–399, 402–403, 424–425.

Americans Represent Many Nations

"You mean English-Americans," he said. "You English constantly speak as if you were the only Americans, or more Americans than others.... The Chicago *Tribune* is written by men who are just over from England, and who yet speak of foreigners when they mean any Americans but English. For instance, in a recent bank failure they said that many 'foreigners' would lose, referring to German-Americans and others who had been in the country for generations. A priest born in Baltimore of Italian parents, speaking English and Italian equally naturally, will see priests, new come from Ireland, promoted over him because he is a 'foreigner.'"

I remarked that if I went to Poland he would not consider me a Pole.

"No, that is different," was his reply. "America was empty, open to all comers alike. There is no reason for the English to usurp the name of American. They should be called Yankees if anything. That is the name of English-Americans. There is no such thing as an American nation. Poles form a nation, but the United States is a country, under one government, inhabited by representatives of different nations. As to the future, I have ... no idea what it will bring. I do not think that there will be amalgamation, one race composed of many. The Poles, Bohemians, and so forth, remain such, generation after generation. Switzerland has been a republic for centuries, but never has brought her people to use one language. For myself, I do favor one language for the United States, *either English or some other*, to be used by every one, but there is no reason why people should not also have another language; that is an advantage, for it opens more avenues to Europe and elsewhere."

He was indignant at the requirement of the naturalization law of 1906, making a knowledge of English a condition of citizenship. I advanced as an argument for it the fact that the proceedings of Congress are carried on in English, and that to vote intelligently a man must be able to follow them. "In our Polish papers," he said, "the congressional debates are as fully reported as in the English-American papers, and politics can be as intelligently followed." I did not feel that I could urge that many English-speaking voters seek familiarity with the debates in full in the *Congressional Record*.

The views that I have tried to reproduce here are, I think, not typical, but they certainly suggest a reconsideration of various questions, among others, "What are Americans?" ...

A NATION OF NATIONS: Americans constitute one nation but proudly preserve customs of ancestral lands. American food offers an international menu with such dishes as sukiyaki, Irish stew, borsch, and even "oriental pizza" (above). Citizens of Chinese ancestry still celebrate the oriental new year — with a dragon parade in New York City (left). Many Americans read more easily in a language other than English. For them foreign-language newspapers are published in this country and others imported (below).

But Americans Also Constitute One Nation

Language wields an influence beyond all calculation, and language has tended to keep the country open to English thought, and comparatively inaccessible to other outside currents. Not only is English generally spoken throughout the country, but it is spoken with surprising uniformity, having much less dialectical variation than the languages of old countries like England and Germany, France and Italy.

Yet granting all that has been said as to the English in the United States, it remains true that the other elements which have made a component part of the country since the beginning have not been either thrust out by the English or simply absorbed or altered over by them into their own likeness. There has been thus far an amalgamation, a fusion, creating a new stock which is no longer English, but something distinctive and different — American. Even our English speech is not the English of England. Our physique, our bearing, still more our tone of mind and spiritual characteristics, not only are distinguishable from the English but mark a national type as distinct perhaps as any.

In spite of . . . [the Polish priest's] belief that America is not a nation, it has in truth the deepest right to consider itself such. It is an organic whole, intersensitive through all its parts, colored by one tradition and bound together not only by love of one material motherland but by one conception of the country's mission and of the means — liberty, enlightenment and prosperity — by which that mission is to be accomplished. . . .

A Program to Harmonize Different Nationalities

What then ought we to be doing for these strangers in our midst? If we ought not to try to "Americanize" them, have we no obligations toward them at all?

It is obviously our plain duty to give the immigrant (and every one else) fair treatment and honest government, and to maintain conditions making wholesome, decent living possible. This is the minimum required at our hands, not by the Golden Rule — that asks much more — but by the most elementary ethic of civilization. Yet as a matter of fact, this simple, fundamental thing we cannot do. It is not in our power.

We can and must do what in the end will be a better thing. We must get our new neighbors to work with us for these things. If their isolation is not to continue, America must come to mean to them, not a rival nationality eager to make them forget their past, and offering them material bribes to induce them to abandon their ideals. We must learn to connect our ideals and theirs, we must learn, as Miss Addams[2] has demonstrated, to work together with them for justice, for humane conditions of living, for beauty and for true, not merely formal, liberty.

Clubs and classes, libraries and evening schools, settlements and, above all, movements in which different classes of citizens join to bring about specific improvements in government or in living conditions, are of infinite value as they conduce to this higher unity, in which we may preserve every difference to which men cling with affection, without feeling ourselves any the less fellow citizens and comrades.

[2] [**Jane Addams:** American social reformer (1860–1935); founder of the first settlement house in Chicago.]

3. Assimilation[1]
✣ Theodore Roosevelt

No word is used more often than assimilation *to describe the process of Americanization. Its meaning has varied but usually comes down to this: an assimilated person is one who loses his ethnic characteristics (those of his ancestral culture) and becomes like everyone else. Unlike the melting pot, this concept does not necessarily envision the creation of a "new man." It rejects, of course, cultural pluralism. Following is what Theodore Roosevelt said on the subject after the outbreak of World War I made him fearful that America's immigrants might have double loyalties.* ■

[1] Theodore Roosevelt, "Americanism," an address delivered before the Knights of Columbus, New York City, 1915. Reprinted in Philip Davis, ed., *Immigration and Americanization* (Boston: Ginn and Company, 1920), pp. 648–651.

There is no room in this country for hyphenated Americanism. When I refer to hyphenated Americans, I do not refer to naturalized Americans. Some of the very best Americans I have ever known were naturalized Americans, Americans born abroad. But a hyphenated American is not an American at all. This is just as true of the man who puts "native" before the hyphen as of the man who puts German or Irish or English or French before the hyphen. Americanism is a matter of the spirit and of the soul. Our allegiance must be purely to the United States. We must unsparingly condemn any man who holds any other allegiance. But if he is heartily and singly loyal to this republic, then no matter where he was born, he is just as good an American as any one else.

An American Is an American and Nothing Else

The one absolutely certain way of bringing this nation to ruin, of preventing all possibility of its continuing to be a nation at all, would be to permit it to become a tangle of squabbling nationalities, an intricate knot of German-Americans, Irish-Americans, English-Americans, French-Americans, Scandinavian-Americans or Italian-Americans, each preserving its separate nationality, each at heart feeling more sympathy with Europeans of that nationality, than with the other citizens of the American republic. . . . The man who calls himself an American citizen, . . . [yet who] shows by his actions that he is primarily the citizen of a foreign land, plays a thoroughly mischievous part in the life of our body politic. He has no place here; and the sooner he returns to the land to which he feels his real heart-allegiance, the better it will be for every good American. . . .

The Men Who Have Fought Our Wars

I appeal to history. Among the generals of Washington in the Revolutionary War were Greene, Putnam, and Lee, who were of English descent; Wayne and Sullivan, who were of Irish descent; Marion, who was of French descent; Schuyler, who was of Dutch descent; and Muhlenberg and Herkimer, who were of German descent. But they were all of them Americans and nothing else, just as much as Washington. Carroll of Carrollton was a Catholic; Hancock a Protestant; Jefferson was heterodox from the standpoint of any orthodox creed;

but these and all the other signers of the Declaration of Independence stood on an equality of duty and right and liberty, as Americans and nothing else.

So it was in the Civil War. Farragut's father was born in Spain and Sheridan's father in Ireland; Sherman and Thomas were of English and Custer of German descent; and Grant came of a long line of American ancestors whose original home had been Scotland. But the Admiral was not a Spanish-American; and the Generals were not Scotch-Americans or Irish-Americans or English-Americans or German-Americans. They were all Americans and nothing else. This was just as true of Lee and of Stonewall Jackson and of Beauregard. . . .

The Men in Roosevelt's Administration

To take charge of the most important work under my administration, the building of the Panama Canal, I chose General Goethals. Both of his parents were born in Holland. But he was just plain United States. He wasn't a Dutch-American; if he had been I wouldn't have appointed him. So it was with such men, among those who served under me, as Admiral Osterhaus and General Barry. The father of one was born in Germany, the father of the other in Ireland. But they were both Americans, pure and simple, and first-rate fighting men in addition.

In my Cabinet at the time there were men of English and French, German, Irish, and Dutch blood, men born on this side and men born in Germany and Scotland; but they were all Americans and nothing else; and every one of them was incapable of thinking of himself or of his fellow-countrymen, excepting in terms of American citizenship. If any one of them had anything in the nature of a dual or divided allegiance in his soul, he never would have been appointed to serve under me, and he would have been instantly removed when the discovery was made. There wasn't one of them who was capable of desiring that the policy of the United States should be shaped with reference to the interests of any foreign country or with consideration for anything, outside of the general welfare of humanity, save the honor and interest of the United States, and each was incapable of making any discrimination whatsoever among the citizens of the country he served, of our common country, save discrimination based on conduct and on conduct alone.

Traitorous to Vote as a "Hyphenated American"

For an American citizen to vote as a German-American, an Irish-American, or an English-American, is to be a traitor to American institutions; and those hyphenated Americans who terrorize American politicians by threats of the foreign vote are engaged in treason to the American republic.

4. Obstacles to Becoming an American[1]
✤ Emily Greene Balch

> *Poverty and prejudice were the chief obstacles to Americanization. No matter how hard non-Anglo-Saxon immigrants and their children tried to link themselves to this country, racists like the Ku Klux Klansmen (page 128) told them that they could never become real Americans. And so long as immigrants lived in poverty, they were cut off from the best in American life. This point is the subject of Emily Greene Balch's piece below. It was written in 1910 about Ruthenians but could apply to any ethnic group living at any time under such appalling conditions in this country.* ■

"My people do not live in America, they live underneath America. America goes on over their heads. America does not begin till a man is a workingman, till he is earning two dollars a day. A laborer cannot afford to be an American."

Degradation, Not Americanization

These words, which were said to me by one of the wisest Slav leaders that I have ever met, have rung in my mind during all the five years since he spoke them.[2] Beginning at the bottom, "living not

---

[1] Emily Greene Balch, *Our Slavic Fellow Citizens* (New York: Charities Publication Committee, 1910), pp. 419–420, 424.
[2] Father Paul Tymkevich, a Ruthenian Greek-Catholic priest of Yonkers. Had he been spared, he could have helped his countrymen and us. See "A Shepherd of Immigrants" for some account of his work. *Charities*, XIII, pages 193–4 (Dec., 1909). [Footnote in original.]

in America but underneath America," means living among the worst surroundings that the country has to show, worse, often, than the public would tolerate, except that "only foreigners" are affected. Yet to foreigners they are doubly injurious because, coming as they often do, with low home standards but susceptible, eager, and apt to take what they find as the American idea of what ought to be, they are likely to accept and adopt as "all right" whatever they tumble into.

I have been in places in Pennsylvania where all one can say is that civilization had broken down. Being in a city, people could not help themselves individually, as they might have done in the country, and the family with the most decent ideas was dragged down by the general degradation of the environment. From the dance hall at one end of the street, to the white door-bells, all up and down its length, which openly denoted kitchen bar-rooms, everything smelled of lawlessness. The water was known to be infected with typhoid, and had to be boiled to be safe — a considerable expense and trouble, and an excellent reason for drinking other things. In the spring the refuse of the winter stood in heaps before the doors. The deep clay mud made some streets absolutely impracticable in wet weather. The neighbors mended them by pouring on ashes and miscellaneous dumpage. Assaults, in some cases ending in death, took place night after night, and although the identity of the offender was supposed to be known, or rather because of that fact, no one dared move in the matter. The mayor stood for "running the town wide open," and was said to have investments not only in saloons but in immoral resorts....

Now consider that it is into surroundings like these that we put our new employees; that this is the example that we set before our new fellow citizens. Under such circumstances the Americanization over which we are so complacent is by no means all gain....

Need for Vision

[Father Tymkevich has said of his people:] "They have no habits. The first step in civilization is to acquire habits, and where can they acquire them? On the streets? In the saloon?

"What my people need most is leaders — leaders to form themselves upon, to give them a standard of ambition. Other people have leaders of their own, strong and influential men among the immigrant body and [also] Americans who know something about . . . [the people of that group] and are ready to take an interest in them."

And again, almost like a cry, the phrase I have previously quoted, "My people are perishing for lack of vision."

"The Slavs are orphans in this country," he said.

The Isolation of Immigrants

And it is in a sense true. It is not chiefly that they have no government of their own, concerned for them as Italy is concerned for the Italians;[3] it is far more that coming to America they are cut off from the life of their old country, without getting into contact with the true life of their new home, from which they are shut off by language, by mutual prejudice, by divergent ideas. To them, both parents are dead, the fatherland that begot them and the foster-mother that supports without cherishing them.

In some ways this isolation is harder for the educated than for the laborer. A man like Father Tymkevich himself is in a position of almost intolerable loneliness. Intelligent, sensitive, separated from his own people by all that separates a scholar from peasants, he was a complete stranger in a community unused to look for friends and associates among foreigners.

[3] [At the time this was written, most Ruthenians lived within the Austro-Hungarian Empire. After World War I, many of them were included in the new state of Czechoslovakia.]

5. A Freedom Fighter Views His Own Adjustment[1]

✤ *Janos Hollo*

Janos Hollo, the author of the following article, escaped to America after fighting in the Hungarian uprising against Soviet domination in 1956. Unlike Father Tymkevich's people about whom you have just read, Mr. Hollo was a well-paid engineer, not a poor laborer. Moreover, he had tastes, values, and hobbies similar to those of the native, middle-class Americans he met. They readily accepted him, and he them. Yet his easy Americanization was no more typical of immigrants in general than the

[1] Janos Hollo, "A Freedom Fighter's Year of Freedom," *The New York Times Magazine* (November 3, 1957), pp. 14, 29. © 1957 by The New York Times Company. Reprinted by permission.

isolation of newcomers trapped by poverty. The most common experience fell somewhere in between the extremes represented by Father Tymkevich and Mr. Hollo. ■

With the anniversary of the Hungarian revolt, my first year in my new country, the United States, is drawing to a close. I am one of those fortunate people who were able to escape from tyranny to the free world and a new life. Now I should like to relate a few of my first American impressions, a few details of the picture that gets clearer and clearer every day.

Easy Adjustment

I am an engineer, and since shortly after my arrival here I have been working in my field at a great chemical enterprise near Cleveland. After a few difficult first months, I found that I adapted myself to American life much more easily than I ever had imagined possible. I had studied English in school, and so I could understand it a bit when I arrived here. Talking was much more difficult, however, and the slang confused me completely. But, with the help of my colleagues on my job, I soon learned the technical terms and, in general conversation, I usually managed to make myself understood. I recall one occasion on which I was very proud. I had gone into a restaurant in Tennessee, and the waitress, after painstaking efforts to understand what I was saying, said smilingly: "I knew all along from your accent that you were a damn Yankee."

A hobby, sailing, brought me my first friends here. At my first opportunity I visited the nearest yacht club. Its members greeted me as warmly as if I had dropped in at a harbor on Lake Balaton . . . [in Hungary]. They helped me not only in resuming my favorite sport, but in settling into my new life. I got acquainted with their homes and customs, and when we talked about our hobby we did not feel at all that we had been born on two different continents.

Misled by Hollywood

Needless to say, I have today a completely different picture of America from that which I had before I came here. From having listened to American radio broadcasts, I knew of the high living standard of this country, as does anyone behind the Iron Curtain who is interested. I knew exactly the minimum hourly wage of an American worker, and was even familiar with the modern jazz of Dave Brubeck. But I thought of the American people in terms of motion pictures and best-selling novels. The men were all devil-may-care gamblers, just between a divorce and a new marriage; the women were all sensualists, ever ready for new flirtations, and in a constant ecstasy over jazz.

The first two weeks showed me the fallacy of this Hollywood-like picture. It is worth noting that, as a result of the moral and material hopelessness of communism, there are relatively many more irresponsible people, many more gamblers, in Budapest than in any of the American communities I have so far had a chance to see.

Americans Sanely Optimistic

I was surprised to discover how early people marry here. I think there is no other country in the world where the life of the society is so firmly based upon the family, and this has impressed me deeply — although I am not married yet.

Naturally, there were social habits which I could not understand. One of them was the conventional question, "How are you?" and the inevitable answer, "Fine." At the beginning I could not believe what I heard. Was it possible that everything was always "fine"? Did they never have a headache or a bad mood? Or, maybe, people were not sincere?

Frankly, I found it rather comic to let everyone know several times a day that I was "fine." It took me months to understand that this was not just a formality, but a philosophy of life, a manifestation of the fundamentally optimistic view of life of the American people.

If I were asked what I like more than anything else in Americans, I would, perhaps, now answer: their youthful . . . [outlook]. I have seen few people old in spirit. They start very young standing on their own feet and assuming their own responsibilities, but in spite of this they do not lose their youthfulness.

I like their goodwill, their philosophy of "keep smiling." I find that their attitude is sanely optimistic; they try to avoid problems and to be as contented as possible.

Too Much Practicality

There are, of course, peculiarities which I am still not used to, although I feel I can explain them to myself. One is the Americans' extremely practical . . . [outlook]. No question about it, this attitude has produced an unmatched technical development, but, on the other hand, the same attitude means that practical considerations rule even in those moments of life when sentiments should prevail. So far, I have met surprisingly few thoughts and needs motivated by an "art for art's sake" attitude.

Soon after my arrival, a new American friend told me: "You must understand that this country always wants something new. If you want to succeed in any field, you have to produce unusual, special new things." This seems to be true. Sometimes I have the feeling that, in the pursuit of the always-new, quality is not always . . . [of first importance].

I consider it a manifestation of the same mentality that almost all aspects of life are more commercialized than in other countries. For example, the enormous amount of advertising I see and hear all about me seems to me very strange. It is so constant that it becomes almost an end in itself. Sometimes I have quite a job putting together the dismembered parts of a newspaper or magazine article. Once I was really astonished to hear advertisements in the short pauses between the movements of a Beethoven symphony on the radio. And I would be really grateful to any cigarette manufacturer who could mention his brand not even once while his television program is going on.

I should like to say just a few words, however, in answer to the well-known European complaint that there is not sufficient cultural life in America. My experience has been that in this country every chance is given people to enjoy culture as much as they wish; they have only to stretch out their hands to reach it.

America Means Self-fulfillment

I am, of course, still at the beginning of my acclimatization. My opinions and my views about American life are gradually changing. Sometimes I find it terribly painful to live in a free country and remember the suppressed fight for freedom of my nation. But at the very instant I left Hungary I irrevocably ceased to be a person playing an active part in the history of Hungary. I manage to get letters to my parents and friends who stayed home, and I correspond regularly with acquaintances now scattered all over the world — a good part of them in the United States and Canada. But my role now is to be a good citizen of my new country, and I am sure there is no other place in all the world where I would have felt my homelessness as little as I did here.

At first, after my arrival, I often tried to give an idea of my experiences to my new American friends, but these lucky people who had never lived under a dictatorship seemed unable to comprehend my feelings. The fact that I am living now in America means to me the possibility of reaching my own individual goals instead of living an untrue life, dictated by commands and slogans. It means security instead of day-to-day fears of persecution. It means the material and spiritual goods of human civilization instead of the poverty and hopelessness of communism. It means being a free member of the community of democratic people. And for all these facts and feelings I am grateful to America.

X. Immigration Policy

Every nation has the freedom to decide the kind of immigrants it wants. For more than a century, until the exclusion of the Chinese in the 1880's, the United States barred no one for ethnic reasons. Next to be denied entrance were the Japanese in 1907–1908. Some fifteen years later, in the Johnson-Reed Act of 1924, restrictionists reduced immigration from southern and eastern Europe to a trickle. Currently, as a result of a law passed by Congress in 1965, American immigration policy conforms again to the original policy of nondiscrimination. The law does, however, limit total immigration to some 300,000 a year. ■

1. Chinese Exclusion[1]
✤ American Federation of Labor

When the Chinese immigrated to the American West in significant numbers in the 1850's, they, like other immigrants, were welcomed. They built railroads, drained swamps, entered the personal service industries, and generally did the dirty work native Americans avoided. During the depression of the 1870's, however, Californians turned on the Chinese and blamed them for rising unemployment. In 1882 Congress passed a law barring them from entering this country for a period of ten years. Thereafter, a combination of California nativists and organized labor had the law periodically renewed. The reasoning was often economic. But the following document shows that the argument also rested on racial prejudice. This document was presented to Congress by the American Federation of Labor in requesting renewal of the 1882 law for a second time. ■

---

[1] American Federation of Labor, "Some Reasons for Chinese Exclusion, Meat vs. Rice: American Manhood against Asiatic Coolieism," *Senate Documents* (Washington, D.C.: Government Printing Office, 1902), Vol. XIII, pp. 29–30.

Experience with Slave Labor

... The Chinese, if permitted freely to enter this country, would create race antagonisms which would ultimately result in great public disturbance. The Caucasians will not tolerate the Mongolian. As ultimately all government is based on physical force, the white population of this country would not, without resistance, suffer itself to be destroyed.

If we were to return to the antebellum [pre-Civil War] ideas of the South, now happily discarded, the Chinese would satisfy every requirement of a slave or servile class. They work well, they are docile, and they would not be concerned about their political condition; but such suggestions are repulsive to American civilization. America has dignified work and made it honorable. Manhood gives title to rights, and the Government, being ruled by majorities, is largely controlled by the very class which servile labor would supersede, namely, the free and independent workingmen of America. The political power invested in men by this Government shows the absolute necessity of keeping up the standard of population and not permitting it to deteriorate by contact with inferior and nonassimilative races.

Our Civilization Is Involved

But this is not alone a race, labor, and political question. It is one which involves our civilization and interests the people of the world. The benefactors, scholars, soldiers, and statesmen — the patriots and martyrs of mankind — have built our modern fabric firmly upon the foundation of religion, law, science, and art. It has been rescued from barbarism and protected against the incursions of barbarians.

Civilization in Europe has been frequently attacked and imperiled by the barbaric hordes of Asia. If the little band of Greeks at Marathon[2] had not beaten back ten times their number of Asiatic invaders, it is impossible to estimate the loss to civilization that would have ensued. When we contemplate what modern civilization owes to the two centuries of Athenian life, from which we first learned our lessons of civil and intellectual freedom, we can see how necessary it was to keep the Asiatic from breaking into Europe. Attila[3] and his

---

[2] [**Marathon:** At the Battle of Marathon in 490 B.C., an Athenian army defeated the forces of Darius, king of the Persians, who had invaded Greece.]

[3] [**Attila:** King of the Huns, an Asiatic people. Under Attila, the Huns invaded Europe in the mid-400's A.D. but were defeated in 451 in a decisive battle in Gaul (modern France).]

Asiatic hordes threatened central Europe when the Gauls made their successful stand against them. The wave of Asiatic barbarism rolled back and civilization was again saved. The repulse of the Turks, who are of the Mongolian race, before Vienna[4] finally made our civilization strong enough to take care of itself, and the danger of extinction by a military invasion from Asia passed away.

But a peaceful invasion is more dangerous than a warlike attack. We can meet and defend ourselves against an open foe, but an insidious foe under our generous laws would be in possession of the citadel before we were aware. The free immigration of Chinese would be for all purposes an invasion by Asiatic barbarians, against whom civilization in Europe has been frequently defended, fortunately for us.[5] It is our inheritance to keep it pure and uncontaminated, as it is our purpose and destiny to broaden and enlarge it. We are trustees for mankind.

Welfare of Chinese Not Overlooked

In an age when the brotherhood of man has become more fully recognized, we are not prepared to overlook the welfare of the Chinese himself. We need have nothing on our national conscience, because the Chinese has a great industrial destiny in his own country. Few realize that China is yet a sparsely populated country. Let their merchants, travelers, and students, then, come here, as before, to carry back to China the benefits of our improvements and experiments. Let American ideas of progress and enterprise be planted on Chinese soil. Our commerce with China since 1880 has increased more than 50 per cent. Our consular service reports that "the United States is second only to Great Britain in goods sold to the Chinese." The United States buys more goods from China than does any other nation, and her total trade with China, exports and imports, equals that of Great Britain, not including the colonies, and is far ahead of that of any other country.

Commerce is not sentimental and has not been affected by our policy of exclusion. The Chinese government, knowing the necessity

---

[4] [**Vienna:** In 1683 an army of Turks who had invaded Hungary and were besieging Vienna were defeated by combined Polish and German forces. This victory turned back a threat to Christian Europe.]
[5] [The writer of the document ignored the fact that the Chinese had developed a high level of civilization centuries before European civilization reached a comparable level.]

of the situation, being familiar with the fact that almost every country has imposed restrictions upon the immigration of Chinese coolies, does not regard our attitude as an unfriendly act. Indeed, our legislation has been confirmed by treaty. Nor are the Chinese unappreciative of the friendship of the United States recently displayed in saving, possibly, the [Chinese] Empire itself from dismemberment. So, therefore, America is at no disadvantage in its commercial dealings with China on account of the domestic policy of Chinese exclusion.

Asks Exclusion for Nation's Safety

Therefore every consideration of public duty, the nation's safety and the people's rights, the preservation of our civilization, and the perpetuity of our institutions, impel . . . [us] to ask for the re-enactment of the exclusion laws, which have for twenty years protected us against the gravest dangers, and which, were they relaxed, would imperil every interest which the American people hold sacred for themselves and their posterity. . . .

2. The Literacy Test Vetoed[1]
✣ Woodrow Wilson

The Immigration Restriction League, founded in Boston in 1894, was the first nativist organization to raise an outcry against the so-called "new immigrants" from eastern and southern Europe. It proposed to keep out these immigrants through a literacy test. Such a measure was enacted by Congress in 1917, amidst the passions of war, even though three Presidents since the 1890's had vetoed similar legislation. On the following pages is President Woodrow Wilson's message to Congress explaining his veto of a literacy test bill in 1915. ■

---

[1] Woodrow Wilson, Message to the House of Representatives, January 28, 1915. Reprinted in the *Congressional Record*, 63rd Congress, 3rd Session (Washington, D.C.: Government Printing Office, 1915), Vol. LII, pp. 2481–2.

It is with unaffected regret that I find myself constrained by clear conviction to return this bill ["An act to regulate the immigration of aliens to and the residence of aliens in the United States"] without my signature. Not only do I feel it to be a very serious matter to exercise the power of veto in any case, because it involves opposing the single judgment of the President to the judgment of a majority of both the Houses of the Congress, a step which no man who realizes his own liability to error can take without great hesitation, but also because this particular bill is in so many important respects admirable, well conceived, and desirable. Its enactment into law would undoubtedly enhance the efficiency and improve the methods of handling the important branch of the public service to which it relates. But candor and a sense of duty with regard to the responsibility so clearly imposed upon me by the Constitution in matters of legislation leave me no choice but to dissent.

A Violation of the Traditions of Asylum and Opportunity

In two particulars of vital consequence this bill embodies a radical departure from the traditional and long-established policy of this country, a policy in which our people have conceived the very character of their government to be expressed, the very mission and spirit of the nation in respect of its relations to the peoples of the world outside their borders. It seeks to all but close entirely the gates of asylum which have always been open to those who could find nowhere else the right and opportunity of constitutional agitation for what they conceived to be the natural and inalienable rights of men; and it excludes those to whom the opportunities of elementary education have been denied, without regard to their character, their purposes, or their natural capacity.

Restrictions like these, adopted earlier in our history as a nation, would very materially have altered the course and cooled the humane ardors of our politics. The right of political asylum has brought to this country many a man of noble character and elevated purpose who was marked as an outlaw in his own less fortunate land, and who has yet become an ornament to our citizenship and to our public councils. The children and the compatriots of these illustrious Americans must stand amazed to see the representatives of their nation now resolved, in the fullness of our national strength and at the maturity of our great institutions, to risk turning such men back from our shores

194   *Immigration Policy*

without test of quality or purpose. It is difficult for me to believe that the full effect of this feature of the bill was realized when it was framed and adopted, and it is impossible for me to assent to it in the form in which it is here cast.

The literacy test and the tests and restrictions which accompany it constitute an even more radical change in the policy of the nation. Hitherto we have generously kept our doors open to all who were not unfitted by reason of disease or incapacity for self-support or such personal records and antecedents as were likely to make them a menace to our peace and order or to the wholesome and essential relationships of life. In this bill it is proposed to turn away from tests of character and of quality and impose tests which exclude and restrict; for the new tests here embodied are not tests of quality or of character or of personal fitness, but tests of opportunity. Those who come seeking opportunity are not to be admitted unless they have already had one of the chief of the opportunities they seek, the opportunity of education. The object of such provisions is restriction, not selection.

No Mandate to Reverse an Historic Policy

If the people of this country have made up their minds to limit the number of immigrants by arbitrary tests and so reverse the policy of all the generations of Americans that have gone before them, it is their right to do so. I am their servant and have no license to stand in their way. But I do not believe that they have. I respectfully submit that no one can quote their mandate to that effect. Has any political party ever avowed a policy of restriction in this fundamental matter, gone to the country on it, and been commissioned to control its legislation? Does this bill rest upon the conscious and universal assent and desire of the American people? I doubt it. It is because I doubt it that I make bold to dissent from it. I am willing to abide by the verdict, but not until it has been rendered. Let the platforms of parties speak out upon this policy and the people pronounce their wish. The matter is too fundamental to be settled otherwise.

I have no pride of opinion in this question. I am not foolish enough to profess to know the wishes and ideals of America better than the body of her chosen representatives know them. I only want instruction direct from those whose fortunes, with ours and all men's, are involved.

3. The National Origins Plan[1]
✤ Ellison DuRant Smith

The Johnson-Reed Act of 1924, which reflected the isolationist views of the 'twenties, was passed by a Congress that disproportionately represented small-town, rural, old-stock America. Except for Asians, who were barred, the law limited immigration to some 150,000 people a year. Through a complicated device ("the national origins plan"), each nation was given a quota in proportion to the number of people of that national origin living in the United States according to the white census of 1920. Like Senator Smith of South Carolina, whose speech is printed below, the proponents of the bill spoke up in favor of "Nordic" supremacy. That is why Italy, Poland, Russia, Greece, and other non-northern and non-western European nations received the smallest quotas — and Great Britain the largest. ■

It seems to me the point as to this measure — and I have been so impressed for several years — is that the time has arrived when we should shut the door. We have been called the melting pot of the world. We had an experience just a few years ago, during the great World War, when it looked as though we had allowed influences to enter our borders that were about to melt the pot in place of us being the melting pot.

Economic Reasons for Closing the Door

I think that we have sufficient stock in America now for us to shut the door. Americanize what we have, and save the resources of America for the natural increase of our population. We all know that one of the most prolific causes of war is the desire for increased land ownership for the overflow of a congested population. We are increasing at such a rate that in the natural course of things in a comparatively few years the landed resources, the natural resources of the

---

[1] Speech by Ellison DuRant Smith. Reprinted in the *Congressional Record*, 68th Congress, 1st Session (Washington, D.C.: Government Printing Office, 1924), Vol. LXV, p. 5961.

country, shall be taken up by the natural increase of our population. It seems to me the part of wisdom now that we have throughout the length and breadth of continental America a population which is beginning to encroach upon the reserve and virgin resources of the country to keep it in trust for the multiplying population of the country.

Threat to American Institutions

I do not believe that political reasons should enter into the discussion of this very vital question. It is of greater concern to us to maintain the institutions of America, to maintain the principles upon which this government is founded, than to develop and exploit the undeveloped resources of the country. There are some things that are dearer to us, fraught with more benefit to us, than the immediate development of the undeveloped resources of the country. I believe that our particular ideas, social, moral, religious, and political, have demonstrated, by virtue of the progress we have made and the character of people that we are, that we have the highest ideals of any member of the human family or any nation. We have demonstrated the fact that the human family, certainly the predominant breed in America, can govern themselves by a direct government of the people. If this government shall fail, it shall fail by virtue of the terrible law of inherited tendency. Those who come from the nations which from time immemorial have been under the dictation of a master fall more easily by the law of inheritance and the inertia of habit into a condition of political servitude than the descendants of those who cleared the forests, conquered the savage, stood at arms and won their liberty from their mother country, England.

The Preservation of Anglo-Saxon Stock

I think we now have sufficient population in our country for us to shut the door and to breed up a pure, unadulterated American citizenship. . . . Who is an American? Is he an immigrant from Italy? Is he an immigrant from Germany? If you were to go abroad and some one were to meet you and say, "I met a typical American," what would flash into your mind as a typical American, the typical representative of that new nation? Would it be the son of an Italian immigrant, the son of a German immigrant, the son of any of the breeds from the Orient, the son of the denizens of Africa? . . .

I would like for the Members of the Senate to read that book just recently published by Madison Grant, *The Passing of the Great Race*.[2] Thank God we have in America perhaps the largest percentage of any country in the world of the pure, unadulterated Anglo-Saxon stock; certainly the greatest of any nation in the Nordic breed. It is for the preservation of that splendid stock that has characterized us that I would make this not an asylum for the oppressed of all countries, but a country to assimilate and perfect that splendid type of manhood that has made America the foremost nation in her progress and in her power, and yet the youngest of all the nations. I myself believe that the preservation of her institutions depends upon us now taking counsel with our condition and our experience during the last World War. . . .

The Quota System Urged

I am in favor of putting the quota down to the lowest possible point, with every selective element in it that may be. . . . We do not want to tangle the skein of America's progress by those who imperfectly understand the genius of our government and the opportunities that lie about us. Let us keep what we have, protect what we have, make what we have the realization of the dream of those who wrote the Constitution.

[2] [Madison Grant was a wealthy New Yorker of colonial British stock who felt the country was threatened by the immigration of non-Anglo-Saxons. His book, *The Passing of the Great Race* (1916), claimed that Anglo-Saxon stock was superior.]

4. The McCarran-Walter Immigration Bill[1]
✤ Time

In the 1950's, when Americans were particularly susceptible to the fear of Communist subversion, Congress passed a new immigration bill — the McCarran-Walter Act of 1952. The racist quotas of the Johnson-Reed Act were retained, despite criticisms of their discriminatory character. The following article from a weekly news magazine not only described the passage of the bill but also quoted one of the bill's sponsors on the need to preserve

[1] "Code for the Melting Pot," *Time*, LIX (June 2, 1952), p. 16. Courtesy *Time*, The Weekly Newsmagazine; Copyright Time Inc., 1952.

the quota system. Congress passed the bill over President Harry S. Truman's scorching veto. ■

[The] torch held by the chatelaine of Bedloe's Island[2] is now used to examine the family trees of would-be immigrants. Since 1924, entry to the United States has been strictly rationed under the principle of national origins. Last week in the Senate, it was made clear that Congress intends to keep it thus.

This principle, which still guides United States immigration policy, takes the 94 million United States white population of 1920, breaks it down into percentages according to foreign ancestry, and applies the percentages to determine how many immigrants may enter from each country. The result, as intended, heavily favors north Europeans, drastically holds down entry of south and east Europeans. Example: out of a total of 154,000 immigrants allowed entry each year,[3] 41.4% may come from Britain and Northern Ireland, 11.2% from Ireland, only 3% from Italy, 2% from Greece.

Last week the principle of national origins came under heavy fire from Senate liberals. Up for debate and disposition was an omnibus immigration measure sponsored by Nevada's Pat McCarran. In essence, the bill proposes no real departure in policy. Product of almost three years of study and hearings by the judiciary committees, it is designed to bring thousands of piecemeal immigration statutes and regulations (accumulated since 1798) into one handy, compact code. In the process, it would remove some glaring inequities, . . . [for example,] all Asiatic immigrants would be eligible for citizenship, where previously Japanese and certain others were barred. But the McCarran bill accepts the principle of national origin without any reservation.

Cry for Equality

New York's Herbert Lehman, Rhode Island's John Pastore, Minnesota's Hubert Humphrey, and Illinois' Paul Douglas led a strong protest against holding to the old rules. The McCarran bill, they agreed, is "harsh . . . discriminatory . . . undemocratic." Lehman called for "a new approach to the whole subject of immigration . . . to demonstrate to the world that we are sincere in advocating principles based

---

[2] [chatelaine of Bedloe's Island: the Statue of Liberty.]
[3] Or one-sixth of 1% of the 1920 white population, a formula which became effective in 1929. [Footnote in original.]

RECENT ARRIVALS: Though immigration will probably never again reach the huge numbers of the early 1900's, America still welcomes several hundred thousand newcomers yearly. Like past immigrants, they come from different lands and for a variety of reasons — to join relatives, to seek opportunity, to find a freer life. Thus, Hungarian freedom fighters who escaped to America after an unsuccessful uprising against Soviet power followed in the footsteps of political refugees like Carl Schurz (page 42). Above, Hungarian refugees about to land in New York City in 1956.

The parents of the Puerto Rican schoolchildren pictured above differed from past immigrants in one respect — they were American citizens who left an American territory to come to the mainland. But these newcomers face problems that immigrants have always faced — learning a foreign language, finding decent homes and jobs, and adjusting to an unfamiliar society. Singing songs in English, as in this schoolroom, helps Puerto Rican children learn the new language. The lesson of the American past is that people of any group can overcome the problems of adjustment and take part in the life of the nation.

on equality of men of all races and nations." Pastore passionately urged: "We should take the roster of the American army in World War II . . . and, upon the basis of those racial strains, judge our immigration law. . . ."

Main changes demanded by the protestors:

❡ Pooling of unused quotas; the McCarran bill keeps the old system under which unused quotas cannot be transferred to countries whose quotas are exhausted.

❡ Updating of population base, from 1920 to 1950, for determining quotas.

❡ Provisions to allow Orientals who are naturalized citizens of Western nations (. . . [for example], Hong Kong Chinese) to immigrate under the quotas of their Western nationalities; the McCarran bill puts all Orientals, regardless of citizenship, in the small quotas assigned to their ancestral countries.

❡ Revamping of deportation rules and procedures; under the McCarran bill, it is at least theoretically possible for a naturalized citizen to be deported for a traffic violation.

Warning of Disaster

. . . Pat McCarran took the floor for what was practically a single-handed oratorical fight against the critics. Their proposals, he thundered, would be "disastrous" to the United States: ". . . opening of the gates to a flood of Asiatics . . . destruction of the national-origins quota system . . . would, in the course of a generation or so, change the ethnic and cultural composition of this nation."

When it came to lining up votes, McCarran swamped his opponents. By 44–28, the Senate rejected a motion to return his bill to committee. By 51–27, it turned down a Lehman-Humphrey substitute bill. Then, the opposition giving up, the McCarran bill was passed by a voice vote.

The House has already given overwhelming approval (206–68) to a similar measure. Next move is up to Harry Truman. Even if he vetoes the bill, basic immigration policy will not change. The United States will still be committed to the principle of national origins, which in many ways is as selfish and unjust as the liberals last week said it was. But in all the debate, nobody has appeared with a substitute principle that has much chance of acceptance by those already in the melting pot.

5. The Repeal of Racism[1]
✤ Lyndon B. Johnson

The McCarran-Walter Act no sooner passed than organizations speaking for over half the American people attacked it as bigoted. President John F. Kennedy took up the fight to have it repealed in the early 1960's. The triumph of striking this law from the statute books fell to the Johnson administration two years later. In 1965 Congress enacted a new law which abolished the quota system and welcomed immigrants according to their skills. On October 3, President Johnson signed the bill, dramatically, on Liberty Island, where the Statue of Liberty stands. The following is what he had to say on that occasion. ■

... This bill that we sign today is not a revolutionary bill. It does not affect the lives of millions. It will not reshape the structure of our daily lives, or really add importantly to either our wealth or our power.

Yet it is still one of the most important acts of this Congress and of this administration.

For it does repair a very deep and painful flaw in the fabric of American justice. It corrects a cruel and enduring wrong in the conduct of the American nation....

The Quota System Abolished

This bill says simply that from this day forth those wishing to immigrate to America shall be admitted on the basis of their skills and their close relationship to those already here.

This is a simple test, and it is a fair test. Those who can contribute most to this country — to its growth, to its strength, to its spirit — will be the first that are admitted to this land.

The fairness of this standard is so self-cvident that we may well wonder that it has not always been applied. Yet the fact is that for over four decades the immigration policy of the United States has been twisted and has been distorted by the harsh injustice of the national origins quota system.

[1] *Weekly Compilation of Presidential Documents*, Vol. I, no. 11 (Monday, October 11, 1965), pp. 364–367.

Under that system the ability of new immigrants to come to America depended upon the country of their birth. Only three countries were allowed to supply 70 per cent of all the immigrants.

Families were kept apart because a husband or a wife or a child had been born in the wrong place.

Men of needed skill and talent were denied entrance because they came from southern or eastern Europe or from one of the developing continents.

This system violated the basic principle of American democracy — the principle that values and rewards each man on the basis of his merit as a man.

It has been un-American in the highest sense because it has been untrue to the faith that brought thousands to these shores even before we were a country.

Today, with my signature, this system is abolished.

We can now believe that it will never again shadow the gate to the American nation with the twin barriers of prejudice and privilege.

America Built by Strangers

Our beautiful America was built by a nation of strangers. From a hundred different places or more, they have poured forth into an empty land, joining and blending in one mighty and irresistible tide.

The land flourished because it was fed from so many sources — because it was nourished by so many cultures and traditions and peoples.

And from this experience, almost unique in the history of nations, has come America's attitude toward the rest of the world. We, because of what we are, feel safer and stronger in a world as varied as the people who make it up — a world where no country rules another and all countries can deal with the basic problems of human dignity and deal with those problems in their own way.

Now, under the monument which has welcomed so many to our shores, the American nation returns to the finest of its traditions today.

The days of unlimited immigration are past.

But those who do come will come because of what they are, and not because of the land from which they sprang.

When the earliest settlers poured into a wild continent, there was no one to ask them where they came from. The only question was: Were they sturdy enough to make the journey, were they strong enough to clear the land, were they enduring enough to make a home for freedom, and were they brave enough to die for liberty if it became necessary to do so?

And so it has been through all the great and testing moments of American history. This year we see in Viet-Nam men dying — men named Fernandez and Zajac and Zelinko and Mariano and McCormick.

Neither the enemy who killed them nor the people whose independence they have fought to save ever asked them where they or their parents came from. They were all Americans. . . .

By eliminating that same question as a test for immigration the Congress proves ourselves worthy of those men and worthy of our own traditions as a nation. . . .

Ellis Island and the Statue of Liberty: American Symbols

Over my shoulder here you can see Ellis Island, whose vacant corridors echo today the joyous sounds of long-ago voices.

And today we can all believe that the lamp of this grand old lady is brighter today, and the golden door that she guards gleams more brilliantly in the light of an increased liberty for the people from all the countries of the globe.

XI. The Contemporary Scene

This book opened with Walt Whitman's characterization of America as a "nation of nations." Now that you have finished reading the historical record, you're in a better position than before to appreciate Whitman's insight. You have seen the extent to which America, over the past three and a half centuries, was peopled from all over the world. You have also noted how the immigrants changed American life, and how America altered the lives of the immigrants. The examination you have just concluded is an examination of one of the great historical forces in the making of our country.

Nor has that process come to an end. Between 1950 and 1970 the United States admitted 5,830,000 immigrants, exclusive of about a million Puerto Ricans who, as United States citizens, are not enumerated in the official statistics as immigrants. To grasp the size of the most recent migrations, remember that when the Constitution was adopted fewer than four million people lived in the United States.

But there are more compelling reasons than numbers for studying the relation of immigration to the contemporary scene. For one thing, the place of minority groups in American life is currently a major social issue. For another, there has been a major rediscovery of ethnic diversity and a growing celebration of its importance for a pluralistic society. Not since the 1920's have considerations of race and nationality loomed so large in the consciousness of Americans.

Keep these things in mind as you read the following documents about the contemporary scene. Also remember that, in a very imperfect world, America's massive ingathering of a bewildering variety of peoples is, on balance, one of the few genuine success stories in the annals of mankind. No other society has taken in so many people, and so many different kinds of people, as has the United States. The big question, still to be answered, is whether the future will look like the past. Much depends on the response of the present. ∎

1. Changing Ethnic Profile[1]
✤ Bill Kovach

In a vast country of over 200 million people, the entry of 350,000 immigrants a year would go unnoticed if they were widely dispersed. But like their predecessors, America's most recent newcomers concentrate in one locality or another. In such localities the newcomers are very noticeable indeed, particularly if they are different in ethnic origin from the receiving people. Below, in an article about Fall River, Massachusetts, and other cities like it, the author discusses the changing ethnic profile that has taken shape since the abolition of the national origins plan in 1965. ■

There is a new Fall River in the making as a result of shifting immigration patterns that are adding new features to the profile of the American population.

Lured by earlier settlements from the Old World, Portuguese immigrants are flocking to southeastern Massachusetts in numbers exceeding 4,000 a year. Since the immigration laws were liberalized in 1965, the Portuguese have overwhelmed older groups from northern European countries and now form the predominant ethnic group of the region.

Shift in Ethnic Makeup Since 1965

Fall River is only one among many cities in the United States undergoing a radical shift in ethnic makeup because of the liberalized immigration laws.

Los Angeles and other West Coast cities have developed entirely new communities of Filipinos; *The Boston Globe* carries a weekly column in Spanish for thousands of new Spanish-speaking residents; Greek and Middle Eastern restaurants are opening in a number of towns across the country.

Indeed, the Immigration Act of 1965, which allowed for the first time large-scale immigration from countries outside Northern Europe, is changing America fast.

The Census Bureau recently reported that nonwhite immigration

[1] Bill Kovach, "Eased Laws Alter U.S. Ethnic Profile," *The New York Times,* June 14, 1971.

reached significant proportions for the first time from 1960 to 1970 — accounting for nearly 14 per cent of all immigrants — for a total of half a million people. Immigration accounted for about 20 per cent of the total population growth of the United States — a total of 3.9 million people — in the decade....

Fall River, an Example

Fall River, which is 15 miles southeast of Providence, R.I., typifies the new immigration patterns.

A few years ago, to serve the needs of the changing population of southeastern Massachusetts, the Roman Catholic Church entered into an agreement with the family of Luciano J. Pereira, a young native of St. Michael Island in the Portuguese-owned Azores. The Church, it was agreed, would educate young Luciano (public education was provided by the Government only through the third grade) if he would agree to serve the needs of the Church.

An assistant at St. Michael Church here, Father Pereira administers to the growing community of Portuguese immigrants.

When Father Pereira came to perform his service to the Portuguese-American community, he was dealing with a small band of people. The Azores had served as a station of cheap labor for the New Bedford whalers and the Fall River packers. Some settled here and each generation lured others to work in cordage factories and later in the textile factories that saved the region from economic ruin in the face of steamship competition.

Twentieth-century immigration from the Azores and the Cape Verdean Islands — as well as the mainland of Portugal — was minuscule, however, under the National Origins Act of 1924, which favored Northern Europeans almost to the exclusion of the Southern and Eastern Europeans and Asians.

In 1965, the last year that the quota system begun by the 1924 law was in operation, 42 Portuguese immigrants came to Fall River. In 1970, there were 700.

Laws of 1924 and 1965 Compared

The Immigration Act of 1965, which became fully operative in 1968, abolished the old National Origins quota system, which tried to keep the same ethnic balance in immigration that was reflected in the population census of 1920.

Quotas were allocated by nations before 1965; Britain, Germany, and Ireland accounted for 70 per cent of all immigrant visas issued for Europe, Asia and Africa. Southern and Eastern Europeans, Orientals and Africans were admitted only in tightly controlled dribbles.

By 1965, a Democratic party campaign for a more equitable system bore fruit. The act passed that year put all potential immigrants on a first-come, first-served basis. Europe, Asia and Africa were granted 170,000 immigrant visas each year; Canada and Latin America were allocated 120,000. No national quotas were imposed and the only limit set was a ceiling of 20,000 from any one country in a year.

At the same time, the law gave a clear priority to relatives of United States residents seeking immigration visas.

The result was like opening a flood gate for those countries whose entry had been restricted. Italians, Chinese, Filipinos and others formerly curbed streamed in. . . . The Philippines and Italy replaced Canada and Britain by 1970 in the top three countries sending new citizens to America.

Ireland, France, the Netherlands, Russia, Sweden and Norway dropped out of the list of the top 25 nations by 1970 to be replaced by countries such as Jamaica, Portugal and India.

Indian and Portuguese communities are springing up in cities that once had Irish and German colonies; Yugoslavs are filling restaurant jobs once dominated by Frenchmen; Spanish is the first language with more and more residents of New York, Boston and Chicago.

Problems

The sudden shift in the character and size of immigration to the United States has created a number of problems, including the following:

Chinatown in San Francisco is bursting at the seams because of immigration that reached a peak of 10,000 in 1969. The new immigrants do not fit into the traditional life style set by the long-time residents.

Chicago's schools are filling with Spanish-speaking and Chinese-speaking youngsters attempting to cope with little in the way of special programs in language training.

Hawaii is receiving unskilled Filipinos and Orientals who compete with local labor and force wage rates down.

Such problems are magnified in places like Fall River, a city of 50,000 population.

Clustering around churches like St. Michael and St. George, named for the home islands and serving communities from those islands, the Portuguese have spread across Fall River, dominating the north and east arms of the city.

Names like Silva, Cabral and Escobar predominate. Restaurants feature polvo (octopus), couves (kale soup) and de bulho (a mixture of tripe and liver).

Inside neat frame houses that reflect the pride in ownership that drove most of the immigrants to invest their first American money in homes, scenes of rediscovery are common. Scenes like the one at 139 Merchant Street, where 72-year-old José M. Silva, tears streaming from his eyes, was reunited with his sisters for the first time in 50 years.

A scene so frequent as to be characteristic of Fall River these days is that of a middle-aged or elderly Portuguese couple, carefully dressed in a dark suit or dress, being led through stores and offices by a young, dark-haired 12-year-old. The youngster, testing his still-imperfect English, is necessary as an interpreter for the newly arrived relatives.

In supermarkets and employment offices the young one transmits information back and forth as his elders begin to cope with the job of becoming Americanized.

John R. Correiro, who in 1967 organized the English as a Second Language Center here to help immigrant children move more smoothly into the school system, has studied the problem in detail.

"Primarily," he said, "it is a problem of rapid adjustment with little or no help. Most come directly from farms, many never wore shoes. Can you imagine the shock? One day you leave a peasant culture by airplane and the next day you're in the middle of a complex, dizzy city."

2. Successful Adjustment in Miami[1]

✛ Bryan O. Walsh

Florida lies about 1,000 miles southwest of the Massachusetts community about which you have just read. It contains about 45 per cent of America's Cuban population, and the majority of

[1] Bryan O. Walsh, "Cubans in Miami," *America*, CIV (February 26, 1966), pp. 286–289.

Florida's Cubans live in Metropolitan Miami. Predominantly refugees of the 1960's from the Castro regime, they constitute one of the newest immigrant communities of genuine size (217,000) in the United States.

In a little while you will be reading about the problems of poverty, but Miami's Cubans suffer from little of that. The reason why is that, unlike immigrants in general, many Cuban political refugees were successful, urban, middle-class folk in their native land. Comprising a disproportionate number of businessmen, skilled workers, and university-educated professional men, they have not only found good jobs and good housing, but have also been a boon to Florida's economy. This last is emphasized in the following article. When the author, a Catholic priest, wrote it, he was chairman of the Commission on Cuban Refugees of the Miami Diocese. ■

The influx of Cuban refugees into South Florida began on Jan. 1, 1959, when Fidel Castro's troops were victorious. It has continued without interruption ever since — directly, by plane and by small boat, and indirectly, via Spain and Mexico. The arrival of so great a number of persons naturally posed formidable problems both for the city of Miami and for the state of Florida. At the same time it has brought definite benefits....

Spanish-Speaking Miami

Because Miami has long had a large Cuban colony (estimated at 30,000) and welcomes more than 240,000 Latin American tourists each year, the impact of the new refugees on Miami was slight. Not until October, 1960, did the community at large become aware of their presence. The resident Cuban colony had done a good job of absorbing their compatriots into their homes and places of business.

When these resources were exhausted, Cubans went to the Church for help. Their chief channel has been the Centro Hispano Catolico, an agency established in 1959 by Bishop Coleman F. Carroll, of the newly formed Diocese of Miami, to welcome Spanish-speaking newcomers. It should be remembered that Miami had and still has growing colonies of Spanish-speaking people (estimated at 12,000) from many Latin American countries as well as 45,000 from Puerto Rico. Some have estimated that there were 100,000 Spanish-speaking residents (10 per cent of the total population) in Greater Miami before the first refugees from Castro's revolution arrived. Long before 1959, there were hotels, restaurants, theatres and shops catering especially to the Spanish-speaking. ...

In the community at large, Cubans face some of the prejudice and hostility that are expressed toward Spanish-speaking persons today throughout the United States wherever there are substantial numbers of them — as, for instance, the Puerto Ricans in New York, the Mexicans in Chicago, and the braceros[2] and migrant workers in the Southwest. It has been my observation, however, that the person of Spanish heritage, whether he be citizen, resident alien, Cuban refugee or tourist, is much better accepted in Miami than anywhere else in the country.

Spanish-speaking persons are to be found in all social circles and at all levels of society. Many of the biggest industrialists, bankers and businessmen in Miami speak Spanish in both their offices and their homes. Except for a certain segment of the white population in borderline economic circumstances, who feel themselves threatened by those who are different, the majority of Miamians respect their Spanish-speaking neighbors, especially if they are Cuban, and regard them as their social equals or superiors.

Cubans an Economic Asset

... Most knowledgeable community leaders, including the newspapers and other media and the Chamber of Commerce, see the Cuban refugee as a real economic asset to the community.

The Miami *Herald* said editorially on Dec. 3, 1965:

"The area has become a home of the cream of a nation in exile. It has seen the creation of a bi-lingual culture of impressing quality. The economy has been helped, not hurt. The *Herald's* own studies show that the Cuban community spends some seven million to eight million dollars a month in Miami. An inventory of new plants, businesses, homes and restaurants will show many Cuban-financed enterprises which have created new wealth."

According to the Miami *News* of Nov. 3, 1965, the Cuban refugee's credit rating has soared 150 per cent. It reports that Miami banks are soliciting new refugee accounts as "sound secure business." Tully Dunlap, of Riverside Bank, is quoted as saying: "It is time the other

---

[2] [**braceros**: Mexican laborers whom a joint United States-Mexican agreement permitted to work in the United States.]

side of the story is told. The Cuban is industrious, aggressive and honest. He definitely is an economic asset to Miami." William Pallot, of Inter-National Bank, declares: "If the refugees were not here, there would be an overabundance of vacant stores and apartments. Miami would probably be suffering economically if not for them."

Last February, the Miami *News* reported that 16 per cent of all homes sold in Miami from July to September of 1964 were bought by Cubans. Some 85 per cent of the Cubans bought homes in the $20,000 and higher brackets. . . .

Unwarranted Fear of Concentration

Many Americans fear that this concentration tends to delay their integration into American society. Yet sociologists who have studied the earlier waves of immigrants report that the newcomers benefited greatly from the "little Italys" and "little Irelands" of past generations. Immigrants' tendency to live close together protects them against loss of identity, and often provides for a family stability and security that far outweighs any delay in rapid Americanization.

Lowered Crime Rate

The Miami police authorities have consistently pointed out not only that the Cubans have not contributed to an increase in the crime rate, but that their crime rate has been so low that it has resulted in a lower over-all rate for the total community. The same has been true of juvenile delinquency (the one exception being the traffic court). According to the most recent FBI figures, the Miami crime rate increased 1.9 per cent during the first nine months of 1965, compared to a 5.1 per cent increase nationally.

Great Thing for Miami

City of Miami surveys have shown that many run-down areas of the city, especially in the southwest section, have been saved and rehabilitated by the Cuban influx. One report stated that no Cuban refugee lives in a slum.

The Cuban refugees have bestowed benefits on Miami that far outweigh any temporary inconveniences and aggravations. Quite apart from bringing $195 million in Federal aid, much of which has been spent in Miami, Cubans themselves by their industry and initiative have created an expanding community, including new restaurants, automobile services, small factories, hotels and new houses. The whole of the city has benefited from their determined effort to support themselves, and from their fortitude and their warmth and gaiety in the face of catastrophe. There is no intention in this article to deny that Miami has its problems. But leaders from every walk of life are to be found in Miami who will agree that, all in all, the influx of Cuban refugees has been one of the greatest things Miami ever saw.

The Airlift Praised

It was on Dec. 1, 1965, that the airlift sponsored by the United States began operations, with one flight a day from Varadero Beach (80 miles east of Havana) to Miami. Each day, up to 90 new refugees now arrive on two flights.

This airlift is particularly significant since it is aimed at reuniting families, such as the parents of the unaccompanied children. By Dec. 1, some 197,000 fathers, mothers, brothers, sisters, sons and daughters had been claimed by refugees living in the United States. At the present rate, it will take several years to bring them all here. The airlift promises to be one of the greatest humanitarian efforts ever undertaken by any government. It is our belief in Miami that we have nothing to fear from this new influx. On the contrary, the reunion of perhaps a hundred thousand families in all parts of this nation is bound to solve numberless problems. To us it is inconceivable that anyone could object to this.

3. Multiple Problems of the Poor

In Section IV of Part Two, you read that, traditionally and with few exceptions, immigrants started out at the bottom of the economic ladder. That is still true today. Yet the problems of being poor are not only the problems of having a low-paying and unskilled job. They also include bad housing, inferior education, broken homes, a violent neighborhood, discrimination, and a low status. The problems of poor people are multiple. ■

A. IN THE SOUTHWEST[1]

✦ Inter-Agency Committee on Mexican American Affairs

You will remember from selection 5 in Section II of Part One that between 1900 and 1930, a huge migration set in from Mexico. Present-day descendants of those immigrants are hardly newcomers to America. But recently a great deal of attention has focused on Mexican Americans, 80 per cent of whom live in the five Southwestern states. The following selection, a government document, reveals that a disproportionate number of them suffer from the multiple problems of poverty.

But the selection does not point out that of 5,073,000 Mexican Americans enumerated in the 1970 census, only 16 per cent are foreign-born. That means that the deprivation discussed below does not merely affect immigrants — it affects an even larger number of native Americans of Mexican ancestry. It means, too, that the cycle of poverty continues, unless broken, into the second and even third generations. The need to break it was the reason for President Lyndon B. Johnson's calling a conference of cabinet officials and Mexican American leaders in El Paso, Texas, in 1967. Below, there is a report of the conference's conclusions. ■

Who Are the Mexican Americans?

There are approximately 10 million Spanish-surnamed citizens in our country, of which six and a half million reside in the Southwest. In 1960, Mexican Americans represented over 12 per cent of the total population in the five Southwestern States; this group is the largest minority in each of these States.

The Mexican American may be a descendant of the Spanish explorers Cortez, Cabeza de Baca, or Coronado. Or he may have recently immigrated from Mexico and may very well be a descendant of the great Aztec civilization. Or he may be a mestizo from the union of Indian and Spanish.

There are others in the United States who have the same features,

[1] Inter-Agency Committee on Mexican American Affairs 1967–1968, *The Mexican American, A New Focus on Opportunity* (Washington, D.C.: Superintendent of Documents, United States Government Printing Office, 1968), unpaginated.

background, language and surnames. For example, there are Puerto Ricans, Spanish Americans (from Spain), Central Americans (from Costa Rica, Panama, etc.), and South Americans. Therefore, among the Spanish-speaking Americans — the second largest minority group in our country — we find a great diversity in origin yet a great commonality in traditions and language. They have also shared the same problems and experiences as citizens of the United States, and in this report the term "Mexican American" is used as a general designation.

As the Anglo American moved out into the frontier lands of our nation, the Mexican American gave way as did the American Indian. He lost lands which he had held for centuries; he lost his footing in his own community. He became the governed in his village. His language, which had been the tongue of commerce, became a mark of the "foreigner." Suddenly this was no longer his land or home.

The Mexican Americans were pushed into menial jobs as the years passed; their children rarely reaped the benefits of education. There appeared in towns, villages and cities certain poor sections, or *barrios* — the ghettos of Mexican Americans. Caught in a vicious circle, the Mexican Americans set the patterns of poverty which their children, to the present, encounter.

Some moved to other sections of the country, to the Northwest, to parts of the East. Their lot has not been much better. The Puerto Ricans, for example, landed on the east coast to find that American citizenship on paper meant nothing to employers or landlords.

Mexican American migrant farm workers make up more than half of the migrant stream in the United States. For example, they account for about 64 per cent of the migrants who come into the state of Michigan. They are also as far away from the Southwest as New Jersey....

A Focal Point Is Created

On June 9, 1967, the President established a Cabinet committee designated as the Inter-Agency Committee on Mexican American Affairs "to assure that Federal programs are reaching the Mexican Americans and providing the assistance that they need, and (to) seek out new programs that may be necessary to handle problems that are unique to the Mexican American community.

The President appointed to the Committee the Secretaries of Agriculture; Commerce; Labor; Health, Education, and Welfare; and Housing and Urban Development; and the Director of the Office of

OPTIMISM AND DESPAIR: The eight young people shown above, refugees from Cuba, have won honors at a Miami high school. Many other members of newcomer groups are less fortunate. The room (below, right) is "home" for a family of eight Mexican Americans in New Mexico. At left, below, is a view of a Puerto Rican slum neighborhood in New York City.

Economic Opportunity, Vicente T. Ximenes, a member of the Equal Employment Opportunity Commission, was appointed chairman of the Committee.

The President created the Committee to help meet the pressing needs of more than 10,000,000 Spanish-surnamed Americans — the Mexican Americans of the Southwest, the Puerto Ricans on the mainland, the Cubans, and others. Often forgotten, although the second largest in the nation, this minority has serious problems.

These problems, at this point in the economic and social development of our people, are unique in dimension, geography, and cultural derivation. Further these are factors which militate for their continuation unless vigorous action is taken. Among these is the continuing contact with the original cultural sources in other countries which other minorities no longer have.

The Mexican Americans in the Southwest, for example, have ties of language with nearby Mexico and this serves to invigorate cultural traditions. Americans of Polish descent, for example, are now long removed from the wellsprings of their ancestral heritage.

And though the problems, if anything, are more complex than those of other minorities, the community's resources are more scarce. Mexican Americans have no colleges or other educational institutions they can call their own, no substantial private institutions, virtually no funding for their organizations, and, until June 9, 1967, no unit anywhere in the Federal government that was specifically concerned with their problems....

Problems Defined, Directions Charted

The specific problems the Mexican American community has faced were minutely examined at El Paso, some for the first time. From this came affirmation of goals long held and some new directions. Typical of the problems:

1. In the five Southwestern states, Mexican Americans 14 years of age and older have only 8.1 years of schooling, compared with 12.0 years for the average Anglo-American of the same age.

2. Mexican American children have a school drop-out rate that is over twice the national average.

3. Mexican Americans in barrios had an unemployment rate of 8 to 13 per cent in 1966 as compared to a national average of 4 per cent for that year.

4. Subemployment rates for Spanish-surnamed residents of the slums were 42 to 47 per cent.

5. Employment of Mexican Americans by the Federal Government was in need of attention. The Civil Service Commission report indicated, for example, that the Selective Service Board had no Spanish-surnamed employees above the Grade of GS-8, and in the Department of Justice, only 62 top-level positions out of a total of 11,695 were held by Mexican Americans.

6. The 1959 family income under $3,000 of *urban* Spanish-surnamed families was 28.5 per cent in Arizona; 17.5 per cent in California; 28.6 per cent in Colorado; 33.1 per cent in New Mexico; and 47.3 per cent in Texas.

7. The 1959 family income under $3,000 of *rural* Spanish-surnamed families was 50.4 per cent in Colorado; 53.8 per cent in New Mexico; and 69.2 per cent in Texas.

In Arizona 32.4 per cent of the dilapidated homes belong to Mexican Americans and in Colorado 24.3 per cent of such housing belongs to the Spanish-surnamed citizen.

Out of discussions by the 1,500 Mexican Americans, Federal officials and other participants of these and a myriad of other problems came more than 1,000 specific recommendations and agreement on the fundamental new directions:

1. The cutlural differences and background of the Mexican American community must be acknowledged and understood.

2. Bilingual education in all phases of instruction should be developed.

3. Federal agencies must develop and practice an "outreach" philosophy in bringing services to the Mexican American community.

4. Federal employment opportunities must be opened further to the Mexican American community.

5. The community must be involved in all aspects of program planning whether it is in school activities or model cities programs.

6. Problem-solving must be undertaken through the co-operation of government, private industry, and Mexican American civic and service organizations.

B. IN NEW YORK CITY[1]

✤ José Morales, Jr.

The author of the selection below, an official of the Puerto Rican Community Project of New York City, was invited to address the El Paso conference. As Mexican Americans concentrate in the Southwest, so Puerto Ricans live most densely in New York City. Properly speaking, Puerto Ricans are not immigrants, for they have been United States citizens since 1917. Yet, as the following selection reveals, they regard themselves as suffering from the same deprivations as immigrants. Note the similarity between the problems of poor Puerto Ricans and poor Mexican Americans. ■

I am pleased indeed to be present today in El Paso at this Inter-Agency Conference on Mexican American Affairs. I bring greetings to my Mexican American brothers from the Puerto Rican Community Development Project of New York City.

Although this conference was convened as a consequence of many years of community organization activity, protest and agitation by Mexican Americans and therefore must rightly focus on their problems, may I note that we Puerto Ricans, who now number more than one million throughout the United States, share many of your problems.

We see this conference a milestone in focusing national attention on the aspirations of the Spanish-speaking people of the United States....

Disadvantaged Migrants

I have been invited to this conference to speak of the housing problems of Puerto Ricans. In order to do so one must see Puerto Ricans in a broader context as migrants and as disadvantaged people in New York City.

---

[1] José Morales, Jr., "The Housing Problems of New York Puerto Ricans," *The Mexican American, A New Focus on Opportunity, Testimony Presented at the Cabinet Committee Hearings on Mexican American Affairs, El Paso, Texas, October 26–28, 1967* (Washington, D.C.: Superintendent of Documents, United States Government Printing Office, 1968), pp. 163–165.

To begin with, Puerto Ricans have been migrants to the United States ever since the turn of the century.

The basic reason for Puerto Rican migration is similar to that which impels most people to move from one place to another. . . . Irishmen cross the Irish Sea to Britain, Algerians from Algeria to France, Spaniards from Spain to Germany, Italians from southern Italy to northern Italy. . . . The search for better opportunity.

Migration figures as published by the Commonwealth of Puerto Rico, Department of Labor, indicate that the bulk of the Puerto Rican migration occurred since World War II. In the decade 1950 to 1960 New York City witnessed a 150 per cent growth in Puerto Rican population from some 246,000 to 613,000 persons.

The Statistics of Deprivation

According to the 1960 Census:

(a) Puerto Ricans, although 8 per cent of the 1960 population, constituted 19 per cent of the poor of New York City.

(b) A young population, median age 22 years, Puerto Ricans have a high birth rate, a reported 40 per thousand.

(c) The 1960 median income for Puerto Rican families was only $3,800; for non-whites $4,400 and for other whites $6,600.

(d) 54 per cent of the Puerto Rican families had incomes of less than $4,000; non-whites 44 per cent; while for the residents of the city as a whole 25 per cent.

(e) Puerto Ricans unemployed were one in ten (9.9 per cent); non-whites one in fourteen (6.9 per cent); other whites one in twenty-five (4.3 per cent).

(f) The average Puerto Rican adult had only 8.3 years of schooling — the average city adult 10.2 years. However, 53 per cent of adult Puerto Ricans over 25 years of age never finished grade school.

Obsolescent Housing

The postwar migration of Puerto Ricans was to a New York City with an increasingly obsolescent housing supply.

A report released by the Department of City Planning after the 1960 Census stated, "In terms of physical deterioration of housing . . . renewal needs (of New York City) potentially involve eight hundred thousand to one million units, approximately one third of the City's entire housing supply."

New York City contains some 40,000 so-called "Old Law Tenements" built before 1901. They contain some 335 thousand apartments and house close to a million people.

On June 29, 1936, more than thirty years ago, *The New York Times* editorialized:

"Built fifty or seventy-five years ago, 66,000 old law tenements still stand, a blot on our urban civilization and a reproach to those men of leadership and genius in our cities who have solved so many other social problems and failed to solve this vital one. In these ancient rookeries men, women and children still live under conditions which are repulsive to every humane instinct and defy all modern housing standards."

A great number of those who live in "old law tenements" are Puerto Ricans. . . .

The Decay of Neighborhoods

The decay of entire neighborhoods is a problem affecting Puerto Ricans and their disadvantaged neighbors in many parts of the city. Block after block has deteriorated as the other residents move out from the neighborhood. The network of organizations, institutions and service agencies that make up an organized community life disappears with them.

Neighborhood social controls that assume safety and tranquility no longer exist. One has only to go to a neighborhood in New York to see an extreme case in point.

Brownsville-East New York was until recently a low middle income Jewish and Italian neighborhood. These families have since moved out.

Brownsville-East New York today looks as if a war was fought there, with house-to-house battles on almost every street. The neighborhood now looks as if the battle is over. The enemy has left the area in possession of the local inhabitants. Fires are prevalent, personal security is at a pretty low state. A community worker of an agency that my project contracts tells me that he doesn't do house-to-house visiting after sundown and points out that on his block there is a grocery store that does its business only through closed gates in the evening; people line up outside the store and receive their goods through the iron barricade. This unfortunately is the quality of life in many of the neighborhoods in New York City where Puerto Ricans live.

The Tragedy of Urban Renewal

Great hopes were once placed in urban renewal, but as far as Puerto Ricans are concerned it has been by and large a tragedy. Relocation to safe and sanitary housing has been largely a myth.

In urban renewal areas Puerto Rican families are promised public housing as a solution to their plight. In many instances, they turn out to be empty promises, and these families find themselves being relocated to substandard apartments in deteriorating or decaying areas, or actual slums, at higher rentals than they paid before. In the name of "progress," the hoax continues to be perpetrated again and again, as low income residents are displaced from the areas where they reside without being provided with adequate substitute housing at rents they can afford. . . .

Poverty Combined with Discrimination

Discrimination is appalling to Puerto Ricans. In Puerto Rico we have been accustomed to dealing with one another as persons rather than [as] symbols. There are no minorities in Puerto Rico: we are all members of the majority group — we are all Puerto Ricans. The "minority" in Puerto Rico is the political party that loses an election.

Race prejudice combined with poverty, however, [has] forced Puerto Ricans to live in the worst housing in New York City. . . .

The housing problems, therefore, of New York Puerto Ricans are decaying neighborhoods, discrimination, poor urban renewal, inadequate code enforcement and a shortage of low-rent housing.

While we are a resourceful and energetic people and expect to struggle our way out of the many problems we face, we know that the resolution of some of these problems lies beyond us.

We submit that what is needed in New York City and all the nation's major urban centers is massive federal and private financial investment in rebuilding neighborhoods.

4. The Response of Government[1]
✤ Inter-Agency Committee on Mexican American Affairs

> The El Paso conference resulted not only in analysis and recommendations but in government action. Recognizing the multiple problems of the Spanish-surnamed poor, official Washington responded with a multi-faceted program. The following selection, a government document, outlines the program. It includes measures for better jobs, better housing, better education, better neighborhoods — and promises a continuing concern with the largest minority in the Southwest. Except for black Americans, no other ethnic group has received as much government attention. ■

Refined by the discussions at the El Paso hearings, the Committee's work of initiating and expediting programs took on new vigor and speed. Set forth below are programs and projects which reflect the new impetus arising from Committee activity during the period of this report.

Manpower and Training

Concentrated employment programs have been established in a comprehensive effort against hard-core unemployment. A total of $30,000,000 has been allocated for the programs in San Antonio, San Francisco, Los Angeles, Phoenix, Albuquerque, Denver, Waco, and Oakland, which account for over 40 per cent of the entire Mexican American population.

More than 18,000 Mexican Americans have been trained or are receiving training through institutional Manpower Development and Training programs. This number included 2,500 specially developed training slots designed to serve the unique needs of the Mexican Americans in various California cities.

In addition to the regular U.S. Department of Labor-funded on-the-job training programs in which Mexican Americans also participate, $3.3 million has been allocated for 3,900 on-the-job training

---

[1] Inter-Agency Committee on Mexican American Affairs, 1967–1968, *The Mexican American, A New Focus on Opportunity* (Washington, D.C.: Superintendent of Documents, United States Government Printing Office, 1968), unpaginated.

slots for Mexican American trainees. Projects are being administered by Mexican American social service organizations in Richmond, Santa Rosa, Fresno, Los Angeles, San Diego, Salinas, Pico Rivera, Santa Clara, California; Denver, Colorado; and Maricopa County, Arizona. For the trainees who speak Spanish, the projects include pre-vocational English classes.

Operation SER (Service-Employment-Redevelopment), created in 1966, is now mounting Mexican American manpower programs in thirteen Southwestern cities in which more than 3,000 unemployed persons, mainly Mexican Americans, will receive job preparation and placement services. Operation SER is directed by Jobs for Progress, Inc., a non-profit organization sponsored by major Mexican American organizations; The League of United Latin American Citizens and the American GI Forum of the U.S. Operation SER has received approximately $7 million in Manpower Development and Training Act funds.

Mexican American youths in the Neighborhood Youth Corps increased to 38 per cent in the Southwest during the 1967 summer work program as contrasted with 25 per cent earlier.

Federal Government Recruitment and Employment

The Post Office Department in the last two years has added Mexican Americans to its staff at about 60 times the rate that it averaged in the last 120 years.

Civil Service Commission survey of Federal employment indicates that during the period of June, 1965, to November, 1967, there was an increase of 41 per cent in Spanish-surnamed Federal employees in the Southwest. Over 9,000 such appointments were made from June, 1966, to November, 1967, with hundreds more being added to the Federal rolls in most recent months.

The number of Mexican Americans in positions paying over $11,000 per annum has virtually doubled in this period in the five-state area.

This trend towards increased representation of Spanish-surnamed Americans in the upper levels is dramatically reflected by the 1967 increase of 185.2 per cent in Spanish-surnamed GS-15 appointees since the 1963 level.

Much of this progress is the direct result of regular meetings and constant communication of the Inter-Agency Committee staff with ranking agency personnel directors and special departmental task forces created to make recruitment and hiring practices more responsive to the Mexican American community.

Activities have included the launching of recruiting drives by member agencies of the committee at schools and colleges with substantial Spanish-surname enrollment. For example, during early 1968, the Department of Health, Education, and Welfare conducted recruitment drives through eleven cities in the Southwest. Since February, the Department has hired 134 Mexican Americans up to and including GS-15 level (paying more than $18,000 a year).

New job element rating techniques and examining procedures are being designed to eliminate unnecessary experience or educational requirements for entry level positions. The Department of Housing and Urban Development has pioneered in new testing procedures which will permit the Government to evaluate the job potential of workers whose abilities might not be reflected by written examinations.

The Inter-Agency Committee is furnishing both technical assistance and information on talented members of the Mexican American community to interested Government agencies through a Committee staff-operated pool.

The Inter-Agency Committee has compiled and published a listing of over 1,400 Spanish-surnamed students who graduated from college during the current year. The first such compilation has been distributed to Federal agencies, private employers and other interested groups. Reports received by the Committee indicate a great interest among these employers. For example, one large national corporation has already hired 22 recent graduates and one school system has mailed applications to over 175 education majors who appeared in the booklet.

The Civil Service Commission is studying a new Federal merit promotion policy to assure fairer consideration of Mexican American employees for advancement and to assure that employees are more fully informed about promotion opportunities. The Civil Service Commission has also committed itself to substantially more emphasis on training for lower level employees to assist their advancement.

The Civil Service Commission, Federal personnel officers, union officials and leaders of minority group organizations are reviewing proposed changes in the procedures for filing, investigating and resolving complaints of discrimination within Federal agencies.

Civil Service Inter-Agency Boards of Examiners in the Southwest regions are working with Mexican American organizations to locate candidates and to identify employment problems. Use is being made of the Spanish language media to advertise job openings and examination announcements.

Agencies are being encouraged to recruit and hire bilingual and bicultural employees where there is a demonstrated need for employees with these qualifications. In the four Civil Service Regions with substantial Mexican American population, the Commission is now especially employing Spanish-speaking persons for public information and testing positions.

Federal-Private Cooperation in Employment

The Inter-Agency Committee, in conjunction with Plans for Progress (a unit in the Executive Office of the President, staffed by executives loaned by industry to intensify private sector co-operation) and the Community Relations Service, sponsored the Southwest Employers Conference on Mexican American and Indian Employment Problems. More than 200 representatives of private industry convened on July 10, 1968, for a three-day conference in Albuquerque, New Mexico. Another is being considered for California.

Efforts to enlist the interest of industry in hiring Mexican Americans include specific assistance to companies in devising equal employment opportunity programs as well as almost daily contact with business executives regarding the employment of Mexican Americans.

Education

In January, 1968, the President signed the Bilingual Education Bill amending the Elementary and Secondary Education Act. The bilingual and bicultural education provisions authorize research, experimentation, demonstration and operating activities. These include the development of curricula, methods, materials, media and administrative procedures relating to bilingual instruction.

Primarily through Elementary and Secondary Education Act funds, the Department of Health, Education and Welfare has sponsored research and demonstration programs for pre-school and elementary students of multi-lingual and multi-cultural backgrounds in San Antonio, El Paso, Travis County, Texas; Northern New Mexico and Las Cruces, New Mexico. Included are the Southwestern Educational Development Laboratory in Austin, the Good Samaritan Pre-School

Bilingual Program in San Antonio, and Project Follow-Through in Corpus Christi.

Related Activities involve the utilization, in Denver, Colorado, and in eleven Texas counties, of televised programs to teach English and to strengthen self-image among Mexican American students through an understanding of their total cultural heritage. Under the Experienced Teacher Fellowship Program, the University of Arizona is training teachers of bilingual-bicultural students.

Through the talent Search Program of HEW, $854,125 has been made available for nine projects in the Southwest to identify talented high school students and encourage them to complete high school with a view toward pursuing a higher education.

National Defense Education Act loans, Economic Opportunity Grants, Guaranteed Loans and the Work Study Program are being utilized increasingly by colleges in the Southwest to help needy Mexican American students. For example, Our Lady of the Lake College in San Antonio has made use of all such aids in its Project Teacher Excellence and the West Texas University combines financial aid to students with an effort to educate non-profit organizations in the uses of Work-Study participants.

A Mexican American Affairs Unit of the Office of Education was established at the urging of the Inter-Agency Committee on Mexican American Affairs. The Unit has conducted a field survey among the Mexican American communities in the Southwestern States, now being analyzed.

Migrant Training and Education

In Florida, Texas, and California, a Migrant Compensatory Education Project has been established to provide basic and remedial education, occupational training, vocational rehabilitation, health and food services and economic support to 1,000 migrant youths and their families.

In Illinois, the Office of Economic Opportunity has established a program of adult basic education service for Mexican American migrants settling out of the migrant stream.

In Arizona, a series of television tapes are being utilized to teach the adult Mexican American migrant of low literate level how to speak basic, simple English.

In Texas, the Department of Health, Education, and Welfare, under Title III of the Elementary and Secondary Education Act, has set up special bilingual instruction for migrant children. The Rio Grande Valley Education Service Center will serve over 70,000 Spanish-speaking and migrant children in four Texas counties.

In Mesilla Valley of Dona Ana County, New Mexico, educational radio is being utilized to increase the communication skills of over 500 children from migrant agricultural families and other disadvantaged children.

In Northern New Mexico, the Home Education Livelihood Program is providing adult basic, general and vocational education as well as assisting in the establishment of farm cooperatives and small village industry.

Eight High School Equivalency Programs have received funding for their second year from the Migrant Division of the Office of Economic Opportunity. Seventy-five per cent of the youths are migrants and over seventy-five per cent are Mexican American. Programs are in Claremont, California; Pueblo, Colorado; Lincoln, Nebraska; Eugene, Oregon; Pullman, Washington; El Paso, Texas; Madison, Wisconsin; and Roswell, New Mexico.

The Migrant Division of the Office of Economic Opportunity has funded twelve information and referral centers for migrants and seasonally employed farmworkers in areas with large numbers of Mexican Americans. Mexican American migrants are in eight of the twelve areas covered by the information centers.

Migrant Labor

The influx of bracero labor, citizens of nearby countries who compete with U.S. citizens for jobs, was reduced during the past year to only 0.4 per cent of its 1959 level in terms of man months of employment, or to 1/250 of its former number.

The Department of Labor has established higher housing standards for farmworkers who are hired through the Employment Services Offices.

The Inter-Agency Committee, in support of community efforts, continues to urge the enactment of legislation extending the right of collective bargaining to farm laborers.

The 1968 Sugar Beet wage rate determination provides a 5.9 per cent to 7.7 per cent increase in piece rates and a 10 per cent increase in the hourly rate. Stricter protective provisions for minors and more stringent regulations governing labor contractors were also approved by the Secretary of Agriculture.

Agriculture and Rural Development

Seven counties in Texas, each containing a Mexican American population of 10 per cent or more, are on a Commodity Distribution Program target list of the Department of Agriculture's efforts aimed at the nation's 1,000 poorest counties — counties which had not previously obtained coverage.

The Forest Service has reallocated $1,000,000 for additional use in revegetation of grazing lands in Northern New Mexico and in Colorado, benefiting the many Mexican Americans in the area who conduct small farming operations.

The Forest Service is dividing its contracts into smaller units so that small village groups can bid, thus creating jobs and stimulating the depressed economy in areas of Northern New Mexico.

The Forest Service has provided funding for the Trinchera Ranch Exchange to provide job and economic development in Costilla County, Colorado, where over 70 per cent of the population is Spanish-surnamed.

Statistical Data

The Bureau of the Census will include in the 1970 Census a notation on the language spoken in the home if it is other than English and other questions to acquire data needed to define and attack problems of the Spanish-speaking.

HEW has changed its surveys so that Mexican American school enrollments will be counted more usefully.

The Civil Service Commission report on minority group Federal employees has been expanded to include more vital information on Mexican American employment in the Federal government.

Housing

The Santa Clara County Housing Authority, in conjunction with the California Better Housing for Mexican Americans Committee, has received a planning grant for public housing units for 450 families and 250 elderly people.

The East Los Angeles Improvement Council has received $1,850,000 for the construction of moderate income rent supplement housing units.

Funds have been granted for the construction of 300 units of low rent and rent supplement housing for elderly people, 50 per cent of whom are Mexican American.

The Home Improvement Project in Albuquerque received an additional $73,000 in March, 1968, to continue its program of rehabilitation of homes and employment for the unskilled unemployed.

Model Cities

The Model Cities Program now includes several cities which contain a high percentage of Spanish-surnamed population: Fresno, California; San Antonio, Eagle Pass, Waco, Texas; Denver, Trinidad, Colorado; Albuquerque, New Mexico; Saginaw, Michigan; and New York City.

Neighborhood Facilities

The first HUD-assisted neighborhood facility, opened in February, 1967, was the LEAP Community Center in Phoenix, Arizona, with a grant of $185,226 and serving nearly 3,000 Mexican American families. Since, many projects have been completed to serve the needs of Mexican American families, including centers in El Paso, Carrizo Springs, Texas; Pagaso Springs, Colorado; Flagstaff, Arizona; Delano, Calexico, California. Grants for these projects totalled $900,700.

5. The Question of Identity[1]
✦ Albert Pena

Don't let the statistics on poverty, and the programs to alleviate it, mislead you into believing that all Mexican Americans are poor. There is a growing Mexican-American middle class, consisting of businessmen, skilled workers, lawyers, doctors, dentists, schoolteachers, social workers, college professors, and government officials. For these people the most troublesome question is a question of identity. In the following selection, by a county commissioner in Texas, the author criticizes the stereotyping of fellow Mexican Americans and describes the image he has of himself. ■

[1] Albert Pena, "The Mexican American and the War on Poverty," *The Mexican American, A New Focus on Opportunity*, Testimony Presented at the Cabinet Committee Hearings on Mexican American Affairs, El Paso, Texas, October 26–28, 1967 (Washington, D.C.: Superintendent of Documents, United States Government Printing Office, 1968), pp. 211–213.

This is one of the things that has always concerned me, the image, the Mexican American image. We're called so many things we don't know what we are. We're called Mexican Americans, Spanish speaking, Spanish Americans, Americans of Mexican descent. I think some nut called us Iberian Americans. So I have come to this conclusion, that I am three things and in this order: first of all, I'm an American because I was born here. Second, I'm a Texan because I was born in Texas, and third, I'm a Mexican without a mustache because no one will let me forget it.

Anglo Stereotypes

It's very difficult for Anglos to erase from their mind the stereotyped serape-draped Mexican sleeping in the shade with an empty tequila bottle to his side and with the burro over here waiting for him to wake up.

Every time I meet an Anglo for the first time, or most of them, they try to impress me first with the fact that they made a trip to Mexico and that they love tequila, they like bullfights, they like Mexican food, and some of their best friends are Mexicans.

Now, this leaves me pretty cold because, first of all, I don't like tequila. I like scotch, and second, I don't like bullfights. I like a good professional football game, the Washington Redskins. But I must confess that I love Mexican food and Mexican women.

Proud to be Mexican and American

The point I'm trying to make is this, that — and we have heard this many times — that we are proud that we are Americans, but we are also proud that we are Mexicans and don't let anybody forget that.

We've got to learn how to identify as a group because when you do this, then you're going to find out that we're going to have more unity. My friend, Maury Maverick, Jr., told me one time, he said, you know what's wrong with you Mexicans and I said, what. "They made white people out of you and now you don't know what the hell you are." Well, we ought to know what we are. We ought to identify with our people. We ought to identify as Mexicans and the problems that are peculiar to Mexican Americans in the United States. . . .

A Matter of Values and Human Rights

My philosophy, and I am sure that most of yours, are the results of two great men. They were sincere men. They were good men. They were religious men. One was the leader of a great nation and the other was the leader of a great religion. One died a very young man. The other died a very old man. And both their names were John.

One was John Fitzgerald Kennedy and the other was Pope John XXIII. The two Johns wrote many things and they said many things. Pope John wrote *Pacem in Terris.* John Kennedy wrote *Profiles in Courage.* And basically, they believed this. They believed first, that all men are created equal in the image of God. They believed that every man was entitled to a good job, decent wages, an education, medical care, and decent housing, but more important than that, they believed that every man should have the equal opportunity to obtain these things and such was the impact of the two Johns that when John Kennedy died, even Republicans, conservatives who never voted for him, cried unashamedly, and when Pope John died, Protestants and Jews declared a week of mourning. Such was the impact of the two Johns. Both said, in different ways, that this generation of Americans has been handed the torch of freedom. Think about that for just a minute. You have been handed the torch of freedom but you're not going to get it until you stop asking for it and demand it.

6. A Plea for Bilingual Education[1]
✤ Nick E. Garza

The foundations of a person's identity are built when he, or she, is a child. Language is important to that process. That is why Mexican-American educators believe that Mexican-American children should be instructed in both Spanish and English in the public schools. Additionally, as the following selection

[1] Nick E. Garza, "Bilingualism in Education," *The Mexican Amercian, A New Focus on Opportunity,* Testimony Presented at the Cabinet Committee Hearings on Mexican American Affairs, El Paso, Texas, October 26–28, 1967 (Washington, D.C.: Superintendent of Documents, United States Government Printing Office, 1968), pp. 117–118.

argues, a bilingual education will assure the child of success in school. The author, of Mexican ancestry, is an elementary school principal in the Southwest. ■

It is my privilege to be here with you to give testimony regarding the importance and need of bilingualism in education.

The Spanish-Speaking Child, a Potential Drop-Out

Literacy in two languages can be a tremendous asset, especially in the Southwestern States where a large majority of the population is composed of Mexican American citizens. We are not taking full advantage of instructing children bilingually, since teaching curricula policies typically advocate instruction only in English, a language foreign to many of the students presently in school who are reared only in the mother tongue that parents have been able to provide, Spanish. The immediate problem is evident, the child cannot understand enough to communicate the experiences of the classroom and therefore loses interest in his endeavors, lags behind, and quickly becomes a potential drop-out.

No Need to Rehash the Need

The need for bilingual education is a well established fact, as indicated by the success of conferences such as the Tucson-NEA Survey on the Teaching of Spanish to the Spanish-Speaking, the Mexican American Conference on Education in San Antonio, the Denver Conference, and the present enthusiasm in bilingual legislation before Congress. We need not rehash the need; it has been most evident for some time.

Teaching bilingualism in the Southwest is recommended and urgently needed. The scope and magnitude of this undertaking will not be easy by any stretch of the imagination, nor will it be completed from one day to the next. It must be a continuous effort on the part of teachers, administrators, and citizens who value equal opportunities for all children, and who are interested in the development of individuals to their highest potential. It would serve to capture the innate, untapped capabilities of the Mexican American and very likely enhance the contributions he can make to the society in which he lives.

Pilot Project in Texas

Some work has been accomplished in this area. More needs to be implemented as soon as possible. Significant progress has been achieved in various parts of the country, with particular note to some cities in the five Southwestern states. In San Antonio, Texas, the Horn Project has taken the initiative in the teaching of bilingualism and has proved to be very successful. This project has been a cooperative effort on the part of the University of Texas and the San Antonio Independent School District, and has received funding from the U.S. Office of Education. New York City schools, as well as others, have indicated they will use the techniques of the San Antonio Language Research Project.

From its rank beginning in the fall of 1964, this project has grown to 111 classes in eight elementary schools, and is providing bilingual instruction for approximately 3,330 children in grades 1 to 4. It has received the co-operation and acceptance of teachers, principals, and administrative officials as well. Most important, it has brought confidence and poise to many youngsters who have demonstrated their eagerness of expression, with words and vocabulary which has provided for them a means of "communicating" with others for the first time. The learning process is most evident in the project children who have participated in this program. The shyness, withdrawal and lack of confidence has been replaced by alertness and the willingness to "take part." San Antonio is one example; I know of several other cities which have excellent bilingual programs in their schools.

Guidelines for Teachers

At this juncture, I deem it necessary to establish guidelines for teachers in bilingual education. "Bilingual teachers for bilingual children" is an adage frequently used by educators and resource people as well. In essence, this may very well prove to be the answer in teaching non-English speakers a second language. The teacher must possess a keen awareness of the cultural background and the environment and have a sympathetic understanding of the problems of the children he teaches. Since teaching is performed in both Spanish and English, he must know both languages well. At times, he may find it necessary to teach through the "mother tongue" first and quickly follow with the second language. This method has helped the non-English-speaking student, for it has shown him that his mother tongue is important too, and above all, that it is used and respected.

In addition, the bilingual teacher must apply the two languages in various subject matter areas. He must teach children a keen awareness of their importance as individuals and of the contributions they can make in the home, the school, and the community. Further, he must encourage children to learn more about themselves, their family, and the society in which they live. The better image of self-concept may well be followed by subject matter areas to include social studies activities, science, and others as they can be fruitfully developed in the learning experiences.

As an educator, I strongly see the need and the demand for bilingual education in the schools of the Southwest. Only in this manner can we ever hope to achieve the full and potential contributions of the second largest minority group in these United States, the Mexican Americans, who seek only the opportunity to help keep our country second to none.

Outline for the Future

To the members of the Inter-Agency Committee, I make the following recommendations and necessary demands!

1. Help us to make bilingual education a reality as soon as possible.

2. Evaluate the good bilingual programs now in operation, and promote full funding to see them through.

3. Establish more teachers' institutes in bilingual education, and encourage more participation by Mexican Americans, who have a natural reservoir of talents in this field.

4. Create an atmosphere where the concept of bilingualism is realized in full.

5. Provide educators and children with materials, books, films, etc., whenever the concept of two cultures is advantageous to our nation, the Southwest, and above all, our children.

6. Amend laws which permit teaching only in English.

The bicultural Southwest needs bilingual education! I urge and encourage all citizens to employ whatever methods are necessary to achieve this goal. The unity of two great cultures will foster and indeed make stronger ties between our citizens. Together we can share the welfare of this great United States of America!

SOME PROMISING SOLUTIONS: *Children of Spanish-speaking immigrants (above) are taught both Spanish and English in a bilingual classroom. At left (below) Mexican-American Cesar Chavez helps to organize migrant workers seeking improved working conditions in the lettuce fields of California. At right (below) the son of Spanish immigrants receives on-the-job training at a Boston bank while attending high school classes.*

7. Uprising in the Barrios[1]
✤ Charles A. Erickson

From what you have read thus far, you can glean that the force to improve the lives of Mexican Americans does not come merely from above, from the government. It also derives from the people themselves. Influenced in part by the example of black militancy, there has been, in the words of the author below, an uprising in the barrios. Barrio is the Mexican American term for a neighborhood most of whose residents are Mexican Americans. Contrary to popular belief, a barrio is not necessarily a slum, since many middle-class people often live there. The militancy of middle-class barrio dwellers is the subject of the following article. It was written by an educator. ∎

In California's cities the natives are restless. The ethnic kin to the Cabrillos and Serras, to Joaquin Murrieta and José de la Guerra are confronting the power structure with demands for educational change. They want it now. They tell you that they don't intend to be stalled or side-tracked or bought off with a job or a raise, a new title or a fingerful of *atole*.[2]

They are activist Mexican Americans. Their awareness of what the American educational system has done to the bilingual, bicultural Mexican American is acute. They know that in California he lags nearly four years behind the Anglo, two behind the Negro, in scholastic achievement. They know that the worst schools in cities like Los Angeles — measured by dropout statistics — are the defacto segregated Mexican American schools.

The day when a lazy "educator" with a glib tongue dazzles them with doubletalk about "language problems" and "responsibilities of parents" is past. They know better. They've done their homework. And while they don't claim to have all the answers, they do know that solutions don't lie with the status quo.

Instant change is the only hope, or many thousands more brown

---

[1] Charles A. Erickson, "Uprising in the Barrios," *American Education* (November, 1968), pp. 29–31.

[2] [**atole:** a thin gruel made of corn and water.]

children of the United States will be destroyed by the system, California's activist Mexican Americans tell you. . . .

The Activists Identified

They are Sal Castro, schoolteacher; Miguel Montes, dentist; Manuel Guerra, college professor; Esther Hernandez, housewife; Moctezuma Esparza, student. The list in Los Angeles alone could fill a book and encompass every trade and profession from newspaper boy to electrical engineer.

The commitment of each varies, of course. In part it is proportionate to the time each has left over from his obligation to job and family, or in the case of some who exploited or downgraded their own race, *raza*, to "make it," proportionate to their personal guilt. Or maybe it is in direct ratio to how much they have been Americanized and made aware of their individual rights.

Some send in a dollar. Some work at it 24 hours a day and go to jail for *la causa*.

The growth of Mexican American militancy in California has been rapid. Its focus is education. Dominated by youth, it moves in spurts. . . .

The Causes for Militancy

Why the sudden shift to militancy?

"The success of the Negro civil rights movement in America unquestionably had a lot to do with it," explains attorney Herman Sillas, a member of the California State Advisory Committee to the United States Commission on Civil Rights.

But Sillas sees other causes: "Today's activist in the Mexican American community is the one who is most Anglo in his attitudes. He's more aware than his neighbors of his rights as an American and more sophisticated in his knowledge of the machinery of our democracy. In other words, he knows what happens to the squeaky wheel."

Sillas and other committee members spent two days in the heart of the East Los Angeles *barrio* last year, listening to the testimony of intense young Mexican Americans about civil rights problems in their community. Typical was the commentary by Rosalinda Mendez, a graduate of an East Los Angeles high school:

"From the time we first begin attending school, we hear about how great and wonderful our United States is, about our democratic American heritage, but little about our splendid and magnificent

Mexican heritage and culture. What little we do learn about Mexicans is how they mercilessly slaughtered the brave Texans at the Alamo, but we never hear about the child heroes of Mexico who courageously threw themselves from the heights of Chapultepec rather than allow themselves and their flag to be captured by the attacking Americans.

"We look for others like ourselves in these history books, for something to be proud of for being a Mexican, and all we see in books, magazines, films and TV shows are stereotypes of a dark, dirty, smelly man with a tequila bottle in one hand, a dripping taco[3] in the other, a sarape wrapped around him, and a big sombrero.

"But we are not the dirty, stinking winos that the Anglo world would like to point out as Mexican. We begin to think that maybe the Anglo teacher is right, that maybe we are inferior, that we do not belong in this world, that — as some teachers actually tell students to their faces — we should go back to Mexico and quit causing problems for America."

Activists Want to Improve, Not Destroy, the System

According to Armando Rodriguez, chief of the U.S. Office of Education's Mexican American Affairs Unit, young people like Rosalinda, who organize and vocalize their bitterness, are our educational system's best friends.

"What is an activist anyway?" he asks. "Our 'conventional' activists are the ones who become involved in the PTA, who get wrapped up in community projects or walk the precincts for one political party or another. Maybe they'll form a housewives' picket line around City Hall to get a street light on a dark block, or maybe they'll bake cakes to raise money for a new church building.

"Whoever they are, whatever they do, they're working to bring about change. They possess special knowledge and have a special point of view. They introduce an idea to the community, and they campaign for it. This is a basic process of democracy.

"Mexican American activists are no different from any other American activists. The issue of education is one that affects them most intimately. They themselves were most likely victims of our schools. They've seen the hopes and dreams of their brothers and sisters, their

---

[3] [taco: a tortilla (thin corn pancake) filled with meat.]

friends, their own children, diminished or destroyed by a system which for years has been indifferent to their needs.

"They want a light in their block too."

Rodriguez contends that these people are vital — just as a PTA is vital — if Mexican Americans are to get their full share of the American educational system.

"Remember," he says, "the Mexican American is not talking about destroying the system. He wants to improve it."

Enter the Federal Government

The Federal Government's awareness of the special needs of the bicultural student is also reflected in comments made by U.S. Commissioner of Education Harold Howe II to delegates attending last April's National Conference on Educational Opportunities for Mexican Americans in Austin, Texas. Howe cited the need to help every youngster — whatever his home background, language, or ability — to reach his full potential. "Such a goal is a lofty one, and it is doubtful that the schools will ever achieve it perfectly," he stated. "What must concern us is the degree to which many schools fail to come within a country mile of that goal.

"If Mexican American children have a higher dropout rate than any other comparable group in the nation — and they do — the schools cannot explain away their failure by belaboring the 'Mexican American problem.' The problem, simply, is that the schools have failed with these children."

Howe pointed out that Federal funds flow through Title I of the Elementary and Secondary Education Act into many school districts in which Mexican-American children go to school. "You and your fellow citizens with a particular concern for Mexican American children should bring every possible pressure to bear to ensure that Title I funds provide education which allows Mexican American children to have pride in their heritage while learning the way to take part in the opportunities this country has to offer. Title I funds are not appropriated by the Congress to promote 'business as usual' in the schools. They are appropriated, instead, to help the educationally deprived get a fair chance.

"The Office of Education," Howe promised, "will join with you to help see that this fair chance is made a reality."

The California State Board of Education requires all school districts to set up advisory committees for Title I funds, which assist in assuring effective programs for the disadvantaged.

"The funds enabled us, for the first time, to focus on the needs of the disadvantaged Mexican American child — to zero in on some of his problems," says Wilson Riles, California's State director of compensatory education. "Students in our Title I programs have averaged about a year's gain for each year of instruction. Before Title I, they averaged about seven tenths of a year's progress in a year."

The problem, Riles states, is in having insufficient funds to reach all of the eligible children with a saturated program. "We require districts to concentrate their programs. We try to reach the most severely deprived areas. Spread the money too thin, and you see no results."

Federal monies or migrant education projects also flow through Riles' office. Ramiro Reyes, who coordinates California's plan for the education of migrant children, says, "We're helping 50,000 children, and 85 per cent of them are Mexican American."

Through special migrant education projects some school districts are discovering that they can structure a regular summer school program capable of attracting significant numbers of migrant children. Reyes cited the community of Mendota, in fertile Fresno County, as an example of this:

"They had never had summer schools there before. They started when our program came in, and the youngsters turned out in droves. Many children of migrants from Texas were able to be absorbed into the program."

English as Second-Language Program

Another federally funded Title I program of importance to California's two million Mexican Americans is English as a Second Language (ESL). Manuel Ceja, consultant in program development in the State's office of compensatory education, sees ESL as the first step which districts take in recognizing that there is a problem and that other subjects should be taught bilingually too.

"Many of today's ESL programs are steppingstones to true bilingual programs," he says.

In September, Santa Monica started using some Title I funds for a 10th-grade bilingual class in reading, math, and English for recent immigrants as well as native-born Mexican Americans.

"We're watching Santa Monica closely," says Ceja. "We're looking to the day when we have Anglos in these bilingual classes too."

Riles points out that there is a strong indirect benefit from the many federally funded innovative programs in use in California. "Through these special programs," he says, "we are continually finding new educational techniques and strategies that are useful and adaptable in the broader system."

Armando Rodriguez cites one of these: "The English as a Second Language demonstration center in San Diego has been very successful in bringing the people into a more effective role in helping determine programs for their districts. Now San Diego's ESL program is moving in the direction of bilingual education."

Rodriguez points out that the Federal Government has made a national legal and moral commitment to bilingual education.

"The commitment must be taken up by the States and implemented, regardless of how many dollars will be forthcoming through the new bilingual legislation, or when they will become available," he says. "There are sufficient monies available now through a variety of other Federal programs. It's up to local school districts to re-examine their priorities as to which are the most effective programs and to initiate bilingual teaching."

California's Miguel Montes of the California school board agrees that true bilingual programs must be given top priority. He sees them as intertwined with priorities for expanded preschool programs and projects to prepare teachers for the cultural differences of the Mexican American child.

"The entire history of discrimination is based on the prejudice that because someone else is different, he is somehow worse," says Commissioner Howe. "If we could teach all of our children — black, white, brown, yellow, and all the American shades in between — that diversity is not to be feared or suspected, but enjoyed and valued, we would be well on our way toward achieving the equality we have always proclaimed as a national characteristic."

Armando Rodriguez sees this as the challenge. "The more completely we develop this bicultural resource — the Mexican American — the better he will serve our nation. That's the goal: to educate the total Mexican American, not just parts of him."

When this happens California's Mexican American activist will stay home and bake a cake.

8. White Ethnic Revival[1]
✤ Roman C. Pucinski

The recent surge of self-consciousness among Black and Spanish-surnamed Americans has led to a resurgence of group pride among ethnic groups of different European origins. If blacks and Chicanos can have their studies programs, it has been argued, then "white ethnics," as they are called, ought to have their programs, too. That kind of thinking eventuated in Congress's passing, in 1972, the Ethnic Heritage Studies Program Bill. The co-sponsor in the House of Representatives, Congressman Roman C. Pucinski of Chicago, tells below why it is necessary for school children to learn their respective ethnic heritages. His remarks are taken from the committee hearings he conducted on the bill. ■

We are starting today on what I hope will be an interesting set of hearings. I have a brief opening statement which I would like to read quickly to perhaps set the tone as to how I feel about this problem.

Two-Fold Purpose of the Bill

There is a growing sense of sameness permeating our existence — threatening to quiet the creative outpourings of the human soul and the gentle sensitivity of one man to the uniqueness and humanity of another.

Clearly, this sustained melancholia has touched all our lives. Perhaps most seriously afflicted by the deteriorating quality of human life are the young. The nation's youth are engrossed in a restless, sometimes tumultuous, and often threatening search for identity. Our young people want to know who they are, where they belong, how they can remain distinctive: special individuals amidst the pervasive pressure for conformity.

Therefore, it is to the young — and to their quest for self-knowledge and human understanding — that we dedicate these hearings on the ethnic heritage studies centers bill, H.R. 14910.

---

[1] *Ethnic Heritage Studies Centers,* Hearings Before House General Subcommittee on Education of the Committee on Education and Labor, 91st Congress, Second Session (Washington, D.C.: Superintendent of Documents, United States Government Printing Office, 1970), pp. 1–2, 4, 93–94, 144.

This important legislative proposal recognizes a twofold purpose: first, that American youth should have the opportunity to study, in depth, about their own ethnic backgrounds — about the rich traditions of their forefathers in the arts and humanities, languages and folklore, natural and social sciences — and the many ways in which these past generations have contributed to American life and culture.

A second and equally vital purpose of the bill is to create greater awareness and appreciation of the multiethnic composition of our society through broadly based study of the readily identifiable ethnic groups in our nation.

Cultural Differences Are Good

There are some who would question the value of studying about differences among human groups — about the ways in which we are culturally unique and in a sense separate from one another. But they overlook the basic fact that diversity has brought strength to our nation; that differences, when understood and valued, can unite disparate groups.

Experience has taught us that the pressure toward homogeneity has been superficial and counterproductive; that the spirit of ethnicity, now lying dormant in our national soul, begs for reawakening in a time of fundamental national need.

The ethnic heritage studies centers bill can create this cultural renaissance. The bill would establish a series of ethnic heritage studies centers, each focused on a single ethnic group or regional group of ethnic cultures, to develop curriculum materials for elementary and secondary schools and to train teachers in their use.

Each center would draw upon the research facilities and personnel of colleges and universities, the special knowledge of ethnic groups in local communities and foreign students in the United States, and the expertise of elementary and secondary schoolteachers....

Homogenization Is Bad

This legislation did not come too soon, because as I said earlier in my remarks, we are in this country trying to homogenize 200 million humans into a single monolith, instead of recognizing that America is a magnificent mosaic, made up of many cultures. It is amazing how we can live in the same neighborhood and work with the same people and go to church in the same community and yet know so very little about each other.

It seems to me that particularly is this true now in the many racial conflicts we witness in the country. Many people have a very distorted view of the nonwhites of America, and too often Americans' concept of their nonwhite fellow citizens is one of recalling that they were brought to this country in chains as slaves, totally unmindful of the deep and rich historic, cultural decades that preceded many of them over the span of history.

No Conflict Involved

So it seems to me that there is a great logic in this bill, and we are hoping that the witnesses that we have today and future witnesses will be able to focus on the fact that there is no conflict between being a very loyal, dedicated, patriotic American citizen and still be fully aware of your cultural, ethnic background.

I think it is in this that we can find our great strength and perhaps make some meaningful contribution toward bringing Americans together and helping them understand each other better as American citizens. I think the brotherhood of man lies in the orderly enactment of this legislation, and in implementing it across the country with the kind of centers that this legislation envisions. . . .

The False Anglo-Saxon Image

We have grown up under the discipline of the Anglo-Saxon image and for 200 years millions of Americans have been molded into that image, whether they like it or not. We ask what is going wrong with the country today. A large part of the problem is that we have tried to put all of these people into one single solitary mold and it so happens that human beings don't like to behave that way. Human beings like to have their own identity and I think that we have tried to deny Americans their ethnicity and we are now starting to pay the price.

Either we turn around with this legislation and face up to ethnicity of this country or the great noble experiment is going to be a much more short-lived experiment than other similar experiments in man's history.

This country has to recognize the fact that we are individual human beings and this effort of trying to homogenize us into a solid single mold, be it puritan, atheist, or Anglo Saxon, or what have you, is a myth and if the country is falling apart at the seams today, it is only because we have tried to deny the ethnicity. . . .

I Don't Want To Be Melted Down

I find the whole doctrine of the melting pot frankly very repugnant. I don't want to be melted down to a monolith. . . .

I don't want to be melted down. For decades we have kept trying to, as you have said, deny people their identity and then we wonder why we have problems. I like that illustration recognizing the fact that there are going to be walls between human beings.

It really is quite a coincidence that my mother happened to be in the United States when I was born. She could have been in France or Argentina, any number of places — it is quite a coincidence that she was here. So thank God I am an American. I am an American of certain cultural backgrounds which I have inherited during the years from my predecessors. I think that you are so right when you say we ought to recognize this in human beings and then see if we cannot build some bridges to bring Americans closer together as one nation of people.

9. Who Are We?[1]
♣ Arthur Mann

Father Andrew M. Greeley, Director of the Center for the Study of American Pluralism at the University of Chicago, has written that there has been "a resurgence of tribalism" in our times. The phrase is apt, but it is one thing to correct a false, Anglo-Saxonized version of American history, and still another to claim that American society is merely a collection of ethnic groups. That objection is the starting point of the concluding document of this book. It is adapted from a lecture by the author-editor of Immigrants in American Life. ■

Urban society in the North is pluralistic, although not quite in the way that Horace Kallen used the term. That kind of society has got

---
[1] Arthur Mann, "The City as a Melting Pot," in *History and the Role of the City in American Life* (Indianapolis: Indiana Historical Society, 1972), pp. 19–22.

to make room for Negroes as equals. But someone will say that "the Negro is not like other ethnic groups." The response to that assertion should be that "other ethnic groups" are not like each other and never were. That is the whole point of pluralism. It took close to half a century to persuade Americans to accept that point as both a fact and an ideal in American democracy. Let us not repeat the folly of the 1920's when men, who should have known better, polarized this country into believing that Americans were merely of "new" or "old" immigrant stock.

We could make still another contribution to clear thinking if we stopped saying "the Negro" as if that term were the plural. It is considered improper to use the singular for any other ancestral group. Who today, for example, ever talks about "the Pole" or "the German" in American history? But getting our language straight is not only a matter of courtesy. Our language should correspond to things as they are. There are Negroes and Negroes. To think otherwise is to fall victim to our own prejudices or to the warped views of those Negro leaders who refuse to recognize and respect the differences among Negroes.

Like other Americans, Negroes have got to have the right to choose. That is the only working definition of liberty that I know. More specifically, individual Negroes must be free to decide whether they want to be total identifiers, partial identifiers, disaffiliates, hybrids, or whatever else makes sense. The essence of an open society is that it encourages its people to keep their alternatives open.

But back to the question with which this lecture started. Has the city been a melting pot in American history? In the Zangwillian sense of intermarriage, it has been for some Americans but not for others. And who is to say that Theodore Roosevelt, of mixed origins, was a more representative American than John Fitzgerald Kennedy, who was of unmixed Irish stock? Yet, in trying to set the record straight, the leaders of the current ethnic revival go too far in asserting that American society is merely a tissue of ethnic groups. It is not, and has not been — and many persons would agree that it ought not to be.

Ethnic diversity has been central to the American experience, but it has defied easy categorization. The theory of Anglo-Saxon supremacy is morally and scientifically unacceptable, and the theories of the melting pot and cultural pluralism have limited applicability to the American people as a whole. But I should like to conclude on a positive note. Towards that end I propose for your consideration the following sketch of an ethnic map of urban America outside the South.

This map — or model, if you will — requires that we start with individuals instead of groups.

Total Identifiers. Such individuals live out their lives entirely within the ethnic group. They reside with their own kind, go to school with their own kind, work with their own kind, pray with their own kind, eat the food of their own kind, relax with their own kind, marry their own kind, vote and campaign for their own kind — they do, in short, what Horace Kallen proposed. Yet such Americans, at present, belong to a fraction of the population.

Partial Identifiers. Individuals of this sort regard the ethnic attachment and identification as important — but not all inclusive. They take their ethnicity in measured and selective doses. Such Americans constitute a larger number than those for whom the ethnic group is the sole touchstone. My guess is that these individuals make up a majority of Americans who still have, and cherish, a memory of their ancestry.

Disaffiliates. These individuals grew up in ethnic or ethnic-religious neighborhoods but cannot go home again because they have chosen not to. They are most often found in the worlds of academia, the media, and show business. They are intellectuals, in a word. In a witty and perceptive article, Father Andrew Greeley called them an ethnic group. That they constitute a tribe of their own is true. They have their own values, rituals, heroes, fears, ways of bringing up children, and so on. Yet, unlike members of ethnic groups, the disaffiliates are not tied together by a common ancestry. Such individuals number in the millions and are likely to become more numerous now that a college education is getting to be more and more accessible. Already, around half the college-age youngsters go to college in America; and the peak has yet to be reached.

Hybrids. Individuals of this kind cannot identify themselves through a single stock. They are of mixed ancestry and come from families that, for a long time, have intermarried. In a course that I give on ethnicity in American history, there are always students in whom the ethnicity has been so completely washed out that they have a hard time getting hold of the concept. Some of them even resent it, thinking that it is a mark of bigotry to sort out people according to their foreign origins. Often these students are Westerners, particularly from California, where it is usual to describe one's self as originating from Iowa, Pennsylvania, or some other eastern state. Such Americans are, in literal fact, products of the melting pot.

The Loneliest Crowd. Finally, there are individuals who have very little sense of self. The most demoralized of them live in skid row. They are the loneliest Americans of all.

Within each of these categories, one would have to make refinements. Ambiguity is the condition of being an American. It's terribly hard to place people in our society, and for people to place themselves in it. Perhaps that's why America has more alienation than other countries.

■ *The Student's Paperback Library*

Certain of the selections in this volume — namely, those by Crèvecoeur, Handlin, Hansen, Kennedy, Plunkitt, Riis, and Steffens — are selections from books available in paperback. Here are some further titles that belong in a paperback library about immigrants in American life.

General: The most detailed but readable and thoughtful history from the seventeenth century to the 1950's is Maldwyn Allen Jones's *American Immigration*. John Hope Franklin's *From Slavery to Freedom: A History of American Negroes*, now in its third edition, is still the best history on that subject. Oscar Handlin's *The American People in the Twentieth Century* is indispensable for that subject. The last seventy-five years or so are also covered with insight in Nathan Glazer's and Daniel Patrick Moynihan's *Beyond the Melting Pot: The Negroes, Puerto Ricans, Jews, Italians, and Irish of New York City*. Oscar Handlin's *Race and Nationality in American Life* is a collection of penetrating essays about a variety of topics, and the same is true of Marcus Lee Hansen's *The Immigrant in American History*.

Special subjects: Jane Addams' *Twenty Years at Hull House* is an eyewitness account by a pioneer social worker of immigrant life in Chicago's slums between 1890 and 1910. Another important autobiography, Frederic C. Howe's *The Confessions of a Reformer*, gives an inside view of federal administrative machinery affecting immigration. The impact of ethnic diversity on religion can be followed in Will Herberg's *Protestant — Catholic — Jew*. There are two excellent histories of the immigration restriction movement, John Higham's *Strangers in the Land*, which covers the subject as a whole, and Barbara Miller Solomon's *Ancestors and Immigrants*, which concentrates on New England. Arthur Mann's *La Guardia Comes to Power: 1933* shows how New York City's first Italo-American mayor overcame the bigotry that stood in his way. For an illuminating account of the theories of the melting pot, cultural pluralism, and Anglo-American conformity, see Milton M. Gordon's *Assimilation in American Life*.

Fiction: One of the most interesting ways of reading social history is in the form of novels. Willa Cather's *My Antonia* is a moving story about a Bohemian girl in Nebraska. New York City's Jewish East Side is the scene of Abraham Cahan's *The Rise of David Levinsky*. Edwin O'Connor's *The Last Hurrah* is a rich novel about ethnic politics in a heavily Irish-American eastern city. For a vivid portrayal of a Greek immigrant father's love for his epileptic son, read Harry Mark Petrakis's *Dream of Kings*. The classical fictional account of Scandinavian immigrants in the Middle West remains Ole Rölvaag's *Giants in the Earth*.

■ *Questions for Study and Discussion*

I. The Colonial Background

1. Why did the trip from Germany to America take six months in the 1750's? What hardships were suffered aboard ship?
2. What did Olaudah Equiano consider the most cruel aspect of slavery? Why?
3. What conclusions can you draw from Peter Kalm's account about New York City in the year 1750? What conclusion can you draw from William Winterbotham's account of Pennsylvania?
4. What misconceptions about America did Benjamin Franklin want to correct? What did he feel were America's actual advantages for European immigrants?
5. Does Crèvecoeur's analysis help to explain why there was an American Revolution? Explain.

II. Migrations of the Nineteenth and Twentieth Centuries

1. How do you account for the relatively large number of immigrants from Great Britain and Ireland? From Canada and Mexico?
2. What does Michael Pupin's account reveal about the financial resources of some immigrants in the 1870's?
3. What were the three major waves of immigration described by Marcus L. Hansen? What were the reasons for each?
4. Why is it difficult to estimate the number of "wetbacks"? What has attracted them to the United States?
5. What have West Indians contributed to the struggle for equal rights? Why?
6. Were John F. Kennedy and Emma Lazarus in agreement on the basic reasons why immigrants came to America? Explain.

III. Some Personal Testimonies

1. What was the chief reason that led each of these men to come to America: Schurz, Andrew Carnegie's father, Mattson?

2. How did each seem to feel about his homeland at the time he left for America?

3. How was it possible for younger members of an Irish family to emigrate from Ireland during the mid-1800's?

4. Why did Jean Baptiste Delusson emigrate from Quebec to settle in Holyoke?

5. Mary Antin saw great contrasts between the life she knew in Russia and American life as her father explained it. What advantages did she look forward to in America?

6. What brought William Scott to America?

7. What did Pablo Mares see as the advantages of living in the United States?

IV. Jobs and Housing

1. Why did the Norwegian farmer in Missouri in the 1830's conclude, "I consider it precarious for everyone to go to America. . . ."?

2. Contrast the working conditions of cigarmakers as described by Gompers and Riis. Why did Gompers fare better than the Bohemian workers described by Riis?

3. Why did so many Italians become "pick and shovel" workers? What was the role of the *padrone?*

4. What does Antoni Butkowski's letter tell about the problems immigrants faced? Was Aleksandra Rembieńska's problem similar?

5. Why did the former black teacher prefer working for the wholesale firm rather than on the construction job? Was money the chief factor?

6. According to the account by DeForest and Veiller, what conditions were characteristic of old-style tenements?

V. Community Life

1. Why was adjustment to farming life in the Dakotas difficult for immigrants of the late 1800's? In contrast, what were the advantages of living in East Harlem during the 1920's?

2. What functions and services did Priest Bójnowski's church perform for Polish immigrants and their children?

3. What services were provided by mutual-aid societies? by the foreign-language press?

4. What were Mary McDowell's suggestions for reducing tension between immigrant parents and their American-born children? Do you think her suggestions would have been effective? Why?

5. What problems does the generation gap pose for Miami's Cubans?
6. What examples of black West Indian immigrants' retaining their heritage are listed by the author? How does this lead to conflict with the next generation?

VI. Politics

1. How did the ward boss obtain the loyal support of the people living in his district? What is your evaluation of such methods?
2. On what grounds did Lincoln Steffens find fault with Tammany? According to Richard Croker, what useful role did Tammany perform? What are your own conclusions?
3. What is your reaction to Fiorello La Guardia's "new school of politics"? to his program for New York?
4. Why were Polish immigrants living in this country deeply concerned about the future of their homeland during and after World War I?

VII. The Achievement

1. In general terms, what contributions have immigrants made to this country's economic development?
2. Why did Lindsborg, Kansas, become a musical center? How did this change the lives of the Swedish immigrants in the area?
3. Why, according to Josephine Roche's account, should the Americanization of immigrants be a "two-way process"?

VIII. Cycles of Bigotry

1. The slogan of the Ku Klux Klan was "Native, white, Protestant supremacy." To what degree was this also the goal of the Know-Nothings of the 1850's? How did each group justify its program?
2. Contrast Al Smith's creed as an American Catholic with the statements of the Know-Nothings and the Klan. What are your conclusions?
3. Why were German Americans persecuted during World War I? Japanese Americans during World War II? What is your reaction in each case?

IX. Concepts of Americanism and Americanization

1. What did Crèvecoeur, Emerson, and Zangwill mean by the term "melting pot"? Why did each of them believe in this concept of Americanization?
2. Contrast the view of the Polish-American priest quoted by Emily Greene Balch and that of supporters of the "melting pot" concept. How did Miss Balch's view differ from each of these?
3. What did Theodore Roosevelt mean by "hyphenated American"? by "good American"? What obstacles to Americanization are brought out in Miss Balch's interview with Father Tymkevich?
4. Janos Hollo stated that "there is no other place in all the world where I would have felt my homelessness as little as I did here." Why was this true? Would it have been equally true for Father Tymkevich's Ruthenians? Why?

X. Immigration Policy

1. On what grounds did the AFL oppose Chinese immigration in 1902? Evaluate the document's assessment of China and the Chinese.
2. Why did President Wilson veto the literary test bill in 1915? Do you agree with his reasons for vetoing it?
3. On what grounds did Senator Smith defend the national origins plan? Evaluate each of his contentions.
4. What changes did Senate liberals wish to make in the McCarran-Walter bill? Why? When the quota system was abolished in 1965, what were the new criteria for immigration? According to President Johnson, what were the advantages of the new system? Do you agree?

XI The Contemporary Scene

1. How is the Immigration Act of 1965 changing the ethnic makeup of American cities?
2. Why has the coming of Cubans to Miami created few problems?
3. What evidence is there that Mexican Americans are disadvantaged?
4. Compare the problems of Mexican Americans with those of the members of New York's Puerto Rican community.
5. What remedial measures have been undertaken by the government? What has been done by education agencies?

Questions for Study and Discussion

6. What did John Kennedy and Pope John XXIII believe was the right of all men?

7. What are the arguments in favor of bilingual education for Mexican-American children?

8. Why are Mexican Americans becoming activists? What are their goals?

9. Why should ethnic education be extended to all groups?

10. Why should blacks or the members of any other group be regarded as individuals? Is there such a thing as Anglo-Saxon supremacy?

■ Acknowledgments

Thanks are extended to the following persons and organizations for making pictures available for reproduction.

25 — top left, Brown Brothers; top right, Photo by Charles Phelps Cushing; bottom, Courtesy of the New York Public Library

41 — top left, Photograph by Byron, The Byron Collection, Museum of the City of New York; bottom, *Harper's Weekly*

65 — top left and bottom, Brown Brothers; top right, The Bettmann Archive

95 — top, Photo by Hine, The Bettmann Archive; bottom left and right, Brown Brothers

113 — top, Culver Pictures, Inc.; middle, Brown Brothers; bottom, The Bettmann Archive

135 — top left and bottom right, Brown Brothers; bottom left, The Bettmann Archive

149 — top, Wide World Photos; bottom, Courtesy of The Boston Symphony Orchestra

165 — top, Courtesy of the New York Public Library; bottom left, Culver Pictures, Inc.; bottom right, Brown Brothers

177 — top, Lisl Steiner; middle, Wide World Photos; bottom, Patricia L. Hollander

199 — Wide World Photos

215 — top and bottom right, Wide World Photos; bottom left, Black Star

235 — top, Wide World Photos; bottom left, UPI; bottom right, Philip Bailey

■ Index

Boldface figures indicate authorship of a selection. A figure preceded by *p* refers to a picture. A figure followed by *n* refers to a footnote.

Addams, Jane, 179
Africans, 3–4, 5, 13–19, *p* 25, 33, 49, 207. *See also* Black Americans
Agricultural revolution, 6
Albanians, 36
Alienation, 248
America, early population of, 2–4; as ideal, 4–5; early voyages to, 8–19; misconceptions about, 24, 80, 185–186; as the land of labor, 26–27, 42, 54; lure of, 55; industrialization of, 68; adjustment to new life in, 80–83; ambiguity a condition of, 248
American Federation of Labor, **189–192**
Americanization, as seen by Crèvecoeur, 29–31; and the foreign-language press, 115; and the generation gap, 116–122, 126; and politics, 127; a two-way process, 151; concepts of Americanism and, 172–188. *See also* Naturalization
American Party, 157, 173. *See also* Know-Nothing Party
American Protective Association, 159
Anglo-Americans, 45, 214, 230
Anglo-Saxon image, falsity of, 244
Anglo-Saxon supremacy, concept of, 154, 155, 156, 164, 195, 196–197, 246
Anti-Catholicism, 53, 153, 157, 159, 164–166, *p* 165, 167
Anti-foreignism, 45, 155, 156, 157–159, *p* 165
Anti-German feeling, World War I, 153, 159–161
Antin, Mary, *p* 65, **71–74**
Anti-Semitism, 53, 72
Apprentices, 28–29
Armenians, 36
"Aryan supremacy," 156
Asia, immigration from, 6, 33, 207
Asia Minor, immigration from, 33, 35

Assimilation, 126, 179–182. *See also* Melting pot
Astor, John Jacob, 144
Attila, 190
Australia, 33, 154
Austrians, 33, 40, 109
Azores, immigrants from, 206

Balch, Emily Greene, **175–179**, **182–184**
Balkans, immigration from, 33, 35, 40
Baptists, 23
Barrios, 214, 216, 236–241
Belgians, 33, 40
Bell, Alexander Graham, 144
Bellanca, Giuseppe, 144
Benevolent associations, 125
Bering Strait, 2
Bethany College, 146–147
Bigotry. *See* Prejudice
Bilingual education, 225–226, 231–234, 240–241
Black Americans, 4, 5, 13–19, 47–51, 74–75, 100–101, 122–126; and British customs, 123–125. *See also* Africans *and* Negroes
Bohemians, 36, 40, 90, 91, 116–119
Border Patrol, Mexico–U.S., 46
Bosses, political, 82, 127–134, *p* 135
Boston, unskilled construction work in, 92–97; Immigration Restriction League in, 192
Braceros, 45–46, 210, 227
Breed, Donald, 150
British Isles, immigration from, 6, 33, 35, 40, 207. *See also* Irish, Scots, *and* Welsh
British West Indies, 48, 49–51, 74, 100, 124–126
Butkowski, Antoni, **97–98**

California, Chinese in, 153, *p* 165, 189, 207; Mexican-American militancy in, 236–241
Calles, Plutarco Elias, 78
Calvinists, 4, 23
Campbell, Sir Gerald, 124
Canadians, 33, 43, 68–71, 207
Cape Verdeans, 206
Carnegie, Andrew, **59–62**, *p* 65, 144

Index

Carnegie, William, **60–62**
Carroll, Coleman F., 209
Castro, Fidel, 120, 209
Catholics, in colonies, 22, 23; prejudice against, 53, 153, 157, 159, 164–166, *p* 165, 167; Polish church, 110–112; Al Smith's creed, 167–168
Ceja, Manuel, 240
"Celtic" wave of immigration, 39–40
Census, of 1790, 4; of 1920, 48
Central Powers, World War I, 140 *n*, 147
Chicago, Bohemians in, 116–119; Spanish- and Chinese-speaking residents of, 207; Mexicans in, 210
Child labor, 81, 89, 90
Chinese, 6, 33, *p* 95, 207; in New York City, 109, *p* 177; in California, 153, *p* 165, 189, 207; exclusion of, 189–192
Churches, in colonial New York, 21; in immigrant community life, 110–112; in Harlem, 123, 124; separation of Church and State, 167
Cigarmakers, Samuel Gompers, 87, 88–89; in tenement factories, 89–91
Civil Service Commission, 224–225
Clark, Barett, 150
Colonial period, 8–31
"Color line," 50–51
Commission on Immigration and Naturalization, **143–145**
Committee on Public Information, 148
Common Sense (Paine), 5
Communism, fear of, 155, 197
Community life, 82, 104–126, 220
Constitution, U.S., 136, 143, 153
Correiro, John R., 208
Corsi, Edward, **108–110**
Cosmopolitanism, 2, 109
Crèvecoeur, J. Hector St. John de, 4, 5, **29–31**, 172
Croatians, 36
Croker, Richard, 131, 132–134
Cubans, 33, 119–122, 208–212, *p* 215
Cudahy, Michael, 144
Cultural Pluralism, 154, 175–179, *p* 177, 243–245
Culture, immigrants' contributions to, 3, 83, 145–147, *p.* 149

Dakotas, immigrant settlers in, 104–107
Danes, 33, 109

DeForest, Robert, **102–103**
Delaware, 4
Democracy, Madison's view of, 127
Depression, 45, 46, 156, 168
Discrimination against Puerto Ricans, 221. *See also* Prejudice
Dmowski, Roman, 140
Domestic work, 98–99
Domingo, W. O., **47–51**
Douglas, Paul, 198
DuBois, W. E. B., 50
Ducharme, Jacques, **68–71**
DuPont family, 144
Dust bowl migrants, 45, 46
Dutch, 4, 20, 22, 33, 40

East Harlem, New York City, 108–110
Economic motive for immigration, 54
Economy, expanding, and immigrants' contribution, 143–145
Edward VIII, 124
Einstein, Albert, 144
Ellis Island, 2, 203
Emerson, Ralph Waldo, **172–173**
Employment, 81, 84–101, *p* 95, 222–225
Enclosure, 35
English, in colonies, 4, 20, 22. *See also* British Isles *and* British West Indies
English as a Second Language Program, 240–241
Episcopalians, 22
Equiano, Olaudah, **13–19**
Erickson, Charles A., **236–241**
Ericsson, John, 144
Ethnic diversity, in early America, 3–4, 22–23; contemporary, 108–110, 204, 205–208, 242–248
Ethnic group conferences, 139–142
Ethnic Heritage Studies Program Bill, 242–243
Europe, immigration from, 6, 33, 34–36, 38–40, 83, *p* 113, 189, 192, 195 198, 207; villages in, 105. *See also specific nationalities*
Evans, Hiram Wesley, **161–167**

Fall River, Mass., 205, 206, 208
Farmers, immigrants as, 27, 81, 84–86, 104–107, *p* 113; and rural development, 228
Fermi, Enrico, 144
Filipinos, 33, 205, 207

Index

Fillmore, Millard, 157
Finns, 33, 40, 109
Fleischmann, Charles L., 144
Foreign affairs, immigrants' interest in, 139–142
Foreign Information Service, 150
Foreign Language Bureaus, 148
Foreign-language newspapers, 31, 82, 83, 115–116, 148, *p* 177
France, end of republic of, 57
Franklin, Benjamin, 4, **23–29**, *p* 25
Fraternal organizations, 112–114
French, 4, 33, 109
French-speaking immigrants, 49
French-Canadians, 68–71
French West Indies, 49
Friends. *See* Quakers

Garza, Nick E., **231–234**
Generation gap, 116–122, 126
German Reformed church, 21, 23
Germans, 4, 22–23, 33, 35, 39, 40, 109, 115–116, 207; persecution of, in World War I, 159–161
Germany, anti-Semitism and anti-Catholicism in, 53; under Hitler, 53, 54, 156; 1848 uprisings in, 56
Goethals, George W., 50, 181
Gompers, Samuel, **87–89**
Government response to needs of Spanish-speaking immigrants, 222–229, 239–241
Grant, Madison, 197
Greeks, 33, 36, 109, 151
Greeley, Andrew M., 245
Guadalupe Hidalgo, Treaty of, 45

Haiti, 33, 49
Handlin, Oscar, 8 *n*, **34–36**, 52, 143 *n*
Hansen, Marcus L., **38–42**
Harlem, New York City, 47–51, 122–126; East, 108–110
Hate groups, *p* 165, 168
Hawaii, 207
Hitler, 53, 54, 156
Hollo, Janos, **184–188**
Homesteaders, 104–107
Horn Project, San Antonio, Tex., 233
Household workers, 98–99
Housing, 81–82, 86, 93, 102–103, *p* 113, 219–220, 221, 228–229
Howe, Harold, 239, 241
Huber, Conrad, 144
Huguenots, 4

Humphrey, Hubert, 198
Hungarians, 33, 35, 109, 184–188, *p* 199
Hungary, revolt of, from Russia, 54; uprising in, 184, *p* 199
Hyphenated Americans, 180, 182

Ibo tribe, 3 *n*, 13
Immigration, statistics on, 2, 32–36, 45, 206–207; reasons for, 6, 51–78; 18th-century, 23–29, *p* 25; 19th- and 20th-century, 32–55, *p* 41; waves of, 38–42, 45; and the contemporary scene, 204–249
Immigration Act of 1965, 156, 206–207
Immigration policy, unrestrictive, 4, 144, 153–154; restrictive, 6, 43, 47, 154–155, 189–200; and quota system, 47, 195, 197, 200, 201-202, 206–207; and 1965 legislation, 156, 189, 201–203; Japanese excluded, 189; limited, 189, 195–200, 202; Chinese excluded, 189–192; and literacy test, 192–194; and national origins plan, 195–197, 198, 200, 201–202, 206–207
Immigration Restriction League, 192
Indenture, 29
India, immigration from, 33, 207
Indians, American, 2
Industrial revolution, 6, 59–62, 84
Industry, immigrants in, 35, 54, 81, 97–98, 144
Inter-Agency Committee on Mexican American Affairs, **213–217**, **222–229**
Inventors, immigrants as, 144
Ireland, famine in, 64–66, 67
Irish, 4, 22, 33, 34, 39, 45, 54, 64–67, 109, 207
Italians, 33, 35, 45, 94, 109, 114, 207

Jamaica, immigrants from, 49, 74–75, 207
Jamestown, Va., *p* 25
Japanese, 6, 33, 45; internment of, in World War II, 153, 168–171; exclusion of, 189
Jefferson, Thomas, 158, 180
Jews, 19–21, 36, 71–74, 109, 114–115; persecution of, 53, 72
Jobs. *See* Employment
John XXIII, 231
Johnson, Lyndon B., **201–203**, 213

260   Index

Johnson-Reed Act of 1924, 154, 189, 195, 197
Jugoslavs, 109, 151

Kalm, Peter, **19–21**
Karelians, 40
Kennedy, John F., 2n, 6, **51–54**, 167, 201, 231
Kennedy, Patrick, 51
Kieft, William, 108
Know-Nothing Party, 153, 157–159, 173
Knudsen, William S., 144
Koreans, 5, 33
Kovach, Bill, **205–208**
Ku Klux Klan, 153, 161–167, p 165, 182
Kyrides, Lucas P., 144

Labor, America's need for, 26–27, 42, 54, 136–137; migrant, 45–46, 210, 214, 218–219, 226–227, 240; child, 81, 89, 90; skilled, 87–89; tenement factory, 89–91, p 95; unskilled construction work, 92–97, p 95, 100–101. *See also* Employment
La Guardia, Fiorello H., 83, p 135, **136–138**
Landholding system, 40
Latin America, immigrants from, 33, 48–49, 207, 209
Latvians, 40
Lazarus, Emma, **55**
League of Nations, 155
Lehman, Herbert, 198
Leinsdorf, Erich, p 149
Liberia, 49
Liberty Island, 55
Lindsborg, Kan., 145–147
Literacy test, 192–194
Lithuanians, 40, 97, 151
Lutherans, 4, 21, 23, p 25

McCarran, Pat, 198, 200
McCarran-Walter Act, 154–155, 156, 197–200, 201
McDowell, Mary E., **116–119**
Macedonians, 36
McKay, Claude, 51
McWilliams, Carey, **43–47**
Madison, James, 127, 144
Mann, Arthur, **245–248**
Manpower Development and Training programs, 222–223

Marathon, 190
Mares, Pablo, **76–78**
Marriage customs, 124–125
Mattson, Hans, **62–64**
Mediterranean wave of immigrants, 40–42, 109
Melting pot, 154, 172–175, 245, 246
Mendez, Rosalinda, 237–238
Mennonists (Mennonites), 23, p 113
Mergenthaler, Otto, 144
Mexican-American War, 44
Mexican Revolution, 76
Mexicans in America, 33, 43–47, 76–78, 210, 213–217, p 215; government response to needs of, 222–229, 239–241; bilingual education for, 225–226, 231–234, 240–241; stereotypes of, 229–230; militancy among, 236–241
Mexico, territory acquired from, 44, 76; compared with U.S., 77–78
Miami, Cubans in, 119–122, 208–212
Migrant workers, 45–46, 210, 214, 218–219; training and education program for, 226–227, 240
Miller, Herbert A., **110–112, 112–115**
Milwaukee *Herald*, 115–116
Missouri, immigrant farmers in, 84–86
Mittelberger, Gottlieb, **8–13**
Model Cities Program, 229
Montes, Miguel, 241
Morales, José, Jr., **218–221**
Moravians, 23
Music, immigrants' contributions to, 145–147, p 149
Mutual aid societies, 112–115, 125–126

Nakashima, Ted, **168–171**
Napoleon III, 57
Nast, Thomas, p 135
Nationalism, Russian, 53; immigrants' interest in, 139, 151
Nationality, concept of, 5, 196; and education, 118–119; and assimilation, 126, 179–182; and melting pot concept, 172–175; and cultural pluralism, 175–179, p 177. *See also* Americanization
National Origins Act of 1924, 206
National origins plan, 195–197, 198, 200, 201–202, 206–207
Nativists, 154, 157–159, 192
Naturalization laws, 5, 47, 176
Nebraska, immigrants in, 104–107

Index

Negroes, immigrant, 47–51, 109; and the open society, 246. *See also* Africans *and* Black Americans
New Amsterdam; New Holland, 20, 108
New Britain, Conn., 110–112
Newspapers, foreign-language, 31, 82, 83, 115–116, 148, *p* 177
New York City, *p* 41, 43, 55; colonial, 4, 19–21; Harlem, 47–51, 122–126; in the 1860's, 87–89; tenement factories in, 89–91, *p* 95; tenement housing in, 102–103, *p* 113; East Harlem, 108–110; and Tammany Hall, 127–134, *p* 135; La Guardia's goals for, 136–138; Puerto Ricans in, 218–221; and bilingual education, 233
New York Times, **119–122**
New Zealand, immigration from, 33
"Nordics," 109, 155, 195, 197
Norwegians, 33, 35, 40, 84–86

Obregón, Alvaro, 78
Occupations. *See* Employment
Ogden, Peter, 49
Olsson, Olof, 146

Pacific islands, immigration from, 33
Paderewski, Ignace Jan, 141
Padrone system, 92, 96–97
Paine, Tom, 4, 5
Panama Canal, 50
Panunzio, Constantine M., **92–97**
Park, Robert E., **110–112, 112–115,** 115 *n*
Pastore, John, 198, 200
Pearl Harbor, 168
Pena, Albert, **229–231**
Pennsylvania, 4, 21–23
Pereira, Luciano J., 206
Philadelphia, 22, 23, 130
Philblad, Ernst Frederick, **145–147**
Philippines, 207. *See also* Filipinos
Plunkitt, George Washington, **127–129,** 130
Pluralism, 154, 175–179, *p* 177, 243–248
Poles, 33, 35, 40, 97–99, 109, 110–112, 139–142
Political refugees, 53–54, 56–59, 184–188, 193, *p* 199, 209
Politics, immigrants in, 82–83, 127–142; issue, 136–138; and foreign affairs, 139–142

Portuguese, 33, 205, 206, 207, 208
Poverty, as obstacle to Americanization, 182–184; problems of, 212–221
Prejudice, against foreigners, 44–45, 155, 156, 157–159, *p* 165; race, 48, 50–51, 153, 156, 162–164, *p* 165, 182, 189, 197, 201–202; religious, 53, 153, 157, 159, 164–166, *p* 165, 167; and fear, 153, 155; and immigration policy, 154–156; cycles of, 156, 157–171; and Know-Nothing Party, 157–159; and World War I persecution of German-Americans, 159–161; the KKK, 161–167, *p* 165; and World War II internment of Japanese-Americans, 168–171; as obstacle to Americanization, 182–184; against Spanish-speaking, 210
Presbyterians, 21, 22
Prohibition, 155
Protestantism, advocates of supremacy for, 164–166
Prussians, 40
Pucinski, Roman C., **242–245**
Puerto Ricans, 81, *p* 199, 204, 209, 210, *p* 215, 218–221
Pupin, Michael, **36–38,** 144

Quakers, 21, 22, 23
Quota system, 47, 195, 197, 200, 201–202, 206–207

Racism. *See* Prejudice, race
Rauschenbusch, Winifred, **115–116**
Reformed Church, 21, 23
Refugees, political, 53–54, 56–59, 184–188, 193, *p* 199, 209
Reid, Ira De A., 74 *n*, 100 *n*, **122–126**
Religious liberty, in colonial Pennsylvania, 22–23; as reason for immigration, 53. *See also* Churches
Rembieńska, Aleksandra, **98–99**
Resettlement centers, 168, 169–170
Reyes, Ramiro, 240
Riis, Jacob A., **89–91**
Riles, Wilson, 240, 241
Roche, Josephine, **147–151**
Rodriguez, Armando, 238–239, 241
Rogers, Will, 2
Roosevelt, Franklin D., 2
Roosevelt, Theodore, 8, 83, **179–182**
Rumanians, 109
Russia, anti-Semitism and anti-Catholicism in, 53; and Hungary, 54

Index

Russian Revolution, 54
Russians, 33, 97, 109, *p* 113, 151
Russwurm, John Brown, 49
Ruthenians, 36, 97, 182

San Francisco, Chinatown in, 207
Sarnoff, David, 144
Saxons, 40
Scandinavians, 33, 35, 40, 107. See also Danes, Norwegians, Swedes
Schick, Bela, *p* 149
Schurz, Carl, 56–59, *p* 65
Scientists, immigrants as, 36, 144, *p* 149
Scots, 4, 22, 35, 39
Scott, William, 74–75
Secret societies, 161–167
Segregation, racial, 48; educational, 236
Shaw, John W. A., 50
Ships, immigrant, in colonial period, 8–19; in 1800's, 36–38, 64, 67
Sikorsky, Igor, 144
Sillas, Herman, 237
Slaves, 3, 13–19; emancipated, 5; in Africa and the New World, 14 *n*
Slavs, 40, 97, 109, 182–184
Slovaks, 36, 97
Slovenians, 112–114
Slums, 81–82, 102–103
Smalley, E. V., **104–107**
Smith, Alfred E., 83, 136, **167–168**
Smith, Ellison DuRant, **195–197**
Smulski, John F., 141, 142
Social clubs, 125
Southwest, problems of the poor in, 213–217
Southwest arc, 43–44
Spaniards, 4, 33, 109
Spanish-speaking Americans, 44, 48–49, 205, 207, 209–210, 214, 222–229, 239–241. See also Mexicans
Stalin, 53
Statue of Liberty, 55, 203
Stead, William T., **132–134**
Steam power, 36–38, 59, 61
Steffens, Lincoln, **130–132**, *p* 135
Survey, **139–142**
Swedes, 4, 22, 33, 35, 40, 63–64, 109, 145–147
Swensson, Alma, 147
Swensson, Carl, 146–147
Swiss, 4, 33
Syrians, 36, 109

Talent Search Program, 226
Talmud, 137
Tammany Hall, 127, 130–134, *p* 135
Tenement factories, 89–91, *p* 95
Tenement housing, 102–103, *p* 113
Teutonic wave of immigration, 40. See also Germans
Thomas, David, 144
Thomas, William I., 97 *n*, 98 *n*
Time, **197–200**
Toscanini, Arturo, 145
Trade unions, 88, 90
Training programs, 222–223
"Tribalism," resurgence of, 245–248
Truman, Harry S., 143, 198, 200
Tunkers (Dunkers), 23
Turks, 33, 109
Tymkevich, Paul, 182 *n*, 183, 184

Ukrainians, 36, 40, 97, 151
Urban renewal, 221

Veiller, Lawrence, **102–103**
Vienna, 191
Virgin Islanders, 49, 125
Volstead Act, 49, 110

Walsh, Bryan O., **208–212**
Washington, George, 5, 158, 180
Welsh, 4, 22, 35, 39
Wendt, Gerald L., **159–161**
West Indies, immigration from, 33, 48, 49–51, 74, 100, 124–126
Westward movement, 42
"Wetbacks," 45, 46
"White ethnics," 242–245
White supremacy, doctrine of 154, 155, 156, 164, 195, 196–197, 246
Whitman, Walt, 2, 3
Wilson, Woodrow, 139, 160 *n*, **192–194**
Winterbotham, William, **21–23**
World War I, 140; and American immigrants, 147–151, *p* 149; anti-German feeling in, 153, 159–161
World War II, 46; internment of Japanese-Americans in, 153, 168–171

Yugoslavs, 33, 207. See also Jugoslavs

Zangwill, Israel, **173–175**
Zwingfelters, 23